Team
Talk

Team Talk

THE POWER OF LANGUAGE IN TEAM DYNAMICS

Anne Donnellon

HARVARD BUSINESS SCHOOL PRESS
BOSTON, MASSACHUSETTS

Library of Congress Cataloging-in-Publication Data

Donnellon, Anne
    Team talk : the power of language in team dynamics / Anne
  Donnellon.
        p.   cm.
    Includes bibliographical references and index.
    ISBN 0-87584-619-X
    1. Work groups.   I. Title.
    HD66.D66   1996
    658.4'036—dc20   95-36810
                                                                  CIP

The paper used in this publication meets the requirements of the American
National Standard for Permanence of Paper for Printed Library Materials
Z39.49-1984

*To my family
for teaching me the joys
and challenges of interdependence*

Contents

Preface

This is a book for team members, managers, change agents, and researchers interested in teams and in language. It offers a different perspective on work teams—a multifaceted perspective that shows teams in their day-to-day realities, firmly situated in their organizational context, doing their work through their talk. Indeed, one of the book's purposes is to demonstrate the centrality of conversation in organizational life and outcomes. My primary goals of the book are to explain why team work, especially cross-functional team work, is so challenging for professional employees and managers—and to offer suggestions for how to meet those challenges.

The research project that produced this book started from three threads. The first was my own longstanding interest in the effects of language and culture on group work; the second was my sense that business requirements (and perhaps practice) for teams were rapidly exceeding the bounds of our academic knowledge; and the third was my interest in seeing how organizations were managing the fit between the bureaucratic concerns for individual accountability and control versus post-bureaucratic requirements for teams, commitment, and creativity. I was also intrigued by the broad implementation of teams in the professional ranks. I had a suspicion that professional employees were likely to find team work more difficult because of having greater expectations of autonomy in their work than the blue-collar workers who responded so well to teams on the production floor.

From the outset, I defined the domain of my research broadly as cross-functional work teams of professional employees who were jointly responsible for some task. Gradually, I came to see that cross-functional teams represent the formalization of two characteristics that distinguish teams from other types of work groups: diversity and interdependence. So, while the insights in this book apply most aptly to cross-functional teams of professionals, they also generalize to other teams of professionals.

My research questions were broad. I sought to understand what the words *team* and *teamwork* meant in practice, how team work was done, and what challenges and constraints it imposed. These research questions required attention to the multitude of details at various levels shaping the meaning and doing of team work. I had to learn how the individual expectations and experiences of team members affected their own actions and others' in the team context. I needed to understand how the organization—its strategies, structures, systems, culture, and managers—shaped those individual and interpersonal experiences and actions. To comprehend this, I needed to observe *and tape record* teams at work, watching and listening as they did their work through their talk.

Many companies were very interested in the research, but few were willing to give me such open access. Finally, I found division managers in four Fortune 200 corporations who graciously agreed to let me study their teams. For reasons of confidentiality, the names (and data) of three of these companies, their managers, and their team members are disguised here. The fourth company was 3M, and in particular, the Occupational Health and Environmental Safety Division, headed by Robert Hershock. I am indebted to all the people in this study who gave me their time and confidences and allowed me to peer at them, follow them, and ask them innumerable questions.

I would like to single out three people who made extraordinary contributions to this work. Robert Hershock and Dave Braun of 3M not only opened up their organization and team, respectively, to my scrutiny; they also showed me what teams could be and what it takes to realize that promise. As they would hasten to add, they did not do this alone and every team member and manager of the Occupational

Health and Environmental Safety Division deserves credit for this extraordinary accomplishment. Joshua Margolis was my research assistant when the field data for this study were collected and the organizational analysis was done. Without his energy, commitment, insight, and intelligence, this project would not have been feasible.

Many of my former colleagues at Harvard Business School gave me help, guidance, and insightful reviews of this research as it proceeded through its various stages. Benson Shapiro inspired me to learn more about the challenges of working across functions, and Kim Clark and Steve Wheelwright helped me with research sites and reviews of my work. I would like to thank Chris Argyris, Herminia Ibarra, Mary Gentile, Rosabeth Moss Kanter, and Dick Walton for their critiques of earlier forms of this manuscript. I also wish to express my gratitude to the Division of Research at Harvard for financing this research.

Several team researchers have also been extremely helpful in reading my work and challenging me to refine my analyses, including Deborah Ancona, Susan Cohen, Dan Denison, Russ Eisenstat, and especially Richard Hackman and Joseph McGrath. I would also like to thank Marcy Crary, Debbie Kolb, and Blair Sheppard for their encouragement, and my Babson College colleagues for giving me the opportunity to learn firsthand the joys and challenges of working as a member of a cross-functional team.

Many people contributed to the production of this book. Barbara Feinberg, Carol Franco, Janet Frick, and Marjorie Williams have each given me first-rate editorial help and assistance. Brenda Barrett, Jan Perry, and Meemee Swofford provided expert word-processing and graphics assistance with graciousness, often under trying conditions and pressing deadlines. Finally, I would like to thank my husband, Ed Ottensmeyer for his love, his thoughtful advice on the substance of my work, his tireless support of my efforts, and his "team work" at home and in caring for our daughter Jane.

Team
Talk

PART I

Introduction

The past ten years of brouhaha over work teams have left managers and professionals in a quandary: we know we need teams (for at least certain organizational tasks), and we've learned a lot about them, but while the demands for high performance teams continue to increase, our ability to create and sustain them has plateaued. Where there should be enhanced capability, greater confidence in the process, and satisfaction with outcomes, there is a growing sense of disappointment, frustration, and cynicism.

This book explains that gap between the ideal and the real by presenting a different perspective on teams—a perspective that shows what is actually happening in teams of professionals and explains how the particulars of organizational design, managerial behavior, and individual preference shape those team dynamics. The perspective focuses on team talk as the medium through which team work is done and through which organizational and individual forces can be observed and analyzed.

In part I, this perspective is explained. Chapter 1 provides an overview of the book. It explains the gap between the ideal and the reality of team work in terms of the paradoxical challenges that team work poses for organizations, managers, and team members. It also explains why organizations need to accommodate their systems, structures, and culture to the requirements of team work.

Chapter 2 develops the argument that to understand teams, we need to understand team talk. This chapter explains sociolinguistics and demonstrates its power as an intellectual approach for analyzing teams. It identifies six key dimensions of team talk that distinguish real teams from teams in name only, and presents the team talk audit, a tool for describing and analyzing team talk.

CHAPTER 1

A Different Perspective on Teams

Team Xerox, Team Disney, the Taurus team, the Mac team, quality improvement teams, customer service teams, new product teams . . . from advertisement to editorial, from management presentation to consulting report, we have been regaled with the language of teamwork for at least a decade. The team concept still has such cachet that teams continue to be adopted by organizations in virtually every sector of the economy. The litany of benefits from teams has become a cliché.

Many managers, struggling to cope with intensifying competitive pressures, claim that the team approach produces higher productivity, lower labor costs, and more committed employees. The success of Japanese companies in ensuring product quality and accelerating development-cycle time has led numerous U.S. companies to emulate the extensive collaborative efforts through which these outcomes are achieved. Self-managing teams are touted as the keystone to leaner and more flexible organizations capable of adjusting rapidly to market shifts and technological advances. Cross-functional teams have considerable currency now as a means to generate more creative, less problem-riddled solutions, faster.

From the perspective of employees, work in teams offers unique benefits. To hourly workers, team work typically provides greater autonomy and job satisfaction.[1] For the professional employee seeking achievement and personal fulfillment, teams provide the significant responsibility and the sense of community so many desire.[2]

The realities of a tumultuous business environment and a demanding work force have converged with organizational theorists' argument[3] that teams are a logical organizational form for getting work done more effectively in today's organization. From this accumulation of support, it would be reasonable to expect that work teams were not only thriving but performing well in U.S. organizations. It does appear that teams of hourly employees are producing the desired results.[4] However, there is no solid evidence that teams at the professional and managerial level[5] have delivered on their promise. Instead there is a mounting sense of disillusionment, skepticism, and even cynicism about team work. Managers privately express frustration with the time and costs associated with development of teams and keen disappointment with the results their teams are delivering. Team members voice their considerable doubts about management's commitment to teams "as the way to do our work," in part to justify their own neglect or counterproductive behavior vis-à-vis the team. Anecdotal evidence is beginning to suggest that companies, teams, and individuals are finding the transition to teams very slow and very painful.[6]

Such disparity between the ideal and the real is not just surprising. In light of the competitive pressures that make team work a necessity and in view of the widespread adoption of teams throughout our society, it is disturbing to perceive inconsistencies between what teams can and should be and what they usually are. The danger is that, as teams fail to realize their potential, the team form will be discarded as just another organizational fad, and the tasks and goals that can best be accomplished by teams will fail to meet managerial expectations—or worse, to meet organizational needs.

THE CRITICAL NEED FOR TEAMS

Clearly, one of the reasons that teams are failing to meet expectations is that they are being used when they are not needed; that is, teams are being used inappropriately to do work that individuals can manage more efficiently.[7] This problem is easily addressed. Far more critical and troubling is the fate of teams assigned to perform the core organizational tasks linked to strategic goals. The now common strategic pressures to accelerate work processes,[8] while improving or maintaining quality and reducing costs, have created a form of interdependency among functional departments that is new to many organizations.

Formerly, most large, complex organizations divided work and responsibility sequentially so that each organizational unit was dependent on the units "upstream" in the workflow, but not on "downstream" units. Now, with acceleration of work processes as an additional strategic goal in so many companies, organizational units require constant communication and continuous mutual adjustment to the information produced in the process of doing the work. For example, to accelerate the development of high-quality products at the most competitive prices, product designers must take manufacturing constraints into consideration, and marketers must respond quickly to design implications of those constraints. Clearly, the most effective means for meeting these requirements and managing this kind of interdependence is a small work team.[9]

The type of task that needs[10] teams of professional- and managerial-level employees is one that requires the continuous integration of knowledge, experience, or perspective that cannot be found in one person but rather is distributed among several people.

Teams of professional and managerial employees are needed to manage such intensified interdependence. It is perplexing why many such teams are disappointing. Culturally, teams are a familiar and valued social structure—at least in the abstract—by Americans. Given the popular interest and participation in team sports and our historical traditions of democratic governance and collective action, teamwork could be expected to develop easily, naturally. Yet in work organizations this appears not to be the case. This is all the more surprising because we know the critical success factors for creating effective teams: clear and engaging direction; specific goals; appropriate membership; agreement on work procedures; team accountability; adequate resources; and appropriate information, education, and rewards.[11] Are organizations not providing their teams with these necessary conditions? Are these factors insufficient?

To understand why this accumulated knowledge is not producing the team dynamics and outcomes that organizations so clearly need, we need a different perspective on teams. We need a way of looking at teams that helps us understand how these important but abstract ideas about interdependence, distributed expertise, and integration are translated in the daily routines of teams. Interdependence of work units is one thing; being dependent on peers you don't know, can't understand, and have traditionally distrusted is a pit-of-the-stomach kind of thing. It's the kind of thing that keeps you awake at night or gives you ulcers. How do teams overcome these feelings and find ways to work together productively? Even the more concrete notions of accountability and rewards have more emotional and social meanings for team members than we have recognized. What does accountability really mean when each team member is juggling too much work and trying to satisfy a demanding manager, needy direct reports, and nebulous team requirements? What's rewarding under such circumstances: a $500 bonus, a weekend in Florida, a step up the precarious middle-manager ladder, or escape from team work?

UNDERSTANDING TEAMS THROUGH THE WAY THEY TALK

We need a perspective on teams that allows us to see and understand what's really happening and what isn't. We need to see how the designs and practices of organizations and managers are shaping the thoughts, feelings, and actions of team members and the dynamics of teams. To get at this, we have to look closely at the day-to-day realities of teams at work. We have to watch them doing their work together; we have to listen to teams talk.

Talk is the sine qua non of team work at the professional level.[12] For teams (though not necessarily for individual team members), the work they do *as a unit* is conversational. The conversations may be face to face, fax to fax, over the phone, or through electronic mail, but regardless of the channel used, teams do their work through language. That is, the work of most professional or managerial teams is to construct new meanings—in the form of new product developments, enhanced processes, or the solution to a vexing problem—by sharing and integrating their knowledge. Team work is essentially a linguistic phenomenon.

Talk plays other powerful roles in team work. Talk reflects people's thoughts and feelings, even those we'd like to hide. It creates thoughts and feelings in the listeners (and sometimes in the speaker). Talk enhances or inhibits relationships, problem solving, and learning, among other things. To understand how team talk does all these things, consider a team member who interrupts others, asks questions but doesn't wait for answers, and makes jokes at the expense of other team members. These ways of talking display a perception that she has greater power than others. With her talk, she reinforces that relationship and probably creates negative feelings in others, thus making it harder for her to influence them. If she can't influence the other team members, her views of what the team should do are unlikely to prevail, which may have positive or negative outcomes for the organization.

Team talk can also reveal the effects of organizational features—like the performance evaluation and reward system, the career system, and the corporate culture—on team members and team dynamics. For example, the way team members talk to one another indicates the extent to which they feel interdependent. Perceptions of interdependence are created through the performance and reward systems (both formal and informal) of the organization. Despite "team player" traits being included in formal performance reviews, teammates may exhibit only moderate degrees of interdependence because career paths make them more dependent on their managers than on their peers. These organizational features thus shape the way team members think and feel about their relationships to, and the way they act toward, one another; and in the case of teams, the acts are conversational. The conversations of teams thus provide a window on the dynamic relationship between teams and their organizations, and on the internal dynamics of teams.

This book looks through that window at the day-to-day realities of a particular type of team—the cross-functional product development team—to offer insight on the experiences of other professional-level teams. The book offers a relatively unobstructed view of such teams at work. It also provides a special perspective for recognizing and interpreting patterns in the dynamics of such teams, including your own. The perspective of this book is based on sociolinguistics, an interdisciplinary approach to understanding human interaction that is part anthropology and part linguistics.

A SOCIOLINGUISTIC LOOK AT TEAMS

Anthropologists study culture, that is, the values, norms, social routines, and structures of particular groups, describing them in rich detail and making comparisons across groups. Linguists study languages, identifying the recurring patterns of behavior and inferring the underlying system of meaning that shapes linguistic choices. Sociolinguistics draws on the theories and methodologies of both disciplines to explain the connections between sociocultural factors and linguistic behavior.[13]

The challenging aspect of both anthropology and linguistics is that culture and language have the same enigmatic quality of being easily interpreted but difficult to explain.[14] In their native culture and language, adults and children can converse with competence and fluidity, but even adults cannot typically explain the grammatical or pragmatic[15] rules that they are following when they talk. In social settings as well, members of the same culture show their shared understandings of what is occurring by acting appropriately, even though they cannot readily articulate all the "rules" shaping such occasions.[16] For example, if the majority of us in the United States were asked to describe a typical American Christian wedding, we'd probably talk about a white dress and a veil, bridesmaids, groomsmen, a cake, and dancing. We might not mention sitting on different sides of the church or what to do in a reception line, yet we know what to say when asked which side, and we know to get into the line and await our turn to greet the married couple and their families.

The sociolinguistic approach meets the challenge of inexplicability by providing analytical methods that identify recurring patterns in the language and the culture of particular groups and that support the inference of the underlying meanings that shape those patterns. The power of sociolinguistics as an intellectual tool for revealing conversational patterns and linking them to underlying cultural phenomena has been demonstrated recently in two best-selling books by Deborah Tannen.[17] In *You Just Don't Understand,* Tannen identifies the conversational styles of women and men, explains how these styles are learned and reinforced culturally, and shows how consequential these stylistic differences may be for relationships. Tannen's *Talking From 9 to 5* focuses on conversation at work, identifying gender-related patterns of talk, and linking them to career and organizational outcomes.

Other sociolinguistic analyses of workplace conversation have also shown the power of this approach in discovering important interconnections among social structure, conversational patterns, and work outcomes. Organizational communication researchers Gail Fairhurst and Theresa Chandler,[18] interested in the process by which formal leaders create different relationships with each of their subordinates, found conversational differences that correlated with differences in the performance level of the subordinates. Linguist Charlotte Linde[19] studied tape recordings of cockpit conversations and found that co-pilots are likelier to use patterns of indirect speech than are pilots. That is, rather than directly asserting an opinion that a take-off or landing should be aborted, co-pilots tended to make observations about weather conditions. These patterns of difference correlate with the difference in the hierarchical rank of the pilot and co-pilot and can be heard in conversations during flight simulations and in those recorded prior to actual accidents. The occasionally dire consequences of these patterns can also be "heard" when that indirectness is followed by a crash.

The sociolinguistic approach produces its interpretations through an interpretive methodology that integrates anthropological information and recorded conversational data. The process begins with the thorough description of the situation,[20] sampling of real conversational episodes, then proceeds to identifying empirical regularities in the talk. The next step is to show how these patterns "contribute to participants' interpretations of each other's motives and intents."[21] *Intent* to sociolinguists refers not to a psychological state but to the observable interpretations of each other's language that participants display when they respond.[22]

The specific research question determines how the linkage between sociolinguistic patterns and interactional effect is made. For example, in an investigation of how ethnically distinct styles of conversation affect committee interaction, Gumperz and Cook-Gumperz[23] identified episodes of misunderstanding, then studied verbatim transcripts to determine how and why these occurred and what they meant to the committee members. Fairhurst and Chandler,[24] who were developing a theory of the leadership process, compared episodes of conflict to learn how perceptions of power and social distance are created conversationally.

Guided by the sense that culture and language were the keys to understanding the disparity between values about and practice of team work, I started this study of the team experience in the field. To understand the realities of team work and to discover what dimensions of team talk were important to study, I stepped into the product development arenas of four large U.S. corporations and immersed myself in their worlds. I watched and listened and recorded numerous cross-functional teams as they expressed their points of view, offered their expertise, argued about differences, and made decisions. I read their team design documents, their procedural materials, their press releases. I asked questions—of team members and others in the organizations— about what they were doing, thinking, and feeling, and why. I listened to them explain the meanings of their actions and their talk.

In effect, I studied their cultures and learned their languages. By this I mean that I learned their corporate cultures and workplace language. Although national cultures[25] and ethnic subcultures[26] play a significant role in shaping workplace dynamics, the teams I studied were all situated in the United States and consisted largely of white males. The cultural differences observed were essentially at the level of corporate culture.

OBSERVING DIFFERENCES IN TEAM WORK

I soon learned the importance of distinguishing between teamwork and team work, for not all team work conformed to the ideal of cooperation and sacrifice of individual interests to group goals connoted by the term *teamwork*. I came away convinced that we would all benefit from greater specificity in our terms. For the remainder of this book, I use the phrase *team work* to refer to the work that teams do and the single word *teamwork* to refer to the ideal defined above. As team researchers Katzenbach and Smith[27] point out, the word *team* itself is overused and lacks clarity, typically because it tends to be used interchangeably with the word *group*. My observations of cross-functional product development teams struggling to accomplish critical organizational tasks led me to create a definition of *team* that distinguishes it from other organizational forms, paving the way for appropriate use and support of teams. A team, as I define it, is *a group of people who are necessary to accomplish a task that requires the continuous integration of the expertise distributed among them.*[28]

The most obvious difference I observed in these organizations was in the satisfaction—of managers and team members—with the cross-functional teams they had created. In three of the four organizations, it was the consensus view that teams were not living up to their potential. In the teams of three organizations, what collaborations I observed were tentative and fragile, threatened by confusion, stress, conflict, and skepticism on the part of team members and their managers. In the fourth company, virtually all those interviewed felt that their teams had exceeded their expectations. The energy and excitement of the teams was palpable. Team dynamics in this organization were markedly different from those observed in the other companies. Team members exploited their differences through collaborative negotiation. Conflicts were common and typically confronted openly. They were resolved by the teams themselves, as they integrated their range of knowledge, expertise, and opinions in the interest of the team task. In short, these teams talked in remarkably different ways from their colleagues in the other organizations.

In comparing the design and implementation of teams in these four companies, I also identified similarities and differences in these organizational contexts that parallelled the patterns in the team talk. In three of the companies, the contexts for team work were variations on a similar theme. The divisional strategic goals, the purposes for creating teams, the basis and process of team membership and leadership, and the degree of actual and perceived interdependence were similar in kind. Furthermore, in none of these companies were teams or managers given training in how to work in or manage teams. Teams were thus interpreted and treated like a black box, matter-of-factly pulled off the shelf of corporate "programs" and used with little or no explicit attention given to the process of team work.

This recognition of the similarities among three organizations came into clearer focus through comparison with the fourth organization, where the sounds of team work were so distinctive. Here the organizational context of the teams was also dramatically different from the other companies. On numerous dimensions this company, a division of 3M, stood in stark contrast to the others. Its unique and deliberate alignment of the numerous organizational factors that influence teams was the result of a thoughtful, incremental accommodation to the requirements of the team process.

When all the data on teams and organizational contexts are taken as a set, a powerful explanation for the gap between the real and the ideal emerges: teams are laboring heroically under a cascade of contradictory pressures, the scope and weight of which few seem to comprehend. These tensions were evident everywhere in my data—in each company, in virtually every interview, meeting, and observation. The tensions of team work occur *within teams* as they grapple with the dilemma of how to integrate their differences, *within individuals* as they try to adjust to being team members, and *within organizations*, as they shift about to make sense of, and room for, teams as a new form of professional work.

A CASCADE OF PARADOXES AND CONTRADICTIONS

The American Heritage Dictionary defines *paradox* as "a seemingly contradictory statement that may nonetheless be true."[29] Organizational researchers Kenwyn Smith and David Berg define *paradox* as a constant struggle between apparently opposing values. They also argue that group experience is inherently paradoxical, in that "individual members experience the group as being filled with contradictory and opposing emotions, thoughts, and actions that *co-exist* inside the group."[30]

Team Work as Paradox

Team work is inherently paradoxical, in that it comprises apparently contradictory elements, each of which is true. Team work requires differentiation among members and integration of members into a single working unit.[31] The differences of knowledge, skill, experience, and perspective among team members are definitional. Without them, the team task (as defined above) cannot be accomplished, yet that task also demands that those different talents or insights be combined or integrated such that the members act as one. This seeming contradiction is nevertheless valid: The paradox of team work is that a balancing must occur between differentiation and integration. As one team member expressed it, "You need multiple interpretations—you can really get myopic within your own functional area—but the process needs to be managed." She alludes here to the problem that the differences required for the task tend to create conflict and divisiveness, which make their integration a constant challenge for teams.

Because team work is so paradoxical in nature, it is both difficult to understand and even harder to accomplish. Comprehending the opposition of differentiation and integration in team work and learning to manage the tension is necessary but not sufficient to guarantee teamwork. This is because, in addition to this central paradox, teams create a host of other paradoxes for team members in terms of their individual relations to and with the team.

Individual Paradoxes

Though the language varied and no one used the particular words *paradox* or *contradiction,* the team members in all four of my research sites described their experiences and interpretations of team work in paradoxical terms. They recognized the ostensible contradictions but seemed also to see that these were actually parts of the truth of effective team work. The cross-functional teams on which they served appeared to evoke four of the common paradoxes of group life:[32] the paradox of individuality, the paradox of identity, the paradox of interdependence, and the paradox of trust.

The Paradox of Individuality. The paradox of individuality as Ken Smith and David Berg describe it, is that the only way for a group to become a group is for individuals to express their individuality and to work on developing it as fully as possible, yet the only way for individuals to become fully individuated is for them to accept and develop more fully their connections to the group.[33]

This characterization is particularly true for teams because the task requirements for differentiation emphasize the individual skills and knowledge that each member brings. In order to add value to a team, a team member needs to draw on her distinctive expertise with the team. For the individual, whether the group is the team or the functional department, the sense of having distinctive value can be achieved only within the context of a group of which one is a member.

The team members I interviewed experienced this paradox as a dilemma of wanting to express and gain recognition for their individual talents and contributions but also wanting to be part of the team and enjoy the credit that the team received. In some cases, team members understood the need for teams but felt dissatisfied with the reality of the experience and wanted to avoid having their own accomplishments discounted by the team's mediocre performance. Here are some of their words on the subject:

> "I'm a team player, but I want rewards to be individual."

> "American culture trains you: here's the goal; you as an individual go out and do it; you win. . . . [Now we're expected to show] a willingness to set aside personal gain for the good of the organization."

> "You have to be able to let go of your own ego. You have to relinquish ideas to the team—let the ideas be the team's, not yours. This is tough."

"In a team, everyone has to give up a bit of himself or herself to make it work."

"I feel tarnished by their lack of performance."

"I want them to feel some ownership in the plan, but I'm not willing to risk achieving my own objectives. So if they go too far, I stop them."

Research suggests that this paradox of individuality may not be a universal experience, but rather a product of one's culture. A study of international differences in work-related values[34] compared countries in terms of their individualism, and discovered a considerable range on that cultural dimension. The United States, as might be expected, had the highest score on an individualism index: 91. The lowest score (12) was Venezuela; and the mean score for the thirty-nine countries compared was 51. To be a member of a team has a very different meaning in Japan (or Venezuela) than in the United States.

Given the weight of cultural pressure—from parents, schools, and other organizations—a person in the United States is likely to find it easier to be an individual and harder to be a team member, while the reverse is likely to be true for a Japanese person. This suggests that American team members facing demanding team work situations will be likelier to resolve the personal tensions they experience by doing what is best for them as individuals. This is the safest, the most familiar, and usually what the organization rewards. In so doing, team members emphasize their differences, making it harder to keep the necessary balance between differentiation and integration.

For cross-functional teams, these tilts toward the individual often overlap with, and are further justified by, one's identification with another group: the functional department. For all teams, because of the inherent diversity of members' expertise, there are always other groups with which team members identify. These multiple identities create another paradox for the individual.

The Paradox of Identity.   The paradox of identity, in Smith and Berg's terms, is that to be an individual, a person must integrate the variety of groups to which he or she belongs. In order to be a group, a collection of individuals must integrate the large array of individual differences that the members represent.[35]

The practical reality of organizational life is that over time people come to identify with their work groups. Research on groups, work roles, and professionalization consistently shows that this identification leads people to adopt the values, attitudes, and work habits of the group. Membership in multiple groups causes individuals to experience internal conflict, stress, and uncertainty.[36] The likelihood that a person will experience such feelings is increased when there is a conflict of values or interests between the groups of which the person is a member.

Cross-functional team work sets the stage for individuals to experience such crises of identity. The training, socialization, and work experience of professional employees contribute to the development of strong identification with their specialty and their functional department in the organization. Yet the assignment to a team charged with accomplishing a meaningful task of greater scope can also motivate personal commitment and identification with the team. Here are some of the expressions of this paradox I heard:

"The power of these teams is to neutralize the different areas people come from."

"If I were a shortstop for the Tigers and a first baseman for the Yankees, I wouldn't know what to do when they played each other."

"As a marketer, I'm supposed to push the customer's interests relentlessly, but as a member of this team, I have to take the others' circumstances into consideration."

"When push comes to shove, I've gotta do what my boss wants, regardless of what the team needs. 'Cause that's what I get paid for."

"Every team member has to have the common goal of the product, not the goal of getting their own job done . . . we want a successful product . . . None of us succeeds unless the product succeeds. The bottom line has to be, 'What are we trying to do here?' The answer is, 'Make a product.' "

"The blur between him and myself, and what we're doing, there's a definite crossover . . . he's straight R&D. I'm manufacturing. [But] I was doing product development work, and now he will be doing manufacturing."

The paradox of identity is especially difficult to manage because of the U.S. cultural emphasis on specialization and the development of professional expertise. This cultural norm has led to a situation in which most professionals enter the workforce with specialized training or degrees and a professional identity as a particular kind of specialist. Upon entry, they further develop the specialist skills, methodology, and identity. They learn how to be successful and effective by being a specialist, which reinforces this identity. When team members encounter conflicts between their functional identities and their team identities, their functional identity—being older, more reinforced, and more familiar—is likelier to win out. Since team members have different functional identities, these identities tend to push team members toward differentiation in times of conflict.

The Paradox of Interdependence. The paradox of interdependence is that, while "a group can function only if members are able to depend on each other . . . [and] ultimately this mutual dependency . . . makes the group a group,"[37] effective team work also depends upon some measure of independence in each member as well. Independence enables and motivates team members to import necessary information to the team and to exercise independent judgment in the face of groupthink.[38] Thus both dependence and independence are necessary to ensure the viability of the team.

For the typical team member, the bigger challenge lies in how to manage the dependency. The difficulty stems in part from the business (and cultural) priority attached to independence—for what professional's job description does *not* include such phrases as "takes initiative" or "capable of exercising independent action"? To express dependency in most business contexts, therefore, is not to measure up to professional standards. To complicate this, in order for the team to achieve appropriate sense of collective interdependence, dependency must precede independence. As Smith and Berg put it,

> there is no way for a group to develop a fabric of reliable interdependencies unless its individual members give expression to their dependency, even when this may mean depending on (trusting) that which has yet to be proved dependable.[39]

The majority of the team members interviewed tacitly understood this paradox. They talked about their dependency but tended to follow this up with assertions of independence, such as, "I depend on him to get me reliable information from customers. But if he doesn't deliver, I just go on basis of my experience, which is pretty good." Typically, this paradox produced the greatest tension when action was called for. Team members did not know how to manage the appropriate balance between their dependence on the team and the independence they had developed as part of their professional responsibility:

> "I have the primary responsibility for the product, but I'm also very dependent on them to achieve my own objectives."

> "When I'm feeling frustrated, it feels like there are two extremes. . . . Is the best thing to do is just be real nice with him, and patient? But then I'd get the ax because I'm seen as not being able to get the deliverables. . . . Or [I could] be a jerk, and say, 'The heck with it, they never deliver.' Then they'll do even less."

> "Another source of frustration for team members is that you're never absolved of responsibility. We're used to finishing our jobs and passing it on. It used to be 'Whose job is it?' It should have been someone else's but now if you really want the whole thing to get done and meet the total objective, you have to go beyond your own job."

> "The team leaders here are not experienced in managing conflict . . . so they don't manage the meetings effectively . . . but I'm not a crusader at this point. . . . My career is in the functional line. . . . It's not worth upsetting people and perhaps sacrificing promotions just to point out that someone's wasting the team's time."

As the last speaker most clearly indicates, another set of dependencies further complicates the situation: the vertical interdependencies between team members and their functional managers. Team members may be dependent on one another to execute their team task, but they are dependent on their functional managers for critical resources: jobs, salary, and promotions. Futhermore, the degree of dependence on the other team members that individuals experienced was a function of how much of their job entailed team work and whether team performance was actually measured and factored into individual performance assessments—in general, how important they as individuals felt the team work was.

In three of the organizations I studied, when team members were faced with situations of uncertainty and conflicting inclinations and emotions, they reported that typically they resolved such tensions in terms of independence from the team. They justified their behavior in terms of their functional responsibilities. Their actions in these situations thus emphasized their differences.

The Paradox of Trust.   The paradox of trust is that in teams, "one needs to trust others . . . where the development of trust depends on trust already existing. Before we are willing to trust others, we want know how they will respond."[40] Team members must trust one another, while at the same time remaining vigilant.

The paradox of trust is particularly acute among professional employees working for the first time with professionals from other disciplines. Having entered the organization with specialized training and education, they have "a 'readiness for directed perception' based on common procedures, judgments, and methods."[41] Through on-the-job training and the strictly functional work assignments that most professionals are typically given, these conventions of practice tend to crystallize into "thought worlds,"[42] systems of meaning of such intrinsic logic and coherence that professionals tend to interpret their work primarily in reference to those meanings. Developing a good product comes to mean developing a product at minimal cost for the manufacturing professional, of highest technical quality for the product engineer, and with the optimal mix of features as far as the marketer is concerned.

These competing interpretations may not be consciously recognized as such, in which case they tend to cause inaccurate attributions about the causes of team conflict or impasse. Drawing on habits and attitudes developed when they worked in isolated, functional worlds, many of the team members interviewed tended to attribute the problems the team experienced to individual incompetence or to competitive, self-centered attitudes prevalent in other departments. In reaction, they felt it their responsibility to defend their departments from the unreasonable demands of the other departments. Even team members who were not antagonistic toward the other functions talked about the importance of maintaining vigilant attention to the essence and implications of other team members' contributions.

Team members often characterized this paradox as the need to strike the right balance among the alternatives of trust and distrust, with the latter amounting to a constant testing or assessment of the others' opinions and expertise. Here is how they talked about disclosure and trust:

> "You need a level of trust that's just not there. Until there's that mutual trust, people won't let their guard down."

"I don't want to tell them they can take more time, because they'll take it."

"From a scheduling standpoint, Engineering's credibility was no good. . . . They were telling us dates that just weren't getting met." (Marketer) "We felt the changes would require more time than the schedule allowed. We went to the head of Marketing and said we needed more time. He said we had to stick to the dates we had." (Engineer)

"My ego can get involved. My job is to come up with ideas, and I've had my feelings hurt when my ideas have been criticized by my teammates. But we haven't had pitched battles, we've had skirmishes."

"You need risk takers at the division management level too. . . . That's real risk taking. He's taking risks on program that he's trusting people on. He knows the people, but he can't know the details about the project."

Typically, the dilemma was resolved with procedures that made trust unnecessary; thorough documentation and assignment of individual "ownership" and accountability relieved the team of the uncomfortable necessity of balancing judgment and trust. However, as the comments above indicate, virtually everyone recognized and regretted the cost of such distrust among team members. Though they did not say so in the same terms, they acknowledged that the distrust kept team members in their differentiated roles and inhibited integration.

The Cumulative Force of Individual Paradoxes

The feelings evoked by the paradoxical experiences that individuals have in team settings have a powerful impact on their behavior. Some of the individuals interviewed appeared to be paralyzed into inertia by their contradictory impulses, making an instinctive choice only when forced to do so. Others vacillated between the two extremes of the various paradoxes. Most of those interviewed, though, seemed inclined to resolve these paradoxes by tilting in the direction that their own individual preferences pushed them. As discussed above, the tilting was toward individuality, functional identification, independence, and distrust. Each of these inclinations led individuals on teams to talk and act in ways that differentiated them from other team members rather than in the ways that would integrate. The cumulative effect was that the teams could not achieve the necessary balance between the two critical functions of team work (see figure 1.1).

Organizational systems and structures can either reinforce those individual tendencies and compound the problems of teams, or they can create incentives for individuals to act differently. Paradoxes in the organizational systems can heighten the sense of paralysis, amplify the vacillation, and produce ineffective or destructive team talk, problematic team dynamics, and disappointing outcomes. Contradictory pressures on teams from the organization can also engender disillusionment with teams and cynicism about management's commitment to the espoused goals of the organization. This is precisely what I observed in three organizations.

Organizational Contradictions

As mentioned earlier, I found that competitive challenges have created a powerful set of contradictory messages and pressures on employees, painfully experienced by professionals working on teams. Trained in specialized fields of knowledge, conditioned to seek individual recognition and independence, led to believe that control is paramount and competition between functions within the organization will yield the best results, they find it extremely difficult to meet new demands for cooperation, information sharing, and joint decision making.

I discovered that these contradictions in the corporate culture that shaped individuals' experience were compounded by contradictions in the organizational environment of teams. Co-existing structures of functional hierarchy and cross-functional teams, and the persistence of evaluation and reward systems based on individual accountability and functional responsibility, created considerable tension in teams and their members. Strategic goals of quality improvement, cost control, and acceleration of the work cycle caused confusion and paralysis. Interim process measures of teams' progress mobilized teams to focus on those targets, often diverting their attention and effort from the desired outcomes. Finally, the focus on teams as the targets of change rather than acknowledging that the whole organization must adapt to the team technology created a kind of double bind for teams. They needed to work differently in order to realize the potential of team work, but the organizations were unwilling to change themselves in ways that would permit change in team members. The pressure of

Figure 1.1 The pressure of individual preferences on teams.

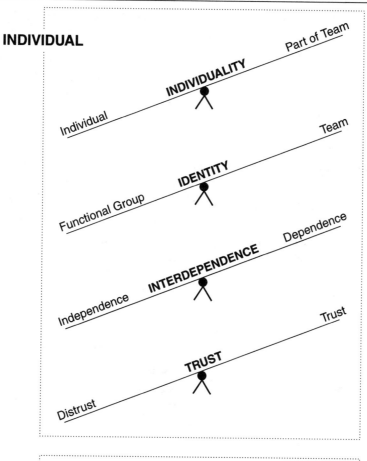

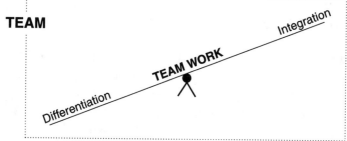

individual paradoxes and organizational contradictions can easily crush teams into a simpler, hardier form of existence. Indeed, most of the teams observed in this research adapted themselves well to their environments. They assimilated, making themselves into the kinds of teams that their organizations would tolerate. Unfortunately, these were not the kind of teams that produced the desired results.

THE CONUNDRUM OF TEAM WORK

These grim interpretations of my observations illuminate the central conundrum of team work: teams both reflect and affect the organizations of which they are a part. The language patterns through which the teams do their work are shaped by the organizational structures, systems, and cultures in which they are embedded. However, insofar as teams are the optimal forum for integrating the distributed expertise required for task accomplishment, the patterns of team interaction that affect the quality of the team work will influence what the organization can and will accomplish.

Thus, to realize their potential, teams require and ensure organizational change. The changes required are daunting, particularly in light of my earlier assertion that both individual interests and organizational designs derive from culture. Nevertheless, for organizations whose tasks demand team work, there is really no alternative.

How can organizations use teams as the vehicle for the required change? How can they keep from reproducing in teams the dynamics of functional competition, antagonism, and distrust they seek to replace with cross-functional collaboration? How do they break the cycle of negative mutual influence?

One drastic solution is proposed by management expert Peter Drucker,[43] who argues, "Gradual change cannot work. There has to be a total break with the past, however traumatic that may be." Radical as this suggested process of change is, Drucker's recommendations for the content of organizational change to produce teamwork stay well within the boundaries of the traditional bureaucratic model. He proposes that team members report to their team leaders only and that rewards, appraisals, and promotions should be wholly dependent on their team roles. Such changes amount to little more than an assimilation of the team form to current bureaucratic design. My research, however, indicates that to assimilate teams into the existing categories of organizational meaning (hierarchical prerogatives, functional division of labor, individual accountability, and an orientation to control) is to gain little from a change that, even if minimally implemented, can cause much disturbance in the system.

ACCOMMODATING THE ORGANIZATION TO TEAM WORK

A very different solution—both in process and content—can be discerned in the experiences of the fourth organization, the outlier in my research. Though the managers and team members did not talk in terms of contradictions, paradoxes, conundrums, or accommodation, their solution to the vexing challenges of team work helped me build the framework that explains how and why they were so different.

The solution started with the determination that teams are required for the achievement of the division's goals. Guided by a willingness to acknowledge and explore the novelty and complexity of team work, the people in this division set in motion a process of continuous *accommodation* of the organization to the requirements of team work. Their initial accommodations to team work included training all team members in this new way of working, assembling teams through recruitment for skills rather than through assignment by position, giving professionals choice over what team(s) to join, and allowing teams to establish their own goals. Over time, many other accommodations were made: training was expanded to include all managers and executives, managerial roles were clarified, and the orientation to control was reduced.

These changes in organizational design enhanced the personal responsibility that the professional employees felt and created strong commitments to the team and the task. This personal commitment provided the motivation for them to manage the conflictual, paradoxical tasks of integrating their differences. These accommodations thus helped offset—and conceivably even altered—the culturally given inclinations that individuals bring to teams. The three organizations that assimilated teams to the existing structures severely constrained the development of those teams by continuing to motivate individualistic and independent talk and action. As a result, the organizations not only failed to offset the individual preferences that create greater differentiation and less integration on teams, they compounded the pressure of the individual preferences. Thus, the teams in three of the organizations I studied found it difficult, if not impossible, to strike the appropriate balance between differentiation and integration.

The dynamics of teams struggling to manage the individual and organizational pressures are revealed in the talk of the teams. Knowing what to listen for, one can readily hear team members differentiating themselves from the rest of the team, hear efforts to resolve conflicts in ways that integrate rather than exaggerate differences, and perceive the organizational pressures that teams feel. In the next chapter, I will explain how talk reveals all this.

PLAN OF THE BOOK

In chapters 3 through 6, the stories of four organizations and four teams are told. Three of these organizations created and supported teams in ways that were merely variations on a single theme. They look too much alike to provide any real insight into the gap between the ideal of team work and its reality. However, in listening to all four teams as they work and talk, and comparing all four organizations and teams in the sample, it becomes clear why three organizations are disappointed with their team work. The contrasts point to a new way of organizing for team work and a new approach for analyzing and shaping team dynamics through talk.

Chapter 2 explains how talk reveals and influences team dynamics. Chapters 3 through 6 present the stories of the four organizations and their teams, demonstrating how team talk and organizational factors shape team dynamics. Chapter 7 summarizes the lessons about the power of language for team members in managing their day-to-day experiences. Chapter 8 summarizes the lessons for managers about listening to teams.

CHAPTER 2

Team Talk

A s established in chapter 1, talk is central to the work of teams. Typically, it is the primary medium through which information is exchanged, decisions are made, and plans are formulated. Beyond these obvious functions, team talk plays other powerful, though subtle, roles. The way a team talks reveals where the team is coming from and where it is headed. More importantly, talk is a tool for changing a team's destination, and it can even alter a team's point of origin. The purpose of this chapter is to explain how to analyze team dynamics through talk. Later in the book, you will learn how to use talk to shape team dynamics and create the capacity to enhance team outcomes and to retrofit the organization for team work.

TEAM DYNAMICS

What are the important dynamics in teams, and how does talk affect these? A common assumption is that a team's character or its typical dynamics are formulated by accumulating the individual traits and values of each team member (see figure 2.1). But it is far more complicated than that. Teams are work groups characterized by the interdependence (and, in the case of cross-functional teams, the diversity) of their

Figure 2.1 A commonly assumed relationship between individuals and teams.

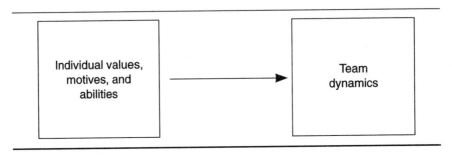

members. These two features create several important dynamics in teams:

1. *Identity crises.* Team members typically come into teams identifying more strongly with their functional group, yet the team's shared goals impose a new common identity on them, which may conflict with their functional identity.

2. *A requirement to manage interdependence.* By virtue of their team membership, individuals who are trained and socialized to think and act independently must learn how to act when they are interdependent.

3. *A requirement to manage power differences.* To manage differences and interdependence without threatening a precarious team identity, teams need to manage the power differences among team members.

4. *A potential for social closeness.* Given the shared identity and diversity of team members, how close are team members socially?

5. *The inevitablilty of conflict.* Differences of perspective, opinion, and interests within a team inevitably create conflict; whether it is constructive or destructive conflict is critical to team effectiveness.

6. *A requirement for negotiation.* To resolve the crises and conflicts created by diversity and interdependence, teams need to negotiate.

Obviously, some of these dynamics start as struggles within individuals, such as the problem of where you identify or how to cope with being dependent on someone who is different from you. Others—like conflict and negotiation—clearly occur among team members. Virtually all these internal dynamics of teams are amplified, if not created, by organizational factors (see figure 2.2 for a depiction of these relationships). For example, organizations with strong functional subcultures amplify the identity crises that team members experience when they join cross-functional teams. Organizations with evaluation and reward systems that focus on individual performance increase the likelihood of conflict in teams, and the probability that team members will use differences in power to influence one another in directions that make their own individual performance look better.

Yet teams typically do not examine their dynamics or diagnose and treat their causes. Instead team members tend to blame one another for the problems the team experiences: "He's incompetent," "She's always got a different opinion from the rest of us," "He talks a good game but doesn't follow through," "She doesn't speak up in meetings but always manages to impose her views." Such judgments of individual

Figure 2.2 Factors shaping team dynamics.

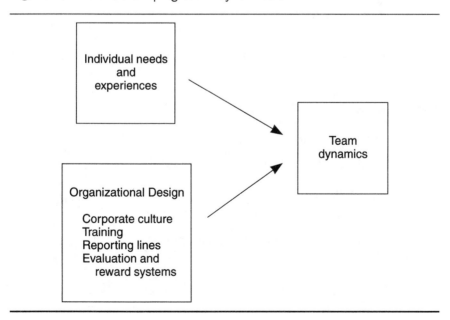

blame are based on the observed behavior of team members, a significant proportion of which is talk. This is ironic because closer attention
to the language that teams use as they do their work would enable
team members to recognize the many factors, other than individual
motives and abilities, that shape the behavior.

Listening to teams as they work, you can hear them struggling with
conflicting identities and using the differences of power among them
to resolve disputes. You can hear and assess the dynamics of the team
by listening to the language the team uses. These dynamics occur in
the talk of teams. Talk thus reveals the team dynamics as well as the
pressures of the organization on the team and its members. But team
talk does more than just reveal team dynamics; it creates them. The
language that team members use as they work together has consequences. If certain team members consistently remind others of their
power differential, those differences create differences in the contributions of team members, as the less powerful defer to the more powerful.
When team members negotiate with one another as if the situation
would create winners and losers, other members adopt similar language.
Language thus creates thoughts, feelings, and behavior in team members, which affect the way the team uses power, manages conflict, and
negotiates. The way this occurs is explained more fully later in the
chapter. Figure 2.3 depicts the distinctive role of team talk in shaping
team dynamics.

Figure 2.3 The role of team talk in team dynamics.

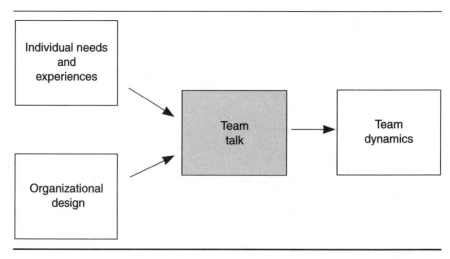

Team talk, because it is so influential in shaping team dynamics, also influences the organization. As teams deliver their joint products or outcomes, organizations are influenced by them. For example, one of the organizations you will meet in the next section of the book overcame stagnant growth through the introduction of teams; it also gradually changed many of its structures and systems in response to team initiatives to ensure that its teams would flourish. In another organization in this study, poor team dynamics not only contributed significant loss of return on investments, they also ended up costing the organization its survival as an independent division. Team dynamics thus shape the organization. Figure 2.4 depicts the full set of relationships among organizations, individuals, teams, and language.

KEY DIMENSIONS OF TEAM TALK

Let's look specifically now at how important team dynamics are revealed and shaped by language. The distinctive dynamics of teams discussed above identify six key categories or dimensions of team talk:

Figure 2.4 The cyclical relationship of organizations, teams, and language.

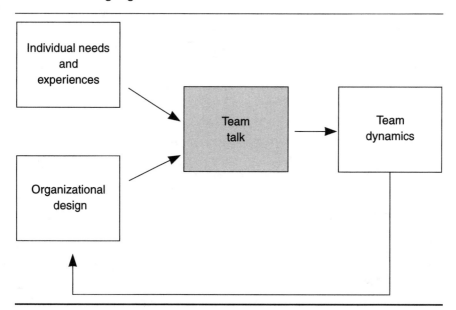

1. *Identification* (with what group team members identify).
2. *Interdependence* (whether team members feel independent from or interdependent with one another).
3. *Power differentiation* (how much team members use the differences in their organizational power).
4. *Social distance* (whether team members feel close to or distant from one another socially).
5. *Conflict management tactics* (whether members use the tactics of force or collaboration to manage their conflicts).
6. *Negotiation process* (whether the team uses a win-lose or win-win process).

The types of words, sentences, and patterns of speech that a team uses repetitively create a sense of how team members think and feel about each other and about their task. Listeners form these impressions often without thinking about what they are hearing or even about what it means. To be more systematic about diagnosing a team's problems, imagine that each of these dimensions is a continuum and that you can analyze a team's talk and place it at some point along each continuum. To do this, you need to know which language or linguistic forms produce the meanings of different points along each continuum. Table 2.1 presents the linguistic forms that research[1] has found to produce specific social meanings. These linguistic forms help us form crude assessments about whether a team is at one end of the continuum, the other, or somewhere between, as figure 2.5 indicates. At one end of dimension is the kind of talk you would expect to hear in a real team, and at the other is the kind of language you would expect from people who were a team in name only.

Doing this kind of interpretive work sounds more complicated than it is. In fact, we make such interpretations of people's talk continually and unconsciously every day. The approach taken here is simply a more mindful and systematic focus on the kind of language that makes a difference in team work. Each of the key dimensions of team talk is explained in greater detail below.

Identification

Organizational groupings provide people with a common identity. From this common identity, group members develop shared values and similar

Table 2.1 Dimension, forms, and examples of team talk.

Dimensions and Forms	*Examples*
I.　Identification	
A. *Functional Identification*	
Inclusive pronouns refer to functional groups	"we" "our" "us"
Reference to functional groups	marketing, engineering
B. *Team Identification*	
Inclusive pronouns referring to team	"we" "our" "us"
II.　Interdependence	
A. *Independence Forms*	
Explicit reference to independence	"We can design this product without your input."
Assertions of individual intent	"I'm going to tell the customer to expect it Tuesday."
Failure to respond to questions	
B. *Interdependence Forms*	
Acknowledgment of mutual interests	"If we can pull this off, our careers will be made."
Expressions of own needs	"I need to know your opinion before I go on."
Soliciting of others' views and needs	"How do you feel about my idea?"
Proposals of joint action	"Let's review our progress to date."
Explicit reference to interdependence	"We need to decide whether this meets our goals."
III.　Power Differentiation	
A. *High*	
Certainty	"I believe we are doing this the wrong way."
Challenges	"Why do you think that?"
Challenges to competence	"Do you have an agenda for this meeting?"
Corrections	"That's not right."
Directness	"I want you to have these data tomorrow."
Interruptions	
Leading questions	"Did you tell us you would have that report today?"
Orders	"Tell me what happens at that meeting."
Repetition of questions	
Topic change	"Moving right along. What about X?"
Verbal aggression	"If you can't do this, we'll have to find someone else."
Excessive or asymmetrical politeness	"Would you be so kind as to . . . ?"
B. *Low*	
Apologies	"Sorry. My other meeting ran over time."
Disassociations of self from request	"The team will need you to take this to management."
Disclaimers	"I'm no engineer, but. . . ."
Indirect questions	"Is there a way this could be done quickly?"
Hedges	"I'm thinking out loud here, but. . . ."
Politeness	"John, could you please tell us more about that?"
Stating one's debt to other	"I am indebted to you for your participation."

Table 2.1 Continued

Dimensions and Forms	Examples
IV. Social Distance	
A. *Social Distance Forms*	
Accounts using formal language	"Our perspectives are convergent."
Formal forms of address	"Mrs. Smith. . . ."
Excessive politeness	"Would you be so kind as to. . . . ?"
Impersonal requests or assertions	"Is it possible for you to review this quickly?"
Literal response to question about relationship	Q: "What does your other commitment do to our 4:30 meetings?"
	A.: "Shortens them."
B. *Social Closeness Forms*	
Casual style, using of slang	"What's up?"
Use of nicknames	
Slurring of pronunciation or ellipsis	"Whatta ya gonna do?" "Dunno."
Claiming commonalities in group membership	"We're all part of the team."
Claiming common views	"I see what you mean."
Displaying knowledge and concern for others' wants	"You're asking whether you need to file that form."
Empathy	"I understand your dilemma."
Expressions of liking or admiration	"I knew you could do it."
Expressions of reciprocity or cooperation	"I'll owe you."
Familiar address	"Pal."
Similar language	
V. Conflict Management Tactics	
A. *Forcing/Avoiding/Accommodating Forms*	
Directives	"Do it in the format she needs."
Threats	"We'll have to take this up with your boss."
Acquiescence	"Okay."
Use of Power Differences	
Voting	"How many think we should pursue this?"
B. *Confronting Collaborating Forms*	
Expression of interest, problem, need	"To get you timely feedback, I need the specs soon."
Questions seeking others' needs	"What do you need to know from us to do it?"
Synthesis of interests	"If you drop that requirement, I can meet your others."
Nonthreatening tone to debates	"We could look at these data another way."
Restatement of dissenting views	"You are saying you're not persuaded we need this."
Analysis of implications or consequences	"If we go that route, what are associated costs?"

Table 2.1 Continued

Dimensions and Forms	Examples
VI. Negotiation Process	
A. *Win-Lose Forms*	
Expressions of positions	"We have always said we need A before B."
Lexicon of debt, concession	"We'll be selling everyone out."
Use of power differences to win	
B. *Win-Win Forms*	
Reframing or reinterpreting in light of others' ideas	"So, as long as I cover the costs, I can speed up the. . . ."
Exploration of implications	"How would it affect you if I . . . ?"
What-if questions	"What if we justified the additional costs?"
Using objective criteria for resolution	"What data would we all need to persuade us?"

patterns of behavior.[2] The challenge for work teams, especially of professional-level employees, is the management of multiple identities.[3] Professionals tend to identify strongly with their disciplines (and functional department), which often have different values and ways of acting and talking, and interpret the cross-functional task in very different, sometimes mutually contradictory ways.[4] On the other hand, the team task creates a new grouping and imposes a new shared identity for team members.

In their interaction, we would expect that members of real teams would display at least as much identification with the team and other team members as with their functional departments. Repeated references to functional groups and identifications with the functional department, especially in the absence of team identification, would usually indicate that this is a nominal team. The primary linguistic forms of identification are the inclusive plural pronouns "we" and "you" and the exclusive, "they."[5] Obviously, analysis of the linguistic context of these forms is required to determine whether such pronouns refer to the team or the functional group.

Interdependence

Interdependence is a central defining characteristic of work teams because team members, by virtue of their shared responsibility, are

Figure 2.5 Key dimensions of team interaction.

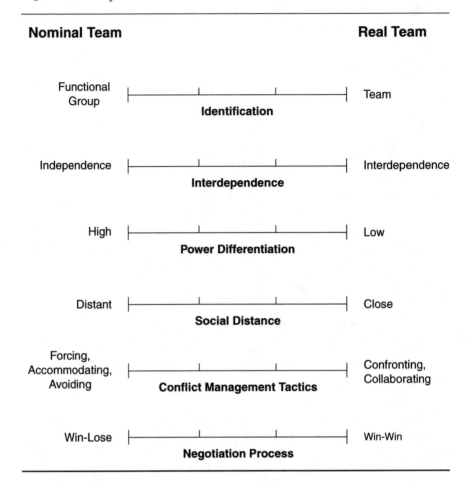

dependent upon one another. However, this interdependence is not always perceived by all of the members of the team. In fact, the primary distinction between a real team and a nominal team is the common perception of interdependence among members of a real team. When team members feel themselves to be interdependent in the process of achieving the task and goals, they not only reflect this in their talk but they also *use it*. The linguistic signs of interdependence remind other team members of their mutual dependencies and solicit appropriate contributions to the necessary integration. Forms that mark such inter-dependence include acknowledgment of mutual interests and expressions of one's own needs,[6] proposals for joint action,[7] and solicitation of others' views, needs, and preferences.[8]

At the opposite end of this continuum, the interaction of nominal teams is notable for both the absence of such interdependence talk as well as the presence of linguistic signs of perceived independence from other team members. Forms that express independence include assertions of individual intent and challenges to the other,[9] and failures to respond to the questions of others.[10]

Distinctions along this dimension are subtle, however, and depend upon the rest of the conversation for interpretation. For example, "expressions of own needs" could indicate independence, even selfishness or defiance of the team, in a statement like "I need that information tomorrow regardless of the team's schedule." To reflect perceptions of interdependence, the expression of one's own needs must occur in the context of expressed mutual interest or interdependency. Similarly, an "assertion of individual intent" could reflect a perception of interdependence if the statement is made *after* a joint team decision, as a summation of one's own role in the plan developed together.

Power Differentiation

Research on groups has repeatedly found that the display of power differences within groups produces numerous negative effects, from the suppression of opinions to conformity of behavior.[11] Given that groups solve problems better[12] and make decisions more effectively[13] than individuals *because* multiple perspectives and sources of knowledge and skill are brought to bear on the problem, the persistent use of power differences in teams is likely to affect teams' performance negatively.

Theoretically, the task interdependence that characterizes teams should motivate team members to contribute whatever they can to the team's efforts, *regardless of their relative power.* Of course, the power distribution within the larger organization is likely to be reflected in the interaction of all teams to some extent, as members employ conversational tactics to preserve their status[14] and to influence others. However, real teams are likely to deemphasize these differences—either deliberately, to avoid suppressing valuable contributions, or unconsciously, because organizational identities are less important than the team identity. Members of nominal teams are likely to use forms that reflect perceived differences of power because they are more oriented to the organization than to the team, more accustomed to using the power differences, and less concerned with threats to the team and its goals. The linguistic forms that show perceptions of power differences (between speaker and listener) are numerous, since this subject has been extensively researched.

The forms of talk that emphasize differences of power between speaker and listener include dominating the floor, interruption, questioning, demands and directives, topic changes, and challenges.[15] These forms are easy to recognize and, when they are repeatedly used by the same people, are typically interpreted as displays and use of power. When team members with greater organizational power refrain from using such forms of talk, they are minimizing the differences of power among members of the team. The linguistic forms that actively minimize the power differences between speaker and listeners include apologies,[16] disclaimers, hedges, indirect questions and requests, and politeness.

Social Distance

Since power differentiation in team interaction suppresses contributions or reduces commitment to team goals, there must be another process by which team members can influence one another. Social exchange theory[17] suggests that linguistic displays of social closeness may fulfill this function. By signaling closeness or inclusion, speakers invite reciprocal feelings and the accommodation that such relationships require.

In one model of social influence, researchers[18] demonstrated how linguistic forms of social closeness produce social calibration and compliance by minimizing attention to disparities in the social exchange. The model implies, for example, that addressing a team member by her nickname signals a closeness that, if warranted and desirable, can distract her from calculating whether the request for support is reasonable and can instead motivate similar feelings of closeness and obligation. In team work, this effect would serve multiple purposes: (1) reducing the attention given to calculating, monitoring, and altering social debts, (2) increasing the attention that could be focused on task accomplishment, and (3) reinforcing team identify.

In the conversation of a real team, where there is a shared identity, a common perception of interdependence and a commitment to the task, we would expect to observe linguistic forms of social closeness.

These include an informal style of speech, claims of common group membership, claims of common views, displays of knowledge of or concern for others' wants, expressions of liking or admiration, nicknames, presumptive requests or statements, similar word use, empathy, and humor.[19]

We might see nominal teams expressing social closeness, for reasons other than a shared identity and the need to influence one another without use of power differentiation. For example, the team members might know and like one another. However, it is more likely that such groups would not display social closeness because even if some team members are close, the presence of less familiar people establishes a level of social interaction at a more socially neutral level. Social distance could be shown by the absence of closeness forms or by specific linguistic forms such as formal language, disagreement, disconfirmation, failure to acknowledge or respond to others' comments, and literal response to questions about relationship.[20]

Conflict Management Tactics

To say that team work inherently involves diversity and interdependence is to acknowledge that conflict is both inevitable and desirable. It also means that conflict management will be a common and critical task for teams and that the amount of conflict does not distinguish real teams from nominal teams. The absence of conflict in a group may be more problematic than its presence.[21] Therefore, it is the tactics for managing the conflict that distinguish a real team from a nominal one.

Researchers[22] have identified five different types of tactics used to manage conflict that vary in terms of their assertiveness and cooperativeness, including avoidance, accommodation, forcing, compromise, and collaboration. Avoidance of conflict in teams is a common but disastrous approach to managing differences: it does not exploit the differences that teams are designed to take into account. Accommodating is the willingness to meet the needs of the other, even at the expense of your own. If team members make concessions that ignore or minimize their own perspective or expertise, chances are that the team's outcomes will be less than optimal. Similarly, if team members try to manage conflicts by forcing their opinions, this behavior will have the same negative effect. Compromise is seen by many managers as the optimal approach to managing conflicts because it seems fair to give up something to get something. Compromise also takes less time than collaboration, which attempts to meet all parties' concerns and needs as fully as possible. In the context of team work, in which differences need to be integrated into a whole that is greater than the sum of its parts, compromise is not desirable because one or more perspectives may not be fully considered. Only the tactics of collaboration can provide the basis for integration, by surfacing differences and discovering overlapping interests.[23]

The linguistic forms that constitute tactics of forcing, avoiding, and accommodating are similar to those that differentiate power. Forcing also includes commands, directives, and threats.[24] The linguistic signs of accommodation and avoidance are typically the absence of self-assertive behavior in the context of forcing behavior. Compromise can be seen in the delaying or redirecting of conflictual decisions, and in voting. Repeated use of such forms identify a team as nominal rather than real. Teams that are focused on integrating their differences (that is, real teams) use confrontation and collaboration tactics of soliciting all members' views and preferences, redefining the problem to take those views into account.[25] Consensus and dissent are explicitly sought. On real teams, we would not expect to find conflicts delegated to the hierarchy for resolution.

Negotiation Process

When teams focus on resolving their conflicts to achieve mutual agreements, they are negotiating. Negotiation theorists[26] have identified two distinct processes for resolving differences among negotiators: win-lose and win-win. The former focuses on the competitive aspect of the negotiation, treating it as a distribution of wins and losses among the negotiating parties. The latter seeks to "integrate the parties and hence yield high joint benefit."[27] These two types of process are the endpoints on a continuum of team negotiation.

Some organizational team work amounts to win-lose negotiation, typically as a result of competitive pressures outside the team, such as resource scarcity or rigid functional accountability. Linguistically, a win-lose orientation is manifest through explicit expressions of positions rather than interests,[28] use of power differences to win, and words that refer to dividing things, or to debt, concession, winning and losing.[29] A win-win negotiation process, especially in the early stages, may include assertions of individual interests that are difficult to distinguish from assertions of positions. However, a win-win orientation ultimately is shown through talk such as the elaboration of the others' ideas,[30] exploration of the implications of the others' ideas,[31] and reevaluation or reframing of one's own interests in light of the others'.[32]

ANALYZING AND ASSESSING TEAM TALK

The process of analyzing and assessing team talk is essentially the same for any researcher, whether that person is an outsider observing the team or a team member assessing how the team functions. (However, a more detailed description of the methodology used in this research is provided in appendix A.) The steps in brief are:

1. Record the data.
2. Describe the data.
3. Analyze the data and assess the team along the key dimensions.

The researcher starts the process by listening to and watching a team at work, while recording samples of specific linguistic behavior during episodes when the team is engaged in lively conversation. The most revealing pieces of conversation are those in which the team is making a decision or debating. You will be more systematic in your description and analysis if you record such conversational episodes on audiotape or videotape and can replay them several times. However, sometimes a team will be reluctant to submit itself to such scrutiny, and taping will create more antagonism and discomfort than additional insight. An alternative is to listen in on and describe several conversations as guided by the team talk audit in table 2.2, answering each question and noting unique forms of talk as they occur. If you have been able to record some conversations, then follow the same procedure for describing the data by answering the questions on the team audit.

Then next step is to analyze what these data mean. For example, do the forms of talk indicate that the team identifies more with their functional groups or with the team? The audit guides your description and assessment by asking you to pay attention to words, syntax, turn taking, topic changing, hesitations, as well as using your knowledge of each person's typical speech style, role, and power in the company.

From these data, the audit helps you to assess your team by placing it at one of three points on the continuum: at one of the endpoints or in the middle. Using the team audit can initially be challenging, and you may require multiple iterations to feel confident of your own assessment. It will probably also be helpful to ask another team member to go through the same exercise and compare assessments. Before using the audit on your team(s), read the next four chapters to observe how sociolinguistic analysis is done.

Table 2.2 Team talk audit for assessing team dynamics.

Listen carefully when the team is talking. Answer each descriptive question (under the letters) first, then the italic interpretation question that follows each set of descriptive questions. On the basis of your interpretation, place the team in one of the three points along each dimension of team talk in figure 2.5. If you find yourself assessing the team as "both" or "somewhat," put your X in the middle of the dimension scale.

I.   **Identification**

A. *Functional group*

When team members say "we," "us," or "our," are they usually referring to their functional group? _____

When team members say "you," is it usually addressed to a single team member? _____

Do team members refer frequently to functional groups? _____

B. *Team*

When team members say "we," "us," or "our," are they usually referring to the team? _____

When team members say "you," is it usually addressed to the whole team? _____

With what group do team members identify themselves?

_____

_____

Table 2.2 Continued

II. Interdependence

A. *Independent*

Do team members make explicit reference to perceived independence? _____

Do they express assertions of individual intent? _____

Do they ignore the questions of others? _____

Are power differences (see III below) highly apparent? _____

B. *Interdependent*

Do team members express their own needs to one another with "I
need you" or "I need us"? _____

Do they express a shared need like "we need to . . ." (which reflects
greater interdependence than "I need")? _____

Do they make explicit reference to their
interdependence? _____

Are power differences deemphasized (see IIIB)? _____

*Do team members act as if they are independent of one another or
interdependent with one another?*

_____

_____

III. Power Differentiation

A. *High power differentiation*

Do the same people tend to dominate the conversation? _____

Do the same people tend to interrupt others? _____

Do those interrupted stop talking? _____

Do the same people tend to ask most of the questions? _____

Do other people typically answer? _____

Do some people tend to ignore questions? _____

Table 2.2 Continued

Do askers wait for answers? _____

Do the questions seem to challenge another's expertise, make the questioner look smarter, or create an opportunity for someone else to look bad? _____

Do the same people always change the subject? _____

Is there a predictable response to such shows of power? That is, are there certain people who always answer, always stop talking when interrupted, rarely try to change the subject, speak less frequently, and never dominate the floor? _____

B. *Low power differentiation*

Are the kinds of behaviors mentioned above exhibited by everyone on the team from time to time? _____

Do team members with higher organizational power refrain from the following:

Dominating the floor? _____

Asking more questions than others? _____

Interrupting others? _____

Do team members with higher organizational power:

Invite or allow others to change the topic? _____

Seek the opinions of all team members? _____

Answer questions others ask of them? _____

Allow themselves to be interrupted? _____

Ask questions to get new information and wait for answers? _____

Do team members with lower power assert their opinions, ask questions, and interrupt others? _____

To what extent do team members call attention to differences in power among them or seem to minimize those power differences?

_____

_____

Table 2.2 Continued

IV. Social Distance

A. *Socially distant*

Do team members use formal forms of address, like Mr. or Ms.? _____

Do team members show excessive politeness to some or all members? _____

Do team members hedge their assertions, for example, "I'm no engineer, but I don't think this design will pass safety tests"? _____

Do team members use formal words or expressions, for example, "This meeting has been convened to assess the team's progress toward desired goals"? _____

Do team members impersonalize requests or assertions by avoiding pronouns and using passive voice, for example, "It has been found during the product review process that the current design fails to meet customer needs"? _____

Do team members apologize before making requests or demands? _____

B. *Socially close*

Do team members address each other with nicknames or in-group names? _____

Do team members use much slang or many colloquialisms? _____

Do team members slur sounds and leave out words, for example, "There's gonna be. . . ." _____

Do team members claim or imply common membership or point of view, for example, "Do we feel good about this decision"? _____

Do team members express liking or admiration for one another? _____

Do team members express their individual needs or feelings, for example, "I just don't feel comfortable with this"? _____

Table 2.2 Continued

Do team members make demands or requests without hedges or apologies, for example, "Hand me that, willya"? _____

Do your team members feel socially distant or close?

_____

_____

V. **Conflict Management**

A. *Forcing, Avoiding, Accommodating, and Compromise*

Do team members use power differences to resolve disagreements? _____

Are there explicit or implicit threats or judgments, met with defensiveness? _____

Do team members tend to avoid conflict by:

Postponing decisions when disagreements persist? _____

Deciding to take problems to their managers? _____

Do decisions get delegated to team "experts" or the leader? _____

Does the team compromise by voting? _____

B. *Collaboration and Confrontation*

Is the tone of team conflicts nonthreatening and nonjudgmental? _____

Is there an attempt to keep conflicts descriptive and/or factual? _____

Do team members express their feelings frequently, openly? _____

Is debate an accepted practice? _____

Does the team listen fully to dissenters? _____

Do team members try to verify understanding by restating dissenting views? _____

Do team members try to integrate dissenting views into the common perspective? _____

Table 2.2 Continued

Do team members examine implications of each point of view in a conflict? _____

Does the team manage conflict through force, avoidance, or constructive confrontation?

_____

_____

VI. Negotiation Process

A. *Win-lose*

Do team members use power differences to win or cause others to lose? _____

Do team members take and argue positions? _____

Do team members use language of loss, debt, or concession? _____

B. *Win-win*

Do team members reframe disagreements in light of others' ideas? _____

Do team members try to understand and articulate the underlying interests of all parties? _____

Do team members try to find objective criteria for resolving their differences? _____

Does the team try to invent new solutions by asking what-if questions? _____

Is your team's negotiation process win-lose or win-win?

_____

_____

PART II

Team Realities

In this section of the book, you will meet four teams and listen in as they work and talk. We'll analyze their talk using the framework presented in chapter 2. You will also see their organizational surroundings from many perspectives: from the team outward, from the top-down viewpoints of the middle managers and the senior executives, and from the perspective of this researcher. You will see a summary description of important features about each organization's contexts for team work.[1] Table II.1 is an example of the kind of descriptive summaries you will find in each of the next four chapters. These multifaceted looks at each team allows us to see the realities of each and to compare the teams and their organizations. From this comparison, we will understand why the conventional wisdom about teams is not helping to close the gap between the reality of team work and its potential.

The stories of the four teams and their organizations are arranged to illuminate different aspects of team realities. Each chapter offers insights and uncertainties. The questions that one story leaves unanswered are examined in the next chapter. By the time all four teams and organizations have been analyzed and compared, you will see how teams need to talk in order to reach their potential and how

Table II.1 Form for describing the organizational context of teams.

Organization	
Feature	*Description*
Recent historical events	
Corporate identity	
Precursors to teams	
Divisional strategic goals	
Initiator of teams	
Expectations of teams	
Nature of team task	
Duration of team structure	
How teams were assembled	
Choice in assignments	
Basis for team leadership	
Size of teams	
Multiple team assignments	
Degree of dedication to team (percentage of team fully dedicated)	
Distribution of stakes	
Mechanisms for assessing team performance	
Hierarchical levels (from teams to top of divisions)	
Role of functional managers	
Liaison to managers	
Training	

organizations need to be designed to encourage that kind of team talk.

Chapter 3 introduces you to the Alpha team, a new team of talented professionals eager to take on more responsibility. Led by a competent and responsive team leader, they have just completed their first cross-functional team task and are hoping to be allowed to continue their work together. Listening to them and analyzing their organizational context will help us draw insights about the importance of the team task, the right people, and team leadership in shaping team dynamics.

Chapter 4 presents the Tech I team, telling a story of a team and an organization at a critical point for all concerned. After many years in development, the Tech I product is just four months from scheduled market introduction. But the product design still has flaws, and members of the team suspect they are way behind in their schedule. Tensions are running very high. Listening to this team at work and to its managers provides important lessons on the influence of organizational culture and design features like managerial incentives and individual accountability on team work.

Chapter 5 describes a very carefully designed team structure and focuses on the experiences of a typical team, the Front-End team. In an organization that has recently gone through massive restructuring and downsizing, the team design provides some of the clarity and specificity that team members seek. Such key features of team design as formal leadership and team accountability are explicitly defined in this system, but the team's talk and dynamics reflect the disappointment and skepticism that are beginning to develop in this organization. By the time you reach the end of chapter 5, you will recognize all the features of teams that are desirable but insufficient to guarantee effective teams. The lessons from the three chapters tell us more about what doesn't work and why than about what does. It will take the story of a remarkable organization and a special team to clarify the picture.

Chapter 6 tells the story of an organization that has committed itself to cross-functional teams and introduces you to the Eurous team, one of its typical high-commitment, high-performance teams. You will see a unique and carefully designed team system, markedly different from the others. You will hear real team talk, signalling mutual identification and interdependence, managing their conflict collaboratively, negotiating for win-win outcomes, minimizing power differences, displaying and using social closeness to influence one another. From this team talk, you will see the significance of the novel organizational context in shaping team dynamics that deliver the desired outcomes.

CHAPTER 3

A Team Task and the Right People

The Medical Products Division and the Alpha Team

This chapter chronicles a division's decision to experiment with cross-functional teams as a vehicle for achieving its strategic goals. Concentrating on the Alpha team gives us the opportunity to listen to a team's ruminations about its early stages while the experience is still very fresh. We hear team members' accounts of taking the raw material the organization has given them—the assigned task, the goals, the people, and the organizational supports—and striving to make something out of it. As we use this case to explore the question, How do you reliably produce teams that will achieve the strategic goals of the organization? we will see that this success was modest at best.

The Alpha team was one of six cross-functional teams formed in the Medical Products Division (MPD) of Greyser Corporation. This division had primary responsibility for distributing medical products to consumer markets. It manufactured its major products—blood pressure measurement kits and pregnancy tests—and purchased others from outside vendors. In 1989 Medical Products Division contributed half of the company's profits, and of that amount the blood pressure product line represented 15 percent. The primary products in that line were fairly mature offerings with high sales volume and good profitability.

Greyser was a large and very successful U.S. manufacturer and distributor of medical products, with 1989 sales of $1.4 billion. Employing 20,000 people in five divisions, one being Medical Products, the company had preserved a "family business culture" up until the early 1980s, when recession braked its rapid growth. The introduction of sophisticated management and strategic planning techniques, along with new efficiencies in manufacturing and other cost-reduction efforts, however, enabled Greyser to retain its market dominance.

The company had significantly downsized as part of these efforts, leaving a professional work force feeling overwhelmed, underappreciated, and concerned about career prospects. At the same time, Greyser was planning to embark on a major globalization drive. Recognizing that this could add intolerably to the load of a work force already laboring under cost-cutting constraints, the firm hired a consulting team to help align human resources with strategic goals. MPD was one of two divisions where the consultants focused their attention.

MPD was functionally organized (see figure 3.1 for an organization chart), with nine directors reporting to the division president and composing, along with him, the operating committee (OC). There were three marketing directors (one each for pregnancy tests, blood pressure products, and new products), a controller, and directors for R&D, operations, quality assurance, sales, and human resources. Because business required most of these directors to travel extensively and make decisions quickly, they tended to operate in isolation; communication and cooperation across functions suffered as a result. This isolation was exacerbated by an evaluation system based on individual, functional performance objectives for professional employees.

The division's 1990 strategic goals were to maintain its contribution to corporate profitability through cost containment, share retention, and global expansion; however, the consultants discovered that conflicts among the functional directors were inhibiting cooperation among their staffs and thereby threatening the achievement of these goals. In particular, the consultants discovered that middle managers believed directors' conflicting interests in quality versus quantity versus bottom line were undermining these managers' initiative, wasting their time, and leading to inappropriate allocation of personnel. The managers were also keenly dissatisfied with their limited decision-making authority. For their part, the directors were not persuaded that the managers had the training or experience to make solid business decisions, as these were traditionally in the directors' sphere of responsibility.

Figure 3.1 Organization chart for the Medical Products Division and the Alpha team.

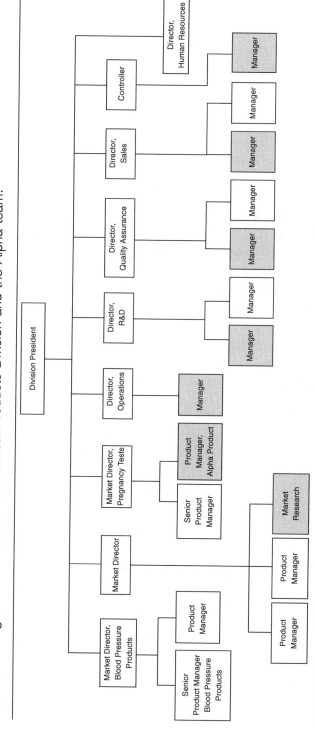

Note: Shaded boxes represent Alpha team members.

To help alleviate these conflicts, the consultants recommended that, among other steps, MPD introduce six cross-functional product management teams, and the operating committee ultimately agreed. The team structure was jointly designed by the consultants, the division president, and the director of human resources.

CROSS-FUNCTIONAL PRODUCT TEAMS

Each team was composed of seven members, one from each function: marketing, market research, R&D, operations, quality assurance, finance, and sales. Although team members were appointed, they could select their leader (called facilitator). Altogether twenty-nine people in MPD served on teams, some on more than one to ensure representation from each function; only team members who were product managers served exclusively on a single team. Beyond team assignments, however, members continued to perform their regular functional tasks. These were delineated in their job descriptions and calibrated in their annual performance plan, which included "standards of performance" against which actual accomplishments were measured. Thus, team objectives might more fully coincide with some members' performance objectives than others, creating a difference in the "stakes" individuals had in the team. Incentive disparities also existed; some product managers, for example, were eligible for bonuses based on the team's performance.

Each team was also assigned two coaches: one for strategy and the other for process. Product strategy was provided by the marketing directors to whom the product managers reported; process coaching was provided by other members of the operating committee.

The Teams' Purpose and Task

The product management teams were introduced at MPD as a multipurpose solution to several of the problems that plagued the organization, threatening the achievement of its strategic goals (figure 3.2). But people tended to attribute different priorities to each potential outcome of team work, depending on their roles. The consultants recognized the multiple benefits of teams and worked with the directors to develop commitment to this concept. The division president saw teams as a way to solve coordination problems created by functional differentiation but exacerbated by globalization:

Figure 3.2 The Medical Products Division: teams and strategic goals.

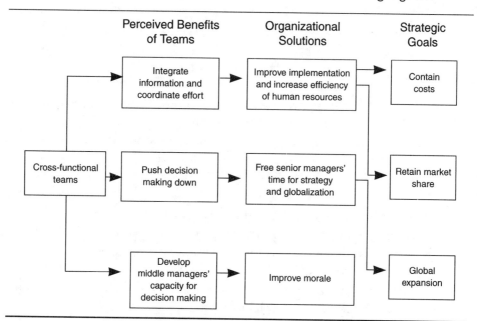

We got to get organized. These people aren't speaking to each other from their own division, let alone across divisions. We're not getting things done. We started a new planning process, a whole new approach to this. So we were getting our strategy down. But I gotta tell you, implementation was really bad. We were a mess, we didn't even have timetables, what we had, they weren't being hit. And plus we were just rushing and we had chaos.

The president also saw teams as a useful vehicle for addressing "the issue of who gets what."

The resource distribution problem that created and fueled functional antagonism: Before teams, we'd negotiate. Then I had to decide, I was the hub of the wheel. It was not working well. Prior to the product management teams, we tried business management teams, but those didn't work because we had no buy-in. We created a structure, then walked away. We think [the product team] is really the key to our success in the future. 'Cause this division badly needs new products, needs badly to be able to work on worldwide teams. . . . We are very, very slim in the resources we have here. We're down almost to bare bones now. So we have to be very efficient with the human resources we have. Also, we are a very profitable division with steep competition now from the Japanese. So we need to be very good at resource allocation. We can't let that slip, 'cause we're the number-one provider of profit to the corporation. So we've gotta be good. We get a lot of attention. So we gotta be good everywhere. Also our superordinate goal, we say we are going to be superior in product quality and in services. So we're setting out to be the best, not just in the company but in the competitive area.

In his mind, teams would provide the opportunity and motivation for cross-functional coordination through the assigned task of developing the division's annual product implementation plan, currently a responsibility of the marketing department.

Some functional directors, however, believed the teams could and should both create and implement product strategy, while others felt team members' lack of business expertise fitted them only for the implementation plan aspect. One director believed this latter viewpoint was based on the directors' personal interest in maintaining control. Another argued that since "these are mature products, there's not much to do, so if you give up strategy to the teams, what's left for you to do?" A third director believed the teams would be a more effective means to distribute information and make good decisions.

The initial task given to the teams represented a temporary resolution of this conflict among OC members. Each team was to develop the strategy implementation for a particular product or product line, on the basis of strategies designed by the marketing directors, and ratified by the operating committee. This task was considered a pilot test of the team concept, yet it was hoped that having teams develop the plan would produce more realistic results as well as the mutual commitment required to realize them. Ultimately, the president hoped to give teams the authority to create and recommend strategy as well as implementation plans.

Team members, for their part, nearly all believed that the purpose of the teams was to push decision making down to their level. Some were concerned, however, that the marketing members would treat the teams as their personal stages for "solo performances with accompaniment," in the beginning at least. Other members saw the formation of teams variously as opportunities to learn about and contribute more to the business, to inform the marketers of the constraints supporting functions faced, or as useless drains of time and energy.

The Operation of Teams

The coaches convened the first meetings of each team, explained the team task and the role of the coaches, and instructed the team to select its own leader. Without exception, the team members from marketing (who were also product managers) were selected. The stated reason was similar across teams: marketing had the most information about the products as well as profit and loss responsibility for the products.

Once commissioned, the teams set off on parallel developmental paths that then began to diverge. The team leaders all began by describing the product and its stage of development. After that introduction, the teams' activities were determined by the product itself and the personalities of the team leaders. Two teams were responsible for products still in development; their planning task was therefore more abstract and open-ended, and one of these team leaders used it as an opportunity to do more strategic and developmental work. That team's meetings tended to be unfocused brainstorming sessions. The other new-product team leader saw his team's task as the development of a plan and a schedule to which each person would commit. He tended to run his meetings like information-exchange sessions in which team members reported their progress toward team goals.

The other teams were responsible for products already on the market. The most mature and significant product line was the blood pressure measurement line. This team met very infrequently. Most team members believed this was because the team leader saw the planning task as his own; the 'team' designation functioned primarily to identify those with responsibility to him. Two of the other teams proceeded to meet on a periodic basis to assemble their data for implementation planning. For no clear reason, these teams were troubled by conflict and lack of participation, although many in the company blamed the team leaders. The Alpha team was developing the implementation plan for one of the home pregnancy tests. By most accounts, the Alpha team developed a very effective team process.

THE ALPHA TEAM

The Alpha team had seven members: the product manager of the Alpha pregnancy test product, a manager of customer service/distribution, a quality engineer, a manager of technical service, a sales manager, a senior budget coordinator, and a senior market researcher. The team met biweekly. The product manager was "elected" to be the team facilitator. Early in its life, its leader played the central role by creating the agenda, running the meetings, taking the lead in opening and closing topics, and soliciting consensus on team action plans and commitment on individual objectives. Team members described the meetings as efficient and effective, and the leader as extremely knowledgeable about the product line and a competent facilitator. However, as the team began to recognize its potential in creating the implementation plan, other team members began to assert their interests in pursuing certain topics and even in negotiating over some of marketing's plans and assumptions. By all accounts, the team leader readily shared responsibility for shaping team meetings and team ideas.

THE ALPHA TEAM'S TALK

Unlike the remaining cases in this section, the linguistic data used to analyze the talk of the Alpha team come from individual interviews rather than from team meeting conversations. This is because the teams were in a hiatus when these data were collected. The interviews with members of the Alpha team provide a fairly consistent picture of its mode of interaction. They also provide linguistic evidence of the team members' interpretations of those experiences.

Irene Belasiac was the product manager for the Alpha product line and facilitator of the team. She believed that the product teams were the result of the feedback generated by the human resource consulting project:

1   There was a consensus among middle managers that we were not being given the opportunity to make decisions and have control over our businesses. The product teams were an answer to that. It's a more

formal method of communication, so everyone is involved in all the projects. It eliminates the problem of some functions not being aware of what's going on. Teams really force the communication.*

In Belasiac's view, marketing benefited more from the teams than the other functional departments. The planning and coordination of resources to design and manage the products had been her responsibility prior to the establishment of teams. She felt that the marketing group was still ultimately responsible for meeting the team objectives,

2   partly because it has not been communicated to the team fully that they are responsible.

The marketing professionals had standards or performance objectives that were more cross-functional in nature, such as maintaining market share or launching a product by a certain date. The other team members' performance standards were more functional in nature.

Belasiac recognized two other disparities in the stakes that teams held for team members. One related to the performance objectives:

3   We have an unequal recognition system. Marketing groups are recognized when they are participating in a presentation to upper managers; it's known what kind of job they've done. But the support groups that help you do your job are not recognized as much. And I think it's important that they receive recognition.

The other difference was that some members were on a bonus plan, while others were not. This affected commitment and contributions to some teams, but less so on the Alpha team.

4   I really see the team members taking a lot more ownership in the projects now. . . . They understand the whole process. We've gone from being a group getting together not really knowing what we wanted to do to really being productive. My last meeting, we decided to move up clinical trials and decided on a different approach that would speed up the whole development process, and the team as a group came to that decision. I see us taking a more active role in the business, being able to plan out earlier. I think we will become more

---

*Each number in boldface in this section refers to a verbatim comment on the team experience by an Alpha team member. Taken from my interviews, each is a single uninterrupted comment in the conversation. Sociolinguists refer to these as conversational turns.

demanding of the operating committee—"You've got to inform us, you've got to communicate." If they're not gonna get their act together, we'll force it. We'll force the communication. . . . It helps all of our workload, it helps us accomplish everything. I think the more active and productive we get as a group, our voice will be heard a little better.

Don Riley was the manager of customer service and distribution and served as the operations representative to the Alpha team, and in this role he was most concerned with efficiency, service, and cost. He felt that the Alpha team was quite effective, and that the team system itself was working:

5   There is much earlier awareness of things that will eventually affect you. Issues are discussed before they become obstacles.

He described the Alpha team's process in the following terms:

6   The product manager reviewed the milestones and objective of that product with the team members. The team members discussed when the product was to be launched, when it is to be available. Based on that, each functional representative prepared their individual time and event schedule as to how they impacted the launch of the product. We reviewed that in the team and we proceeded from there, and there was a tremendous amount of dialogue about how we interface with one another, on how it impacts someone. For example, something may impact me what someone from another area is doing. But if that functional representative is there, we can talk and try to come up with some kind of an agreement, and therefore it proceeds much more smoothly.

Riley did have several concerns. The foremost appeared to be the considerable time demands that teams created, especially for members who served on multiple teams, as he did. He felt that the Alpha team leader was particularly effective because she recognized the constraints team members faced and managed the team's time together very effectively: "She knows how to obtain information from the product team members," how to focus the group on issues relevant to all members, and how to table a discussion for a subgroup meeting. Some teams he served on took a considerable amount of time without improving the quality of the product or the service.

Riley felt that facilitators of other teams tended to go to functional directors to obtain information, rather than working through the team. But he also recognized that part of the problem originated with the team members, some of whom were not participating adequately, not voicing their opinions, especially concerning problems of team process. He characterized the attitude of those people as:

7 Why bother? What I have to do is come in at a certain time, and stay till a certain time. The project will still be launched on a certain date however much time we spend.

He was unimpressed with the coaching that teams were supposed to receive from members of the operating committee. He had seen no evidence of it: "Coaching may occur through the team leader, but this is not observed by the team."

Perry Picceli was a quality project engineer and served on two teams. While he had a favorable assessment of the product team concept, he was more satisfied with the Alpha team:

8 I think it's [the team has] made us think more and more about what we're doing and how we're gonna do it, and how to take a request from management and figure out how we could do it. Whereas before, we would just say it can't be done. Now we're sayin', "Okay, can we do it and how do we do it?" All of a sudden we're talking we can do this and this and this. It has been good. . . . In the long term, it may make my job easier 'cause I'm not the bad guy who on the last day before the launch has to say, "Wait a minute, that's wrong, you gotta throw that out and start again" and stop the whole launch. It may save a lot of frustration and animosity in the long run because all the issues theoretically have been reviewed and authorized. There's not that last-minute surprise.

He was, however, concerned about the lack of coordination among teams. Teams increased the demands on his time and created conflicts between him and his colleagues when he could not accomplish everything as quickly as they wanted.

Vic Glassberg, manager of technical services, served on three teams. He saw teams as more beneficial to marketing, while everyone else now had more to do:

9   Teams are working. You have to have teams, no one person can do it. But now there is more stress on the appearance of being organized than on the substance of getting things done. There is too much emphasis on artificial milestones. We need targets but don't need constant tracking. . . . The emphasis on schedules creates the appearance that OC is saying "Without these schedules, you dummies couldn't get this done."

In Glassberg's view, the Alpha team was working better than the others. He characterized those team members as talking in terms like

10   'Here's what we have to get done.' They are dependent on one another. Rather than 'Here's what you have to do for me.'

Glassberg was highly critical of operating committee members as coaches, feeling that they provided no real value to the teams, but served mainly to symbolize the hierarchical distance between the directors and the professionals: "The signal it sends is 'We're coming down from the great OC to help you out.' "

John Kassarjian, a sales manager, was currently serving on two teams and generally had a positive assessment of the team concept:

11   I can see this team concept starting to click. It's amazing how productive, how efficient and how we can dovetail all our activities and also get a different perspective on whatever our functional area is. . . . I see this thing as just a fabulous way to operate. . . . We're going to be able to meet deadlines better.

Kassarjian believed that team process and performance were largely influenced by the team facilitator. He was somewhat critical of the Alpha team leader for exerting too much control over the team, but he recognized that there was a learning curve for the product managers attempting to manage what had been their own business as part of a group.

12   The Alpha team seems to operate well but is somewhat dominated by the marketing person, who's really controlling closely but then again is also very competent, so . . . with Alpha, it's a team leader [not a facilitator]. A team leader has more control, controlling the agenda, cutting off discussion, guiding the discussion, establishing outside meetings, making most of the decisions. A facilitator guides the discussion, tries to get a group consensus. [You need a] little bit of both; that requires lot of versatility. But ultimately marketing does seem to have ultimate responsibility.

Despite some reservations about the progress that the Alpha team had made in managing the task together, Kassarjian was convinced that the team could and would develop the cohesion necessary to counter the negative influence some operating committee members had on the business:

13 Some people still cling to the old ways. They feel threatened . . . and want to be the one to set the deadlines and to drive the business. But we as the team members have to make them realize that "Fine, we can do that, but it's at some cost. It means that something else is being pushed aside." Or maybe we need to give them more information before they make these sweeping decisions. We feel that we ought to be the group that supplies them with some of the information in order to make their decisions.

Like Belasiac, Kassarjian was concerned about the senior management's commitment to developing an effective team system:

14 I'm not sure how sincere they are about fixing the problem. They seem to be sincere about diagnosing it. But I'm not so sure that they're willing to make any drastic changes or spend the money to fix it. . . . [If they] continue to keep expenses down, salaries down, raises down . . . the risk is that the people are not as happy, the products are not as good, and that morale goes down a bit.

Rick Swanson from finance was a senior budget coordinator, whose role on the team was to "put everything into numbers and pose the question, Is it feasible?" Very enthusiastic about the team, he felt that participation had given him a much better understanding of the whole business, as well as a sense of where his contribution fit into the whole. As a result, he felt more involved with and more committed to the organization. He also believed that the teams had enhanced the working relationships among professionals. Using the example of finance and R&D, he pointed out that the relationships that teams developed led to a reduction in the tensions that naturally occurred as people performed their functional responsibilities. He believed that the Alpha team had made significant progress in learning to work together effectively:

15 Initially a lot of people were not sure what their roles were. Everybody was very confused. . . . The product manager explained what the product team is, what we're going to be doing, and presented the milestones, and everyone else was saying, "I'm not sure what I'm supposed to do." . . . With time, people understood better what their role was. We were meeting . . . understanding what needed to be done. . . . In the first meeting, only the facilitator was talking. Now everybody is talking, bringing things which the product manager never thought of. Initially the facilitator had this role [of managing the team conversation]. If the conversation became too technical or she felt maybe the whole product team would not benefit from this, maybe she'll suggest "If you feel you need more conversation, maybe you could sit down together yourself." [But now] we do that. Initially, it was we would look to the leader and say, "Hey, you gotta stop this." But now people say things themselves. Everybody's now in the group. It's no longer a leader, it's a team. Now people are working together.

Swanson was persuaded that the team had developed sufficient cohesion to be able to act in concert to offer sound business advice to the division's senior manager:

16 We are providing a basic tool to the management, what they should be doing. We recommend based on what we've been doing, saying "This is what we feel is the right approach and if you disagree, give us more feedback as to what your concerns are."

Ed Montenegro was senior market research analyst and served on three teams. In general, he assessed the product teams positively, feeling he benefited from getting a "more global view of the business" and that teams enhanced the communication among functions. However, he too was concerned about the additional demands that teams placed on his time:

17 Teams reduce my productivity. Teams are a good move. But they have to do something about time—there are too many meetings if you're on more than one team. We need more definition of what our roles and responsibilities are.

He was most impressed with the Alpha team:

18 This team works best, basically because the product manager is very

organized, so it's easier to work with her. The facilitator needs broad knowledge, so the product manager seemed logically to be the person. The facilitator is very good; she keeps everything moving. She has key issues that she wants to talk about, boom, boom, boom. What's nice then is that the product team members all pretty much play their part, and participate when there needs to be an answer from their specific area. Seems to be a good group of people and the meetings tend to go very smoothly.

In describing the way the team operated, Montenegro's account differed from other members'. He suggested that most of the integration of team expertise was handled not by the team but by the team facilitator:

19 Each functional area has made up its own time and event schedule, then submitted it to the product manager, who then made a master. I did not have to do any integration. I didn't have to do the integration with any R&D or manufacturing requirements.

LINGUISTIC ANALYSIS OF THE INTERVIEWS

The linguistic analysis of these snippets of the Alpha team's talk is guided by the team talk audit presented in chapter 2. To assess where the team fits on the key dimensions of team talk, we must first describe and analyze the patterns of each type observed in the data. This process, as explained in chapter 2, requires the auditor to listen (or look, in the case of transcribed talk as we have here) for both function and form. That is, you look for both specific meanings, like interdependence or conflict avoidance, and for the forms of language that typically create that meaning. The process is demonstrated in the analysis of each dimension of talk that follows. The analysis is summarized in the audit form in table 3.1.

Identification

The linguistic data from these interviews with the Alpha team members have patterns of both functional group identification and identification with the team. Explicit references are made to the functional groups (turns 3, 12, 18, 19), indicating that team members are identified with

Table 3.1 Audit of the Alpha team.

Dimensions	Samples of Team Talk	Your Interpretation	Score
Identification	"Marketing groups are recognized. . . . but the support groups that help you do your job are not . . . important that they receive recognition" (3) "things that will eventually affect you" (5)	Groups other than team identified (3, 12, 18, 19), boundary between self and other team members noted with "you" (3, 5) and "they" (2, 3) and "I" (19) and "my" (17).	Team Identification
	"I see us taking a more active role in the business, . . . We'll force the communication. . . . our voice will be heard." (4)	"We," "us," "our" used by virtually every team member to refer to the team (4, 6, 8, 9, 11, 13, 16, 17).	
	"This is what we feel is the right approach" (16)	The use of "our" and "we" with words that have a singular meaning, like "voice" and "feel," shows even stronger identification with other team members.	
Interdependence	"My last meeting" (4) "Teams reduce my productivity." (17)	Some independence (4, 17, 19).	Moderate
	"[The team] may make my job easier" (8) "You have to have teams, no one person can do it." (9) " 'Here's what we have to get done.' They are dependent on one another. Rather than 'Here's what you have to do for me.' " (10)	Lots of interdependence recognized explicitly (6, 8, 9, 10, 11, 13, 16).	
Power Differentiation	"My last meeting" (4) "the (leader) . . . keeps everything moving. She has key issues that she wants to talk about, boom, boom, boom. What's nice then is . . . team members all pretty much play their part, and participate when there needs to be an answer		Moderate

Table 3.1 Continued

Dimensions	Samples of Team Talk	Your Interpretation	Score
	from their specific area." (18) "The Alpha team . . . is somewhat dominated by the marketing person. . . . controlling the agenda, cutting off discussion, making most of the decisions. . . . guides the discussion, tries to get a group consensus. . . . But ultimately marketing does seem to have ultimate responsibility." (12)	Team leader shows her perception of power differences: it is "her" meeting, not "ours." Others also see her as having and using her greater power to influence the team (12, 18). Yet there is a shared sense that although the team leader initially dominated the team talk, when other team members began to assert their own opinions and preferences, she refrained from using power-differentiating behavior (6, 8, 11, 15).	
Social Distance	Absence of closeness forms, presence of distance forms.	Not much social closeness, but this is probably a result of using data from an interview with a stranger.	Indeterminate
Conflict Management Tactics	"[Team leader] keeps everything moving. . . . team members . . . play their part" (18) "team leader . . . controlling the agenda, cutting off discussion . . . making most of the decisions" (12)	Slight evidence of avoidance and accommodation (12, 18), forcing (12, 18).	Collaborative
	"Issues are discussed before they become obstacles." (5)	Expressing own needs and interests (5, 6, 8).	
	"we would look to the leader and say, 'Hey, you gotta stop this.' But now people say things themselves." (15)	Confronting differences (8). Not avoiding conflict (15).	
	"the team as a group came to that decision" (4)	Integrating differences into common perspective (4, 16).	

Table 3.1 Continued

Dimensions	Samples of Team Talk	Your Interpretation	Score
Negotiation Process	"a tremendous amount of dialogue on how we interface . . . on how it impacts . . . someone (6) "we can talk and try to come up with some kind of an agreement" (6)	Slight evidence that power differences are used to win at the expense of other team members (12, 18). More evidence that team members are trying to understand each other's underlying interests (5, 6, 8, 10, 12), and are jointly examining the implications of those (6, 8), and are trying to find new ways to integrate (6, 8, 11).	Win-Win

those groups by others. For example, the manager of sales training, in explaining why the team leader acts as she does, says "ultimately marketing does seem to have ultimate responsibility" (turn 12). Several team members also show a lack of identification with other team members by noting implicitly a boundary between themselves and the others with their use of pronouns that distinguish between themselves and other members, like "they" (2, 3), "my" (17), "I" (19), and "you" (3, 5).

On the other hand, virtually every team member used inclusive pronouns repeatedly, identifying themselves with the team and the other members (turns 4, 6, 8, 9, 11, 13, 16, 17). For example, "I see us taking a more active role. . . . we will become more demanding. . . ." (turn 4). Two of the team members use forms of talk that reflect identification with others even more strongly: the use of a plural pronoun with a word that has a singular meaning. The team leader does this when she says "our voice will be heard" (4). The team member from finance does the same when he says "this is what we feel is the right approach" (16). This combination of words signals strong identification because many people cannot have one voice or one feeling unless they see themselves as one.

The evidence from the team talk analyzed here indicates that this team identifies more with the team than with the members' functional groups. This would put them near the team endpoint of the identification dimension (see figure 3.3).

Interdependence

The Alpha team members explicitly refer to their interdependence frequently (turns 6, 8, 9, 10, 11, 13, 16). For example, one argues that "you have to have teams, no one person can do it" (9); "they are dependent on one another" (10). Another tentatively points out that the team may "make my job easier" (8). A third person expresses the

Figure 3.3 Assessment of the Alpha team's talk.

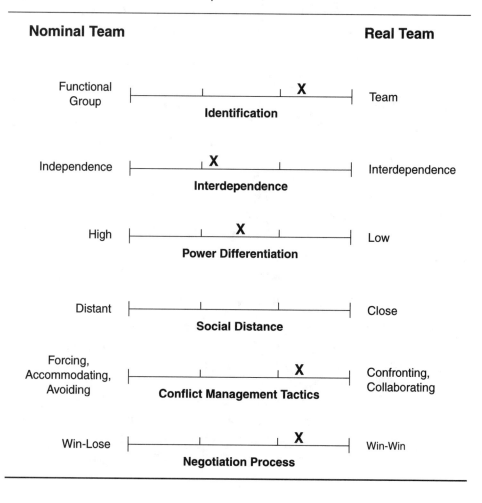

interdependence in terms of a shared need, "we [as a team] need to . . ." (13).

There is also evidence that, while team members do perceive themselves to be interdependent, they also display some independence and resentment about the constraints that this interdependence imposes on their independent actions. For example, one team member claimed that members of other teams deliberately withheld opinions from the team because others took action independent of those views: "why bother? . . . The project will still be launched . . . however much time we spend [in discussion and debate]" (7). A member of the Alpha team shows mixed feelings with the statement, "Teams reduce my productivity" (17).

The team leader reflects a similar perception of being both independent and interdependent in her curious phrase "My last meeting" (4). "My" is a singular possessive pronoun suggesting that something belongs to the speaker alone, suggesting independence. A "meeting" cannot exist without the involvement of at least two people, thus making the attendees interdependent, at least for some period of time. Another common way of referring to such an event would be "our meeting." A single person "owns" a meeting when he or she takes independent action to convene and manage it, typically with the agreement of the others. This form also implies a perception of having the power to call such a meeting and expect others to attend and participate.

Taken as a whole, the linguistic behavior of the Alpha team with regard to interdependence indicates that team members feel moderately interdependent. This assessment puts them in the middle of that dimension (see figure 3.2).

Power Differentiation

In this organization whose strategic function was to distribute products, marketing was widely known to have significantly greater informal power than the other functions. This power difference was re-created in the teams when marketers were elected by their teams to be team leaders. The leader of the Alpha team viewed herself as having greater power than the other team members as a function of her strategic expertise (2, 3), as her comments and the phrase "my . . . meeting" (4) indicate. The other team members recognized this power difference and its basis (12), and they deferred to it, allowing her to use that power difference to manage the team dynamics (12, 18, and implied in 7). For example, one team member says: "the leader keeps everything moving. She has key issues that she wants to talk about, boom, boom, boom. What's nice then is . . . team members all pretty much play their part, and participate when there needs to be an answer" (18). This description suggests that the team leader dominated the talk and asked most of the questions, while others with less power awaited their turn to answer the questions. This view is corroborated by another team member who describes the team leader "controlling the agenda, cutting off discussion, guiding the discussion, [and] making most of the decisions" (12).

However, most of the team members described a process in which the team leader used these behaviors in the beginning but as other team members began to speak up and ask questions, her behavior changed (turns 6, 8, 11, 15): "In the first meeting, only the facilitator was talking. Now everybody is talking, bringing things which the product manager never thought of. Initially the facilitator had this role [of managing the team conversation]. . . . now people say things themselves." The kind of talk they describe as typical of the team reflects more power balance: "We reviewed that in the team and we proceeded" (6); "it's no longer a leader, it's a team" (15).

These comments together suggest that the team talk was characterized by a moderate use of power differentiation (see figure 3.3). Though we do not have data on subsequent team interaction, it would not be unreasonable to assume that in the future, this team's talk would involve less power differentiation because the leader has already distributed her power to other team members.

Social Distance

The Alpha team does not exhibit social closeness in its talk. However, this may be because the linguistic data used to analyze the Alpha team's talk comes from interviews with the researcher, a relative stranger. On the other hand, there are some forms of social distance: the use of impersonal words rather than names to refer to team members (e.g., "the product manager" and "functional representative") and the use of formal expressions like passive voice ("the product will be launched").

However, under these circumstances, it is not possible to determine how close the team members felt to one another on a social basis.

Conflict Management Tactics

Conflict management tactics often parallel power differences among team members. That is, when there is a difference in the organizational power of team members, conflicts tend to be managed by the use of power; the person with the greater power forces the others to accommodate him or her. Two members of the Alpha team emphasize the use of power differences among team members and imply that the team leader forces her point of view and others accommodate her, and possibly avoid topics of conflict (12, 18). However, there is another team member who compares the Alpha team favorably with other teams in which conflict is avoided (7).

The majority of the team talks as if the team typically used the tactics of confrontation and collaboration to manage their disagreements (4, 5, 6, 8, 15). Team members talked about people's expressing their own needs and interests: "Issues are discussed before they become obstacles" (5); "all the issues theoretically have been reviewed" (8). There are open expressions of feeling and conflict is not avoided: "Initially, it was we would look to the leaders and say, 'Hey, you gotta stop this.' But now people say things themselves" (15). Differences are confronted: "I'm not the bad guy who on the last day before the launch has to say 'Wait a minute, that's wrong, you gotta throw that out and start again' " (8).

The team members talked as if they were also able to integrate these differences into a common perspective: "The team as a group came to that decision" (4), and "this is what we feel is the right approach" (16). These patterns of perceived behavior lead to the assessment that the Alpha team's typical conflict management tactics are confrontation and collaboration (see figure 3.3).

Negotiation Process

As with conflict management tactics, the negotiation process of a team can parallel the use of power differences within a team. When a team emphasizes the power differences among the members, it is often done in order to win regardless of the expense to other team members. As discussed above, two of the Alpha team members indicate that power differences were used to control the team (12, 18), and one specifically attributes this behavior to the desire to achieve the marketer's goals (18). However, again most of the team's talk reflects a negotiation process directed at achieving wins for all parties concerned, including the team and the organization.

There is considerable evidence that the team members tried to understand each other's interests and needs (5, 6, 8, 10, 11). For example, one member describes "a tremendous amount of dialogue about how we interface . . . on how it impacts . . . someone" (6). Others too described the joint process of examining the implication of individual interests on the team: "made us think . . . what we're doing and how. . . . [and] may save a lot of frustation and animosity" (8), "how . . . we . . . get a different perspective on whatever our functional area is" (11). Team members also talk about finding new ways to integrate their differences: "It's amazing how productive, how efficient and how we can dovetail all our activities" (11); "we can talk and try to come up with some kind of agreement" (6). The majority view of this team and the words they use to describe their typical behavior indicate that their negotiation process is more win-win than win-lose (see figure 3.3).

TEAM TALK AND ORGANIZATIONAL CONTEXT

The accounts the Alpha team members provide of their team interaction reflect somewhat greater identification with the team than the function, moderate degrees of interdependence and power differentiation, indeterminate social distance, conflict management tactics of confrontation and collaboration, and a win-win negotiation process. This analysis puts the team at various points on each of the key dimensions of team talk[1] (as shown in figure 3.3), making it more than just a nominal team, but suggesting the team is not fully realized. This assessment of the team through its talk reflects the powerful countervailing forces at work in the organization. Table 3.2 summarizes the data on the organizational context and team design at the Medical Products Division.

Several organizational factors worked against the Alpha team's development of effective team dynamics (see figure 3.4). The most palpable pressure affecting the team's identification and their perception

Table 3.2 Description of the Medical Products Division's organizational context.

Medical Products Division	
Feature	*Description*
Recent historical events	Downsizing
Corporate identity	We *were* Family. Now?
Precursors to teams	Early attempts at teams, human resource consulting
Divisional strategic goals	Cost and share
Initiator of teams	Consultants
Expectations of teams	Efficiency, delegation coordination
Nature of team task	Closed, near-term
Duration of team structure	6 months
How teams were assembled	Position-based assignment
Choice in assignments	No
Basis for team leadership	Lead function
Size of teams	7
Multiple team assignments	Yes
Degree of dedication to team (percentage of team fully dedicated)	14%
Distribution of stakes	Formally variable
Mechanisms for assessing team performance	Formal periodic report, functional reporting
Hierarchical levels (from teams to top of divisions)	4
Role of functional managers	Unchanged
Liaison to managers	Senior manager coach
Training	None

Figure 3.4 Major forces shaping the Alpha team's dynamics.

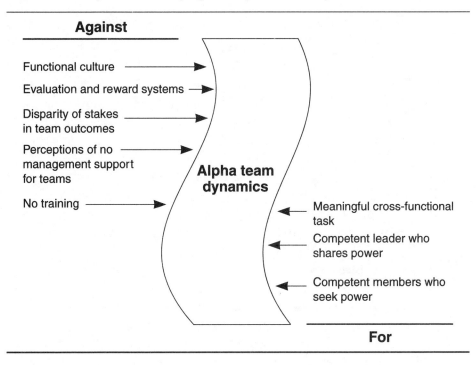

of interdependence came from the functional directors to whom team members reported. Both the functional division of the organization and the preferred management style of the president contributed to a strong sense of functional isolation and competition among the senior managers. Prior to the human resource consulting project, the division president had typically dealt with his directors one to one, rarely convening the operating committee. His own description of the division's mission and mode of operation suggests that far greater attention was given to the distribution of resources than to the integration of efforts:

> So we have four independent strategy centers. . . . It is my job as the president of this division to try to manage these four businesses, strategically and financially. . . . We have these staffs who have to work with each of these marketing directors in order to have these businesses succeed and grow. So the issue in the past has been who gets what, in terms of time. How do we go about determining who gets what, and addressing issues. . . . So then they said, "Well, what

we'll do is, uh, negotiate." . . . So when I came here we had people negotiating, debating, and when that debate took place and it couldn't be resolved, who had to resolve it? One guy who's responsible for it all—me. So our day was spent, so we saw ourself as a hub of a wheel.

Though the president had recently come to see that this functional competition was creating serious implementation problems and believed that product teams were the way to solve "our management style around here," he recognized that it would take some time for the old habits of behavior to change. He and his consultants were working to develop patterns of productive exchange and power sharing within the operating committee and between the committee and the teams. Although progress was perceptible in both arenas, persisting conflict in the committee as to the teams' role augered poorly for their future.

Two other powerful factors pushing against interdependence were the performance appraisal and reward systems. As noted earlier, professional employees were evaluated on the basis of "standards of performance," or objectives established between themselves and their functional directors. For some functions these tended to be more cross-functional in nature. For example, the product manager's standards included objectives, such as a certain product launch date, that were highly dependent on the efforts of people in other functions. However, other professionals were typically evaluated on the basis of their functional subgoals, for example, on-time delivery for wholesale customers or containing manufacturing costs. Annual pay increases, and occasionally promotions, were based on the functional director's assessment of how well a professional had met these objectives. Both these systems thus created incentives for professionals to resist solutions to team problems that would negatively affect their function's subgoals.

The disparity in compensation also influenced Alpha team members' perceptions of interdependence, as evident in the interviews with the team leader and the representative from customer service and distribution. Those whose individual standards of performance were dependent on the team's accomplishments would experience even greater dependence on the team if they were eligible for a bonus. Those who were not bonus-eligible had less to gain and so felt less dependent.

Considering the forces working against interdependence and identification with the Alpha team, the extent to which the members displayed these qualities is surprising. Several factors working for the team's moderate sense of interdependence and identification with the team include the nature of the task, the competence of the team leader, her willingness to share power, and the team members' interest in assuming greater responsibility.

The task of this team accounts for much of the perceived interdependence and team identification. Objectively, the task of the Alpha team was compelling. The product line was mature, and so there was an immediate and concrete quality to the task of planning implementation of the product strategy. It was also clearly a cross-functional task, requiring input and, in light of the deadline, continuous mutual adjustment to the information that each team member brought to the task. The output would also affect not only the organization, but each of the team members fairly directly, so the task itself was meaningful to each person.

The transformation of these objective qualities into a task that was so meaningful that it elicited identification with the team and willing interdependence occurred through the behavior of the team leader. Team members repeatedly characterized her as extremely knowledgeable, well prepared, and a highly competent team facilitator. Her expertise about the product and her ability to coordinate ensured that the task of planning would produce results. Her willingness to accept the contributions and expertise of the other team members and to share her power as team leader and product manager allowed team members to see the task as cross-functional and made participation in that task significant and meaningful to individuals.

One final force contributed to the Alpha team's interdependence and team identification: the membership of the team, specifically the competence and readiness of team members to assume greater responsibility for the business. Their interviews corroborate the findings of the human resource consultants that these professionals felt keenly dissatisfied with the level of decision-making authority and responsibility they had. As several team members explicitly stated, they saw the team work as a fitting response to this complaint. They eagerly took up the challenge of developing the annual plan as a group and felt that they had earned the opportunity to take the next step in managing the business together. This shared mind-set, galvanized by the team task and shaped by the team facilitator and heightened by the recent team experience, counteracted the external pressures for independent, functionally oriented action in teams.

Regarding the power differentiation dimension, initially the facilitator exhibited high power and the other members, low power. The immediacy and familiarity of the planning task made it reasonable for her to take the lead. Given that by design the marketing team members had greater responsibility for the task and higher performance-contingent benefits, both her taking power and others' acceding to this were predictable. However, it appears that militating against the power differentiation was her recognition of her dependence on the other team members.[2] Team members' accounts indicate that, after the team had reached a level of understanding of the team task, there was a shift toward power sharing within the team. When team members exhibited an interest in shaping the discussion and agenda, the leader displayed a willingness to share power.[3]

The social distance among team members, though impossible to assess, appeared to be moderate. Their interviews display few, if any, signs of either social closeness or remoteness, and the predominant relationship is clearly professional. They are polite, cordial, and speak of one another in terms of their knowledge and responsibility. There is little indication of personal familiarity or interest in one another, or of animosity. The functional design of the organization and the workload led to their having had little connection with one another in the past and therefore, not much opportunity to become acquainted with one another. It would be reasonable to expect that, if they continue to meet as a team, assuming that they preserve the more recent trends of perceived interdependence and lower power differentiation, they will experience more social proximity and use the display of it as a means of influencing one another.

The collaborative conflict management tactics and win-win negotiation process that we observed in the team talk are unexpected in an organization where so many forces are working against interdependence among the functions. However, they are the likely outcomes of a common identity and a willing interdependence, the dynamics created by the cross-functional task, and the readiness of the team members and leader to share power.

This examination of the Alpha team's talk and dynamics in light of the Medical Products Division context suggests that these dynamics are the joint product of the organizational forces and this particular team. According to the Alpha team members (most of whom served on other teams at the same time), the Alpha team was the only one that did real team work, that truly integrated the team members' expertise to accomplish the task. According to the directors who commissioned the teams, the Alpha team—like the others—achieved its task of producing a cross-functional plan for implementing product strategy. However, that task was very focused and time-limited, and it was unknown whether the team could continue to work effectively together on tasks of greater scope critical to achieving the division's stated, multiple strategic goals.

The Alpha team members also felt that their collaboration was fragile. They felt that they had constructed an entity that was highly susceptible to pressure from functional and divisional management, and was therefore very dependent on significant change in the organization.

The Alpha team leader summarized the predicament that the Medical Products Division would face in the future of product teams. She observed that there was "too much waffling over strategies, too much tinkering with plans, then changing plans." This, she asserted, produced an overload of work that had become constant, in exchange for which the corporation offered too little compensation. There was a serious morale problem in the corporation, she claimed, because professionals were underpaid and were experiencing truncated career development. She felt that the high performance and sense of accomplishment that the Alpha team experienced had produced a sense of satisfaction that would not persist if the division's promises of greater responsibility and career progression were not met in the near future.

Most team members also expressed skepticism about the willingness of the division's senior management to give teams the authority, resources, and moral support that they would require in the future to realize their potential.

> Prior to teams, MPD was autocratic. Everything was mandated from the top . . . teams were mandated to us. Upper management didn't try to convince us. . . . At first, people were just going through the motions, but lately a greater commitment to teams has developed. There's a willingness to give it a try. . . . The real problem facing us is that the OC doesn't communicate well . . . because they have different goals, strategies, interests and so they can't agree. . . . There's no indication yet that the division will allow the team to control resources. Teams must be allowed to fail. Tons of decisions are made outside of teams, and some of those should be made at team

level. Teams have no experience of making decisions. Are you going to let mistakes be made or are you going to masquerade that teams have decision-making authority?

Resources, especially in the form of professional employees, were not increased with the introduction of teams. For employees who were already feeling overworked and underappreciated, the addition of new team responsibilities exacerbated their cynicism about the division's intentions. Those who had experienced the downsizing of the mid-1980s were already dubious about the company's commitment to its employees and its products. Adding teams in the context of the corporation's strategic human resource initiative without removing any functional responsibilities (and, as some pointed out, without any investment in training) or increasing the staff was interpreted by many as a hollow gesture.

The implementation of the team system also failed to inspire confidence in the operating committee's commitment to teams. The functional and hierarchical orientation of the organization was unaffected by the team system. The distribution of stakes in the team's performance mirrored the distribution of resources and status across the functions. Giving the teams the right to choose their own team leader was purely symbolic in light of the persistence of these other distributions of power. Assigning members to teams on the basis of their positions in the functional hierarchy heightened their functional identifications and created the potential for conflict based on divergent functional interests.

That the Alpha team, among others, was able to buffer itself from the organizational pressures that worked against team work at the Medical Products Division is impressive and instructive. In a short period of time (just six months), despite the organizational pressures against effective team dynamics, the team created a clear demonstration of the enormous potential of teams, and for the observant, an illustration of the power of language to shape team dynamics.

LESSONS FROM THE ALPHA TEAM

The experiences of Greyser's Medical Products Division in designing and implementing product teams and the particular experience of the Alpha measurement team offer several useful insights into the challenges of team work. First, the Alpha team demonstrates that cross-functional teams can develop effective team dynamics despite organizational pressures that emphasize the apparently contradictory values of hierarchy, individual performance, and functional performance.

Second, key conditions for creating effective team dynamics under such circumstances include a meaningful, cross-functional task and the right people in leadership and membership positions. This case suggests that the criteria for identifying "the right people" go well beyond the usual prescription of the right skills; it indicates the positive effects of a leader who is seen as being very competent technically and as a coordinator/facilitator, and who shares power with the rest of the team. This case also indicates the importance of a competent membership that is eager to share the power and the responsibility for achieving the team task.

Third, this case shows the power of linguistic analysis in assessing team dynamics. By examining both the forms and functions of certain types of language, we were able to identify recurring patterns in the perceptions and behaviors of Alpha team members. In the chapters that follow, we will apply this analytical frame to transcripts of actual team conversations, and we will find even more revealing details about the dynamics within the teams and between the teams and their organizations.

Fourth, this case illustrates the complex and fascinating relationship between structure and process in organizations. When the Medical Products Division introduced the product teams, it created a new structural form but altered virtually none of its other major structural features, like its reporting lines, its evaluation and reward system, and its managerial hierarchy. The cross-functional teams were a small experiment. In most of MPD's teams, the team process never overcame the structural constraints of the organization. The Alpha team process, however, was on its way to becoming a force powerful enough to challenge those structural barriers in the organization. However, as so many of the players in this divisions reported, that team process was extremely vulnerable. Given the organizational forces working against effective team dynamics, it was widely believed that even the Alpha team would not be able to sustain the process it constructed. We see in this story the power and fragility of team talk.

The case of the Medical Products Division and the Alpha team also led to many questions about organizing for effective team work. How can an organization manage to establish strategic goals that do not place contradictory demands on the functions? How is it possible to maintain control without having evaluation and reward systems that focus on the individual? How much does the commitment of the operating committee or senior management team to the team concept contribute to team work? Does a significant team task enhance the commitment of team members to the team and task? Can a committed senior management group and a significant task overcome the problem of insufficient resources? In the next chapters, we will try to answer these questions.

CHAPTER 4

Functional Hierarchy and Individual Accountability

The Building Controls Division and the Tech I Team

This chapter tells the story of a team and an organization at a critical point for all concerned. The Tech I product, after many years in development, was within four months of its projected market introduction. The project was the most ambitious in the history of the Building Controls Division (BCD). The problem now was that the Tech I team was already behind on both the design and the production schedule. The pressure everyone felt was intense, exacerbating the functional antagonisms that were the legacy of both the organizational structure and the old, sequential product development process.

THE BUILDING CONTROLS DIVISION

The Building Controls Division of Spackler, Inc., was formed as a separate division in 1981, following a corporate overhaul that included several waves of downsizing, consolidating the locations of the engineering, manufacturing, and marketing/sales organizations, and establishing a parallel product development process and cross-functional teams. By 1988, BCD's 1,250 employees produced and sold climate controls and systems for four market areas: heating, ventilation, and air-conditioning (HVAC); burners and boilers; lighting; and water products. Its 1988 sales were more than $150 million. The division dealt with two types of customers: original equipment manufacturers (OEMs) and trade customers. OEMs incorporated Spackler products into their own products, which they in turn sold to the market; trade customers sold Spackler products directly. BCD placed highest priority on the quality of its products, on its flexibility, and its response to customers. Profitability and return on investment—both well above industry averages—were sources of pride.

Parallel Development and Cross-functional Teams

When BCD abandoned sequential development in the mid-1980s, it embraced a new process called parallel development, whereby people from the three critical functions—manufacturing, marketing/sales, and engineering—worked together on teams to guide a project from the conceptual stage all the way through final production. (Figure 4.1 depicts the division's map of relationships between teams and divisional

Figure 4.1 The Building Controls Division: teams and strategic goals.

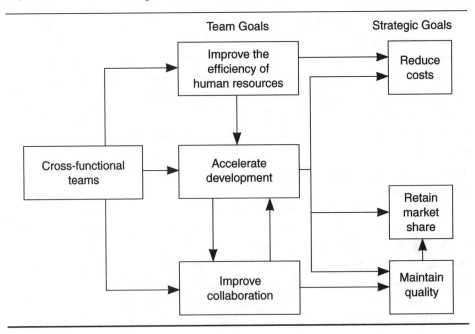

strategic goals.) These team members still reported to their functional managers, who continued to supervise and evaluate all employees, and each functional area continued to perform its specialized role on the project; yet all areas now worked on the same project simultaneously. The team guided and tracked the development, coordinating efforts across functions and addressing issues of mutual concern. A program manager was assigned to secure resources for the team, orchestrate its work, keep an eye on the complete project, and serve as a liaison to senior managers. There was, however, no formal team organization, and teams were appointed as needed, primarily according to skill and experience. Teams were assembled as a result of a negotiation between functions and business teams regarding the allocation of functional resources.

Seen in the division as highly effective forms of collaboration, the business teams were small, consisting of four to six middle managers. Their common goal was to decide upon the strategic direction and operational means for their business segment. Their commitment to this joint goal was at least partially related to having established "shared objectives"—interdependent goals written into their individual annual plans, the accomplishment of which would make each business team member bonus-eligible. These business unit teams commissioned product teams like Tech I, part of HVAC.

As BCD made the transition to parallel development, it had to confront its history and discard old habits. Marketing had always enjoyed a sacred position at BCD, as the general manager explained: "Marketing called all the shots, controlled the purse strings. Engineering felt it worked for marketing." Thus, to make the team system work, each functional area had to see itself as an equal partner and contributor. The Building Controls Division held a formal monthly review for each of its product teams, which typically entailed participation by the entire team as well as the division's senior managers. Team members' contributions were evaluated in these reviews, but members were held individually accountable for these activities by their functional managers. Their compensation and careers continued to be largely determined by these evaluations. Moreover, people had to accept additional responsibility— responsibility for the success of the entire project, not just for their functional role. Team members now had to attend team meetings whether relevant to their functional area or not. A manufacturing engineer, for example, had to attend team meetings even if the project was only at a design stage. Since people were accustomed simply to completing a task and passing the project on, they felt that team meetings stole time from doing actual work and added to their total work load. As people gradually adapted to parallel development and teams, they continued to struggle with their expanded roles and responsibilities. Several team members described the pressures they felt and what they perceived to be their sources:

> "We have to make a decision on the deployment of resources. When it comes to choosing between things to do, the answer from above is, 'Do both'—with no added resources. Or if we get additional resources, we're just stealing them from another project."

> "The system is heavily loaded, especially since we're learning a new way of working. There are many things to do with little head count and no relief with the project schedule. Engineering doesn't have a realistic schedule. This puts stress on the system. Teams could help but there are obstacles to having a team work on a project. You need true support from management. If somebody's supposed to be dedicated to a team, management has to be willing to let that person spend all of his or her time on the project. Logistics also need work. You have to be able to work out the fractions of people's time. You need one fully dedicated person from each function, but you also rely on the entire functional group. So people working on multiple projects have to know how to split their time. How do you prioritize projects? *All* work is high priority. And how do you reward people?"

The division's general manager commented:

> I can't be autocratic and dictatorial to my people, as I tended to be when I was vice president of marketing with Spackler Asia. All other things being equal, I'm a pretty good dictator. I'm very comfortable with that style. Part of the problem is, I grew up in this business. I understand HVAC. It's real easy for me to tell people what I think they have to do on almost any issue. But if I do that, and my staff does that, it goes right down the line, and we don't have teamwork. We also don't benefit from the ideas and perspectives of the whole work force.
>
> So I've tried to learn to have patience, change my style, look for consensus, have involvement of my staff as a team, share more information, be more open. I've had to learn that you take a risk with

this and not everything comes out the way you want it, but the potential payoffs far outweigh the risks.

I don't know how you legislate dedication, creativity, or motivation into people. I don't think you can. You can't tell people they have to do it a certain way. What you do is create the environment and the responsibility and be flexible.

But those are all new things for me. I didn't come to this as a natural team player. I got into this because it looked like the way this business could run best.

Using parallel development, BCD management believed that the division was now in a position to make better products—and in less time. Indeed, according to the division's estimates, the new system had reduced development time from an average of thirty-eight months to fourteen. The general manager saw speed as BCD's weapon for reclaiming competitive prominence, and he campaigned tenaciously to cut the time it took to get products from "concept to carton." Nonetheless, although people attributed much of the division's resurgence in the 1980s to the close working relationships that now existed between different functional groups, antagonism had not evaporated entirely, and finger pointing still occurred. A marketer and an engineer gave separate examples:

"From a schedule standpoint, engineering's credibility was no good. They were telling us dates that just weren't getting met. We [in marketing] tried to arrange shared goals and objectives, and it was like pulling teeth from engineering. They said they had their own milestones. The first shared deadline they suggested wasn't valid since we needed things from them well before that."

"We in engineering thought we had a minor design problem that we could solve as we worked on other problems. However, the problem didn't go away, so we moved it up on our list of priorities. Finally, we had to blow the whistle on ourselves because we felt the changes would require more time than the schedule allowed. We went to the head of marketing with our position. We said we were making progress but did not feel we would make our introduction date and needed more time. He said we had to stick to the dates we had. It's his prerogative to demand that the target dates be met, so the target dates were not changed, even though the team knew we weren't going to make it. Insisting that a date not change, though, can lead to a project problem. I'm not sure what's accomplished by insisting on unrealistic dates."

THE TECH I TEAM

With its new strategy for product development, BCD approached the Tech I project intent on "making the dates happen." The general manager explained the project's urgency: "Two competitors have introduced new products and retooled. They have overcapacity and are just waiting to steal market share. We cannot make a mistake." BCD was spending $19 million to develop Tech I, a motor used in heating, ventilation, and air conditioning (HVAC) applications, and planned to have it replace products accounting for over 30 percent of the division's profit. These figures led one senior manager to call Tech I "our golden egg."

The History of Tech I

In 1981 Jack Palmer, process engineer on the current Tech I team, was asked to examine how the company could improve the quality of its motors and reduce their cost. His study turned into a cost-reduction, quality-improvement initiative executed in three phases. Tech I represented the final and most ambitious phase. Although inspired by engineering, Tech I promised the most dramatic innovations in manufacturing and therefore was deemed a "flexible manufacturing project." With the one Tech I motor line, BCD planned to automate its entire assembly process and replace four families of motors—a total, per year, of more than 200,000 motors and over $20 million in revenue. The project promised to reduce costs and improve profit margins, making it attractive to the manufacturing people. But some marketers were concerned that customers would not accept this new motor and BCD would lose share, thereby reducing revenues, the primary index of marketing's contribution to the organization. The team, however, intended to offer a product with features and enhancements attractive to customers, and price incentives to encourage them to convert to the Tech I.

BCD began work on Tech I in 1984, prior to the introduction of teams and parallel development, but the same design and process engineers had worked together on Tech I from the beginning. They had even carved out an open office area, nicknamed "the bullpen," by removing partitions between cubicles and setting up a central conference table. Manufacturing engineers were frequent visitors to the bullpen and initiated many of the impromptu meetings. Design, process, and manufacturing, however, did not collaborate closely with marketing until 1986, when the current Tech I marketing people began replacing their predecessors on the project. One team member, an engineer, spoke about marketing's involvement:

> The marketing people have changed since the project began, while the engineers have been the same since the beginning. Marketing decisions changed each time the marketing people changed. We had to do two rounds of market research. This has had a negative psychological effect. It leaves the impression that the rationale developed in marketing is only as good as the people who developed it. So we lived through a change of direction. Not one marketing person is the same as when the project began.
>
> For a long time, marketing didn't buy into Tech I. They were force-fed enthusiastic. Now they're enthusiastic because it's a better product, but it's been a lot of extra work for them. They would have been better off with the combination of the old product and the absence of this extra work.

In 1986 Lisa Jensen became director of HVAC Controls (see figure 4.2). As the senior marketing person for the Tech I product line and with primary profit and loss responsibility for the product, she could see the impact any delay would have on her area's performance. She understood the pressing market need to have Tech I contain attractive features, and she knew that marketing had to play a more active role in the product's development. She had collaborated closely with her peers in other functional areas and described her role as HVAC director this way:

> I feel that it's a mini general manager position. I think that's the way business-unit directors are expected to perform. Of all the players, we have ultimate responsibility for the P&L. And I am responsible for my engineering deliverables. The engineers do not report to me, but I am accountable for telling them what projects to work on and in what order. Likewise, sales does not report to me, but my marketing group controls the revenue plan and unit-sales targets they must

Figure 4.2 Organization chart for the Building Controls Division and the Tech I team.

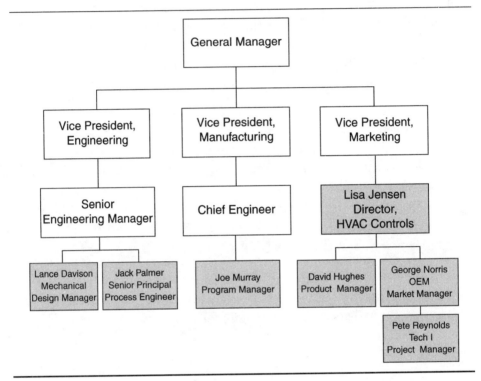

Note: Shaded boxes represent Tech I core team members.

achieve to earn bonuses. We're also responsible for developing their programs for customers and for authorizing special deals. We're responsible for defining the product road maps and introducing the products. We provide the technical support to customers—the training, the hot line, the technical support for the field reps. We're in charge of pricing, advertising, and sales promotion activities. We're also responsible for arbitrating unresolved delivery problems and for determining delivery codes and lead times. It runs the gamut.

She explained how marketing had to make up for lost time on Tech I:

Marketing was uninvolved for a long time—for two reasons. First, it was never a marketing-driven development, which is highly unusual. Second, marketing was so Johnny-come-lately. By the time we had a solid marketing team established, engineering and manufacturing were entrenched in the way they believed it should be done. That made it much harder when we did come along.

The new marketers' concern led the team to revise the project's scope, but marketers still had some lingering uneasiness. A marketer explained:

> Tech I is replacing our bread and butter for no market-driven reason. Sure, it's a cost reduction and a quality improvement, but our motors already are very high quality and provide high margins, so from a marketing standpoint, it didn't have to be done. The customer benefits derived from Tech I, including modules, could be developed for our present motor lines.

Team Issues

Since fall of 1988, the Tech I core team of seven members (see figure 4.2) had been meeting Friday afternoons to discuss major issues and to resolve cross-functional disputes. Although team members interacted almost every day, the meeting guaranteed joint discussion and allowed the team to delve into issues, address all concerns, and come to a resolution with all parties present. In addition to Lisa Jensen, core team members included the following people:

Joe Murray—Program Manager. He served as a program manager while also supervising the project's manufacturing efforts and several other manufacturing activities. Murray had recently joined the Tech I team, and although he had known all of the project's engineers for ten years, he called himself "the new kid on the block." He described his role as program manager:

> I try to keep all ends tied together for the net result. Where are we on tooling dollars, engineering design, order and delivery of the production machines? I tie all the pieces together to make sure they hit the floor at the same time. I make sure communication is happening so that all things are getting done. I make sure we don't get one of these things where we get all done and someone says, "You didn't tell us about that."

Jack Palmer—Senior Principal Process Engineer and "Father" of Tech I. His 1981 study led to the development of Tech I, which he now worked on.

Lance Davison—Mechanical Design Manager. In charge of all engineering efforts on Tech I, Davison supervised all seven design engineers working on HVAC Controls products. Six of those engineers were working on Tech I, and Davison himself had worked on the product since it began in 1984. Although he rarely let the pressure of a situation disturb his demeanor, he acknowledged the history of tension on the project:

> The impetus for the program was increased profit. The project is attractive to manufacturing because they're profit-driven. Marketing is revenue-driven, and this product may reduce revenue. Since it will cost less to make the Tech I, customers will want it for less, and that will reduce revenue. Engineering's objectives are to deliver at cost, on time, and with the specified features. Dates are our driver. Engineering is neither revenue- nor profit-driven. We're market-driven, but we respond to manufacturing as well. To bring the product to market, engineering has to do certain things and marketing has to do certain things. What marketing has to do is often dependent upon engineering support. But what marketing needs engineering to do is not necessarily the next thing on the list of priorities for engineering.

Pete Reynolds—Tech I Project Manager. As the only marketer working full-time on Tech I, Reynolds was marketing's "field marshal" on the project, responsible for the product's smooth introduction to the marketplace. However, "It's [Tech I is] kind of scary. I'm feeling reasonably comfortable, but there are some things that make me feel uncomfortable." He attributed the tension between marketers and engineers to the project's history: "It's somewhat a power struggle because this has been engineering's baby. Engineering saw marketing as just getting in the way."

David Hughes—Product Manager. As product manager, he supervised all technical content of HVAC Controls products, serving as the liaison between field sales and engineering. Hughes joined marketing in 1986 and had worked on Tech I thereafter.

George Norris—OEM Market Manager. Norris supervised marketing efforts directed at OEMs. He maintained a focus on customers, whereas David Hughes focused on products. Although Norris devoted his time to many projects during the week, Tech I was the most important product he had to introduce, and the weekly team meeting gave him an opportunity to learn about the project's progress, provide input, and voice his concerns. He described the role marketers played on the team:

> Marketers with an engineering background have a tendency to tell engineering how to do things. People on our team are getting better at not doing that. Marketers are forced to be confrontational to make things right for the customer. We've all had to play the bad guy at times. But Pete [Reynolds] has had to make sure that the product can be introduced. That has put him in the role of "lead bad guy."

By April 1989, Tech I was behind on both the design and the production schedule, although the team was fighting to meet its August 1989 date for introducing Tech I to the marketplace. The marketers were busy preparing a training video for Tech I users. The engineers had their hands full with a noise problem. And the manufacturing engineers were ordering parts and arranging the assembly lines. The team as a whole still had to decide about control modules, a volatile issue that had inspired heated debate. A module could be added to a standard motor to change its function, thereby providing increased flexibility and eliminating the need to have distributors stock separate motors for different applications. The motor's flexibility would also appeal to customers.

One competitor had introduced control modules in its new motor, and another had followed with an even better modular system. Pete Reynolds, marketing project manager for Tech I, concluded, "Motor customers expect Spackler to come out with a better module provision." The Tech I business plan did mention modules, but marketing and engineering interpreted the commitment to modules differently. He explained:

> Engineering did not have a module provision and intended to solve the problem by having the distributor stock a large number of different circuit boards. We can't give distributors—our customers in this case—the impression that they have to stock extra components because it saves us money. Engineering doesn't consider modules important. They see modules as peripheral. They say that only the

most sophisticated units need them, and that's only 10 percent of volume. But the varieties within that 10 percent account for over half of the total varieties of Tech I motors. That's why the distributors don't want to stock extra motors or circuit boards.

Reynolds believed the Tech I had to include a module to provide a feature customers desired. Although a module did not have to be available for the initial product introduction, he did not want to make this suggestion. Engineering, he felt, had dismissed the importance of modules for too long and might be tempted to use the offer as yet another way to postpone work on them. Reynolds wanted to get the engineers' commitment to develop modules.

Lance Davison (mechanical design engineering manager) understood the marketers' interest in modules, but with limited resources at his disposal, not to mention other design problems confronting him and his staff, he felt he could not actively develop them at this time. He outlined his concern with modules:

> As we wrote the Tech I business plan, modules were defined in concept but not in detail. The number of modules and their specific functions weren't detailed in the business plan.
>
> At times, marketing establishes criteria that are very difficult for engineering to meet. Marketing defined a Tech I case that is small enough to fit the product strategy but not big enough to fit the module, as we normally produce it, and everything else that has to go into the unit.
>
> With regard to space inside the unit, we might be able to split the module into two parts, which would make it fit into the unit. That's not how we normally produce a module. It means additional plastic parts and therefore added cost, so I haven't entertained it as an option.

Davison and his staff were concentrating on solving a noise problem with Tech I. The motor was producing excessive noise, and the engineers were trying to determine its source and correct the problem. He was confronting a classic engineering dilemma:

> If there are design changes that involve a manufacturing tool, there is no way to test that change until the tool is completed, and that's

a long lead-time proposition. Final testing of the change cannot be done until final production parts are available, and that happens precisely when we're also trying to move the product into production. So pressure mounts at that one time. There's also pressure up front when a designer suggests a change of this sort.

Lisa Jensen also found herself in a difficult predicament:

It's sometimes really hard for me to figure out what is the right thing to do. Getting new products out when we do requires prodding and nagging and pushing and cajoling and pleading. I'd prefer not to do all that because I see the tremendous loads engineering and manufacturing have, and I feel bad about bothering them. But if I don't keep after them, my revenue plan suffers. I understand the pressures they face, and if I push too much, I'll only alienate my colleagues in the other functional areas, and things will get worse. As it is, they're beleaguered. They're just stressed to the max. Putting more stress on people doesn't get any results.

Surveying the challenge facing the team, David Hughes concluded:

Pressure on schedule originates with return on investment (ROI). If the schedule is strung out, ROI decreases. That's a good reason to have milestones chiseled in stone—leverage, since things must be done by certain dates to achieve that ROI. It also lets customers know when things will be ready. But it's not good to insist on a chiseled date when it's clear you're not going to meet the date.

Added Jack Palmer:

I worked on the biggest "It-will-happen" project in the history of the United States—the Apollo project. They said, "You will get to the moon." But we couldn't go until we were ready. And Apollo had unlimited funds. If management thought someone or something could help, the project got it. Tech I doesn't have that luxury. I can understand why BCD management can't run over on cost or schedule. . . . It's blind, though, to think that just by saying something's going to get done by a certain date, it's going to get done.

BCD's general manager was aware of the difficulties confronting Tech I:

We have several problems going on right now, and I'm not really happy about them, but no one expects me to be happy about them. But I know all those people are really working hard to resolve the problems. Now if you jump in there and shout, or accuse, then what you're basically saying is you don't have faith in the people you've assembled to get the job done, or you don't think that they're giving it their best effort. We may lack some skills in the technology we're in, but basically I think we have a good set of people, and I think they're working really hard. My job is to support them rather than shout at them.

My highest priority on this project is quality. I know it's $19 million and the clock's ticking on the cash flow and all that, but our bread and butter is the motor line. This new motor has to be equal to the performance of the old one, has to be, because we have such a good reputation, and we have two competitors out there just waiting to take our market share. So I can't risk performance problems on the new motor, even if we have to say we'll never run the $19 million investment. It would be better to do that than to risk our share.

We sometimes hasten to assume that people want to be directed. I try to listen to a team's problems, make them feel empowered, and suddenly they feel they can climb mountains. It gives them an emotional lift.

If I think they're giving it their best shot, and problems are occurring because of the technology, or because of resources, or because of vendors, then let's go work those problems. Work the things, the issues. Don't blame the people. I think we have good people. They're working hard, doing the best they can. If there's a problem, maybe we didn't select the right ones for the team, maybe we haven't trained them right, maybe we haven't given them the right resources. Let's go work those issues.

In hindsight, if I had it to do all over, I wouldn't try to implement a new design and a new line simultaneously. I thought we had laid out sufficient time between phases that we could manage it. But it's too much to ask. It's too many variables for one team to manage. . . . That's what I've learned. I'll never make that mistake again. I take that as my fault. That's not the team's fault. I never had a project this big before.

THE TECH I TEAM'S TALK

On cross-functional teams, communication is often a major problem, since different disciplines tend to develop their own languages and values. The Tech I team was no exception, as two team members commented:

> "We've had a lot of problems with language on this project. We've had a lot of semantic issues with the differences between what's literally required in the application versus what's required in order to position the product in our distribution channel. What's been hard about that is we haven't known we've disagreed."

> "We asked distributors whether they would need more single-shaft or more double-shaft motors. The distributors said, 'The majority of applications will be single-shaft.' Engineers and marketers were sitting in the same room, listening to the same distributors say that. Engineers took that information and prepared to make primarily single-shaft motors. When marketers found out, they felt it was a disaster. Regardless of where the majority of applications fall, the distributor always wants to make sure either case can be handled, so the distributor will stock double-shaft motors, which can also be used for single-shaft applications. We all heard the same piece of information in the same setting. Engineering was listening for the literal application. Marketing was listening for the customer's buying preferences."

However, different dialects and focus were the least of their problems with language, as the following section on the team's talk shows. What follows are excerpts and linguistic analysis from a Tech I team meeting that reveal many of the difficulties team members expressed in their interviews.

The excerpts below were taken from a single meeting that lasted *five hours*. It was scheduled at the insistence of Pete Reynolds because two previous weekly meetings had been canceled by Lance Davison due to other, pressing demands. The subject is the thorny issue of control modules, and the team members, in order of appearance, are: George Norris (OEM market manager), Lance Davison (mechanical design manager), David Hughes (product manager), Pete Reynolds (project manager, marketing), and Lisa Jensen (director, HVAC controls). Jack Palmer and Joe Murray did not attend this session.

It is important to note that people do not speak the way they write. They repeat themselves, they leave things out, and they don't always speak in grammatically correct sentences. Sometimes these "mistakes" are meaningless and irrelevant to the conversation. Often, we don't even notice them. Frequently, these behaviors are meaningful and they provide the attentive listener with clues for interpretation. For the purposes of this transcription and the interpretation, I have faithfully recorded what the speakers actually *said,* using the following conventions:

****	where utterances have been deleted
//	overlapping talk or interruption
. . .	a pause of one second or less
(3.2)	a pause of more than one second, length indicated in seconds
[ ]	an explanatory insertion
.	a falling intonation marking end of assertion, even if it is not a grammatically complete sentence
?	a rising intonation marking question form
italics	emphasis

Excerpts

Several members of the team enter the meeting room where an engineering meeting has just ended later than scheduled.

1 George: You mean we're ready to start the Tech I meeting, now?

2 Lance: Sorry . . . we're scrambling so much because we got so many things **** our purpose is to further converge on the features that are kind of peripheral to the main design, the modules and the accessories and . . . we have developed [some mild group laughter] . . . peripheral, all the pieces that go together [laughs] to make it up. We have developed what is a final configuration model **** The things that are on the list to talk about are the box, the modules, the auxiliary switches, the things that go in the box. We also have the mounting hardware to show you. So I think we probably want to start with modules. We had a good meeting on the twenty-seventh where we talked concept and I think we converged on requirements and things

we can provide, and this is the next step in further refining that discussion.

[Brief discussion of the module design ensues]

3 David: Lance? Uh, you know, maybe it's because I'm not as much up to speed as everyone else here is, but it seems to me that we've jumped right into solving problems. Do we have a list is there a list of the accessories we're gonna review today and how we're gonna step through 'em?

4 Lance: Yeah, there is//

5 Pete: I have a list of things that we need.

6 Lisa: Kinda like an agenda that we can have in front of us?

7 David: So we can see where we are? And what we are and what we're trying to cover?

8 Pete: Let me make copies of this.
     [Silence (3.4)]
     [quiet talk]

9 Unknown: Pete's ordering lunch.

10 David: That's what he told me. Box lunches.

11 Lisa: Marketing pays again?

12 Unknown: Sure.

13 Lisa: Engineering hasn't offered to pay for a midyear lunch. Production paid. Marketing paid twice.

14 Lance: We bought pizza.

15 Lisa: Yeah, right. One pizza for twenty people.
      [group laughter]

16 Unknown: Everybody's on a diet.

17 Lisa: Speak for your*self!* [Group laughter] You're on a diet when you're eating on engineering's budget.

18 David: So are we gonna go through these in the order that Pete has 'em? And just go through so we have a list of what we're checking //

19 Pete: Yeah, this is just a list. Lance, I don't know if you have a certain order or format or structure of how to review this? Er //

20 Lance: I'd prefer to review the modules first as you have on the list here //

21   David: The interface modules?

22   Lisa: Number eight?

23   Lance: No, this list that came out with the meeting notice.

24   Pete: So everybody has a list of the items needed. Let's look at that.

25   Lance: Okay.

26   Pete: When you say that modules. And you mentioned before as being a peripheral part of the motor. Really this is where all the pieces of the motor come together. These are the parts that is the human customers and end-users come into direct contact with and the part that they are going to see. So I think this is as important as the heart of the motor is. And I think how we review it, what order we take, will really help structure the review and make the best use of the time. So if we really start at the right point**** But I think we should try to set an approach and follow that through. You know, rather than just hit items at random. Does anyone have any questions?

27   David: I guess the question I have is, this is a lot of people, is this gonna be a formal review where we all go back like we did the critique sheets? Or is it gonna look at the motor in front of us and more or less comment as it comes around, and then there's no plans to break off into three disciplines or anything like that?

28   Lance: Nuh-uh. This needs to be a working session and we need to come out of here with a resolve are we on track, are we off track and if we're off track, and where are we missing if we're off. And we've got to turn it around as fast as we can go. That's our purpose in being here today is to check where we are on track and redirect where we're off.

29   David: Okay.

30   Lance: We have *no* time and this is extremely critical timewise. The box is our most critical part and revising puts us in extreme jeopardy of our August date.

31   Pete: And I think we all agreed that it was going to be an informal review. The question just is if we come up with some things that are really wrong, then we are gonna have to make it right.

32   Lance: Well, *yeah,* that's what we're here for.
    [Silence (2.7)]

33   Lisa: Since everyone from marketing is talking, I'll add to the wordiness. I understand from a *design* point of view that these are peripheral issues, the auxiliary, accessories and the //

34 Lance: That was a poor choice of words if we're gonna get hung up on that.

35 Lisa: No, but I just do want to clarify that all these things are central to the introduction, and I would also agree that the order in which we address them is also quite significant. We all are driving to an August framework; we need to not let that get in the way of making the right decision //

36 David: That's true.

37 Lisa: So while I may, I'm here saying, "Well, let's not worry about August," I don't want anybody to quote me outside of this meeting, 'cause I don't want to lose my job, which may drive you to do so. [group laughter] But I really do think in this context that first of all we ought to be thinking about what's the *right* thing to sustain the **** business long-term//

38 David: Uh-huh.

39 Lisa: And *then* figure out, is it or is it not doable by August. I don't mean to imply that August isn't important, I just want to say we need to keep the primary objective around here.

[Silence and sighs]

40 Pete: Let's start by looking at the list we have in front of us and see if there's a certain order. Again I just numbered the items and put 'em on. It wasn't meant to be in orderly structure. But this should be fairly inclusive of everything we have to talk about today, and may include things we don't have to talk about. And I do agree that the box is really the crucial item we have to talk about now, so we should probably talk about items that affect that and we should probably leave off things like ****** I think we should make sure we discuss those things before we go on. Now, of those items, I don't know if there's a certain order that you think is most effective?

41 Lance: I think we should start with the modules 'cause those are the most critical thing.
****

42 Pete: (As Lance begins to gather up his papers) I guess you're about done?

43 Lance: I'd like to wrap up.

44 David: Are you leaving?

45 Lance: I'm gonna try. I wanna see my daughter play ball.

46 David: Softball?

47 Pete: I hope these aren't weekly games, Lance? . . . Does she play at four o'clock every Friday?

48 Lance: Three a week. Yup. I'm gonna be scarce as I can be.

49 David: I was gonna bring my daughter along.

50 Pete: What does that do to our 2:30 to 4:30 meeting?

51 Lance: Shortens it.
   [group laughter]

52 Pete: Well, if you're leaving at 3:20, does that mean that you'll want to, should we try to //

53 Lance: It would be nice if it could be earlier. [some group laughter] Maybe you have it without me and get something done too.

54 Pete: Should we change to a different day?

55 Lance: No. 'Cause the day is . . . maybe we could do it earlier.

56 Pete: I don't know if we could get started before 2:30.

57 Lance: Yeah.

58 George: An alternative would be to meet right after your morning meeting. 10 to what—11:30.

59 Lance: Trouble is, our morning meeting doesn't really control itself to one hour. We often need more than that.

LINGUISTIC ANALYSIS OF THE EXCERPTS

The linguistic analysis of these excerpts from the Tech I team's talk is guided by the team talk audit described in chapter 2. As we did in our analysis in the preceding chapter, we will listen for both function and form in each of the key categories of team talk. Table 4.1 presents the audit of the Tech I team.

Table 4.1 Audit of the Tech I team.

Dimensions	Samples of Team Talk	Your Interpretation	Score
Identification	"our purpose is to. . . . we probably want to start with modules" (2) "We have developed . . . a final . . . model. . . . we also have . . . hardware to show you." (2) "Pete's ordering lunch." ". . . Marketing pays again?" (9–17) "everyone from marketing is talking" (33)	Many inclusive references to the team, many references to functional groups, frequent identifications of people with functional group nouns. Using language strategically (26–27).	Mixed, Functional
Interdependence	"I have a list of things that we need." (5) "Let me make copies" (8) "we should try to set an approach" (26) "we need to come out of here" (28) "we all agreed" (31) "we need to keep the primary objective" (39) "I have a list" (5) "I'd prefer to review" (20) "I think we should" (26) "I'm gonna be scarce" (48)	Considerable expression of shared needs, implicit and explicit (5, 8, 26, 28, 31, 39). Some expression of individual intent (5, 20, 26, 42, 48). But lots of power differentiation (see next categories).	Mixed
Power Differentiation	"You mean we're ready to start . . . ?" (1) "You're on a diet, when you're eating on engineering's budget." (17) "I don't want to lose my job, which may drive you to do so." (37) "That was a poor choice of words" (34) "Do we have a list?" (3) "Kinda like an agenda . . . ?" (6) "are we gonna go through these in the order that Pete has 'em?" (18)	Humor as a weapon (1, 2, 11–17, 37, 42). Apologies shows deference to power (2, 34). Questions of engineering by marketing (3, 6, 7, 18, 19, 31, 26, 27, 42, 44, 47, 50). Leading questions (3, 6, 7). Challenges to competence (19, 40). Assertions of individual opinion or intent (8, 26, 35, 40, 45, 48). Interruptions of engineering by marketing (4).	High

Table 4.1 Continued

Dimensions	Samples of Team Talk	Your Interpretation	Score
	"I think this is as important. . . . I think. . . . I think"(26) "we need to come out of here" (28) "I just do want to clarify . . . I would also agree" (35) "I'm here saying . . . let's not worry about August" (37)	Dominance of talk by same people (marketing has 37 turns to engineering's 19).	
Social Distance	First names (3, 18, 19, 47) "You're on a diet when you're eating on engineering's budget." (17) "our purpose is to . . . converge on the features. . . . We had a good meeting . . . next step in further refining" (2) "I just do want to clarify that all these things" (35) "Lance, I don't know if you have a certain order" (19)	First names indicate proximity but are not used frequently (only five times), no nicknames. Humor is sarcastic and implies negative evaluation (11–17, 50–53). Formality and politeness. No slang but some slurring of sounds. No expression of admiration or liking, no common membership claimed. No peremptory demands or requests.	Distant
Conflict Management Tactics	"Let me make copies of this." (8) Lance makes no response when Pete insists on copying his list for others. "we are gonna have to make it right" (31) "that's what we're here for" (32) "from a *design* point of view" (33) "a poor choice of words if we're gonna get hung up on that" (34) "I'm gonna be scarce as I can be." (48)	Displays of force (power) are repeatedly met with either avoidance or accommodation.	Forcing, Avoiding, Accommodating

Table 4.1 Continued

Dimensions	Samples of Team Talk	Your Interpretation	Score
Negotiation Process	"this is as important as the heart" (26) "I. . . want to clarify that all these things are central" (35)	Team members argue from positions. No attempts to find underlying interests or to invent new mutually beneficial options.	Win-Lose
	"Marketing pays again?" (9–17) "I understand from a *design* point of view" (33)	Orientation to distribution of credit and blame.	

Identification

The linguistic evidence for team members' primary identifications is mixed, though it shows stronger connections with functional groups than with one another. There are numerous uses of the plural first-person pronouns "we," "us," and "our" to refer to the team and to the functional groups, as well as many references that are ambiguous. For example, Lance's turn 2 reveals both identifications with twelve pronouns including ten "we's," one "our," and one "you." In five instances, these refer to the team and appear in the first and last two sentences. The evidence for the team as referent come from the participants in the two meetings he mentions. In the other instances, the word "we" refers to engineering and "you" to the other members of the team, the evidence here being the group who participated in the development of the product model and the identity of those who will be seeing it that day for the first time. Lance's identification as evidenced in turn 28, where the pronouns are very ambiguous, might be said to be with the team. However, reference to the event itself would suggest that he is identifying here with the engineers who are submitting their work to the team for review and advice.

In five turns (3–7) at the beginning of this meeting, three team members from marketing use "we" and "us" eleven times, and every reference is to the team. This is typical of these members; in this episode, there is not a single use of a plural pronoun by one of these people referring to their function. However, two other aspects of this conversation suggest that this use of plural pronouns to include the other team members may be a strategic projection of image rather than unconscious reflections of their psychological identifications. The first aspect is Lisa's explicit identification of people with their functional groups in specific and negative comparisons, suggesting that at a deeper level, she identifies herself and others more with their functions than with the team as a whole. In turn 11, Lisa clearly identifies Pete (turn 9) with his group, and she continues to do this in turns 13–17. She makes a similar identification in turn 33 by characterizing people by their functional affiliation, both the marketers and the "design" engineers. In both instances, Lisa calls attention to the boundary that separates the team members and implies a negative evaluation of the engineers.

The second type of evidence suggesting that the marketers may be using the pronouns with team identification strategically is very subtle and appears in Pete's response to Lance's statement of the meeting's purpose (turns 28–31). Pete's use of the inclusive pronoun with an idiomatic verb of compulsory action ("we are gonna have to make it right") must be interpreted in light of the fact that several speakers including Lance are interpreting this meeting as a review by marketing of engineering's latest designs. In this context, Pete's "we" seems inappropriate given that he is not an engineer and does not have the skill to design or redesign a part. An alternative interpretation is that this pronoun and verb form reflect Pete's sense of the team as an integrated unit in which some people do the work that others review and direct. This presumption of power differences again emphasizes the boundary between marketing and engineering and is indicative of a stronger identification with functional groups than with the team.

Interdependence

Numerous expressions of individual and shared needs indicate that this team recognizes its interdependency at one level. Yet the occasional expression of individual intent and the significant use of power differences show that at least some of these team members also experience themselves as independent of the others. For example, Pete (turn 5) and Lance (turn 28) both talk about what "we need." Even if Lance's pronoun is interpreted as referring to engineering, his whole comment here reflects a perception of engineering's dependence on other team members. Lisa (turns 35, 37, and 39) makes explicit reference to the team members' interdependence in meeting the business objectives.

This perception of interdependence, though, is balanced by behaviors that exhibit independence in a variety of ways. For example, while David and Lisa are asking or possibly inviting Lance to shape the meeting's agenda (turns 3, 6, 7), Pete interrupts Lance to put his own agenda forward: "I have a list of things we need" (turn 5). Despite Lance's repeated attempts to provide the structure requested (turns 4, 20, 23), Pete persists in putting his independent views before the group (turns 8, 19, 24, 26).

In turn 20, Lance shows some signs of independence. He interrupts Pete to reiterate his preference to start with a discussion of modules. While it is not entirely clear from his words whether he is simply asserting his independence or has not understood that the marketers were seeking not a first topic but an overview of the day's topics, the interruption reflects perceptions of power equality. Lance's reference to an alternative to Pete's list as the authoritative one (which becomes clear in the subsequent confusion of turns 20–23) support the interpretation of his assertion as an act of independence. In turn 23, Lance clarifies that he is referring to another list and counters the impression that he is not prepared by pointing out that the list he refers to had accompanied the notice about the meeting. In light of Lance's current insistence on using an alternative to Pete's list, it is difficult to interpret his allowing Pete the time to copy his list for everyone; he might have been distracted and not heard Pete or was perhaps avoiding conflict.

In the concluding section of the excerpts (turns 42–59), Lance exhibits an unusual degree of independence, both verbally and physically. Without seeking anyone's approval or agreement and even without comment, he prepares to leave the meeting. When asked about this, his answers take the form of intentions to take individual and independent action: "I'm gonna try," "I wanna see my daughter," and "I'm gonna be scarce." When Pete expresses his disapproval through the powerful form of questions and expression of his personal feelings (turn 47), Lance displays independence and social distance by answering the question literally while ignoring Pete's expressed preference and asserting his intention to pursue this independent action on a regular basis in the future (48). When Pete acknowledges his dependence on Lance by referring to "our meeting" and asking Lance to consider the implications of his independent action on the team, Lance uses humor and a literal response again, showing independence and social distance (turn 51). Lance persists in this tactic, which might be called passive aggression, through four attempts by Pete and George to find solutions that would integrate his interests and theirs (turns 52–57).

This incident also epitomizes the extensive struggle for power in this team, which reflects the team's tensions about dependency. Because they feel independent of one another, they utilize power differences, yet their very use of these tactics to accomplish team work reveals their sense of being interdependent to some degree. The next section analyzes the way the team employs power differences in their talk.

Power Differences

The talk of the Tech I team reflects vividly both the differences in the organizational clout of the Tech I team members and the ambiguity of power in the context of team interdependence. The marketers display and use their power as the lead function in this "market-driven division" by asking all the questions (turns 1, 3, 6, 7, 11, 18, 19, 21, 22, 26, 27, 40, 42, 44, 46, 47, 49, 50, 53, 54) and by dominating the floor. Some of these questions can be interpreted as leading questions that challenge the competence of the engineers (3, 6, 7). Apologies (2, 34) and accommodation (8, 25) by Lance are indicative of his perception of having less power than the marketers. Yet, subtle aspects of the team's talk show that the power relationship is complicated by the dependency of marketing on engineering to get the product out. Indeed, this excerpt is bracketed by two exchanges in which power differences are displayed and used through humor.

In turn 1, George looks to Lance and expresses mock surprise that the scheduled team meeting is going to begin. Reference to the social context of Lance's having just ended another meeting late and thus kept the other Tech I team members waiting to start their meeting indicates that George is not really surprised or confused about Lance's behavior in trying to convene the Tech I team. His comment is ironic, and despite his first person plural pronoun reflecting a team identification and the humor that might signal social proximity, it produces no laughter. The team does not respond to it as if it were a signal of social proximity. Lance's subsequent apology and explanation for the late start (turn 2) acknowledge the humor as a negative sanction from someone with equal or greater power. The subsequent struggle for control over the agenda and the apparently superficial use of team identifications makes George's comment feel like the sarcastic jibe of someone trying to mask ill will and/or manipulate.

In the exchange at the end of this excerpt, it is Lance who uses humor to display his power (turn 51). His literal response to Pete's question about the consequences of his independent intention to leave the meeting early is obviously seen as inappropriate and thus is treated as humorous by some on the team (group laughter immediately followed it). As a reaction to a team member's concern, it displays a lack of empathy, independence, and a perception of having the power to reject the others' requests.

A third example in which humor reflects the power struggle within this team occurs in the discussion of who is paying for the team's lunch (turns 11–17). Here a common type of workplace joke develops into a boundary-marking occasion, as well as another opportunity to have a laugh at engineering's expense. The round begins with Lisa identifying Pete with marketing, rather than with the team (turn 11), and her question expresses a complaint about unfair distribution of resources: "Marketing pays again?" She then recounts previous contributions, while identifying people by their functional department, and concludes with an assertion that her group has contributed more than others. Lance adopts this distributive focus and expresses identification with his functional group (turn 14). In the final turn of this round, Lisa turns someone's joking account of being on a diet into a sarcastic generalization about engineering's meager contributions (turn 17). Her imperative verb in the first sentence of this turn is clearly a powerful speech form, and both the cleverness of the rejoinder and the disparagement of engineering create social distance within the team, orienting the members toward the other groups with which they identify.

The most obvious feature of power relationships in this team is the ongoing struggle here to control the agenda. In the process, team members from marketing dominate the floor, taking 37 turns compared to engineering's 19, ask all the questions, and ignore the answers they receive. (This disparity is partly due to the fact that Lance is the only team member from engineering at this meeting, but this pattern of dominance in the team talk is also reflected in the functional make-up of the team.) The stuggle begins with Lance's opening comment (turn 2), in which he mentions a list of topics to be addressed in the meeting and proposes beginning the discussion with the subject of modules.

Several minutes after that discussion begins, David asks Lance whether he has a plan for structuring the meeting (turn 3). At the content level, this would seem to challenge Lance's competence in running the meeting; however, David's linguistic choices minimize the accusatory nature of his questions and his observation that they have "jumped right into solving problems." He opens by addressing Lance by first name, which signals social proximity. He then follows this with a disclaimer, "I'm not as much up to speed as everyone else," and finally hedges his observation as a personal perspective, "it seems to me." He also identifies with Lance and the team by using the first person plural four times, including himself in the group of people apparently doing the wrong thing, then asking whether the team has a list of topics to review and make progress on. Although he might have directly impugned Lance's leadership by using the second person, such as "Do you have a list?" he does not do so.

The advantages of such a display of identification, interdependence, and social proximity on David's part are suggested by Lance's immediate response in turn 4, "Yeah." However, Lance has no chance to remind David that he has already mentioned the list, before Pete proffers his list (turn 5), with Lisa and David reiterating the question and desirability of an agenda (turns 6 and 7). This repetition of questions, *all from marketing personnel*, seems to silence Lance, for he does not mention his list again for several turns (until turn 20). The questions, in light of Pete's immediate substitute and Lance's acquiescence, take on the quality of leading questions. This impression of entrapment persists despite the use of the inclusive first person pronouns in three turns (turns 5–7), which seem to draw the boundary around the team and signal identification with it. In a much later turn (34), Lance will display a similar interpretation of being trapped. For the time being, his silence may be interpreted as the reaction of the powerless.

Meanwhile David, perhaps motivated by his prior experience of working on numerous engineering projects with Lance, refocuses the conversation on the task at hand by offering Lance the right to say how the meeting will proceed (turn 18). He does this with a question form. Before Lance can answer, Pete reiterates the question (turn 19). As if this "double-teaming" weren't challenging enough, Pete's linguistic form subtly questions Lance's competence: his introductory words, "I don't know if you have a certain order," imply a doubt that Lance has prepared to run an organized meeting, and his repetition of synonyms, "format or structure," hammers this point.

Pete appears in turn 24 to concede to Lance, as "the list" of earlier remarks becomes "a list" here. He also uses a proposal verb form and inclusive pronoun, "Let's," displaying interdependence and social proximity. But this conciliatory demeanor is not maintained. In turn 26, Pete challenges Lance's earlier characterization of modules as peripheral, using powerful and distancing linguistic forms that express certainty, directness, and disconfirmation such as the adverb "really" with the assertion forms "this is" and "these are," and beginning three sentences with assertions of his opinion, "I think." A team member sensitive to criticism might also be disturbed by Pete's framing of the alternative to his own agenda-setting proposal as "just hit[ting] items at random." His concluding remark, "Does anyone have any questions?" takes the ritualistic form for controlling a discussion.

In David's response (turn 27), he again signals identification with the team through his plural pronouns and again addresses questions to Lance as if acknowledging his right to control the meeting. David's final question about plans to break into three subgroups by discipline reflects the group's history of breaking down into coalitions, a practice that might account for the team's inability to forge a common agreement.[1]

Lance's confident assertions (turn 28) of team goals and needs appear to satisfy David (turn 29); but Pete (turn 31) seems still to be unconvinced ("the question . . . is if we come up with some things") of Lance's commitment to the team. In his response (turn 32), Lance signals that this forcing is unnecessary, since the whole team has convened for the purpose of review and adjustment: "Well, *yeah*, that's what we're here for."

The silence that follows Lance's assertion is notable for the absence of confirmation by other team members. In fact, the next comment not only signals identification of team members with their functional areas but also reintroduces a distributive orientation. Lisa (turn 33) creates these impressions by identifying herself with the marketing coalition and characterizing Lance's use of the word "peripheral" as deriving from his "design point of view" on the team task.

Lance (turn 34) concedes to her argument and her display of power and distance with an implicit apology for his "poor choice of words." Lance's "if we're gonna get hung up on that" implies that she is playing verbal power games. But Lisa (turn 35) declines his retraction with an initial "No," followed by an emphatic assertion of independent intent ("I just do want to clarify") and a seconding of Pete's view. She also echoes Pete's condescension through her use of inclusive "we" with verbs of compulsion ("we need to" and in turn 37, "we ought to"). In turn 37, Lisa also differentiates herself as having the power to relax constraints on the team, "I'm here saying 'Well, let's not worry about August' " and to dictate what they can and cannot say outside the room. She does have some real claim to this power as the person with profit and loss responsibility for the Tech I product. Others on the team have their interests as well, which accounts for much of the struggle for control that we have observed here. The silence and sighs that follow Lisa's repetition of the team's obligation in turn 39 suggest recognition of joint responsibility but a lack of commitment to joint action.

Despite this evanescent recognition of their interdependence, the team quickly reverts to a common pattern of using power differences to achieve desired ends. Pete picks up the conversation (turn 40) with a proposal for joint action on his suggestion for setting the agenda. He bypasses an opportunity to show solidarity with Lance by making it explicit that it is Lance's opinion about the importance of the box that he is agreeing with. He repeats his opinion of how the meeting should proceed and concludes by asking Lance a question that Lance has already answered twice. Lance, nevertheless, responds to the question (turn 41), and this display of compliance or power neutrality finally produces what he wants, a focus on modules rather than a discussion of the agenda.

Social Distance

The Tech I team shows very few indications of feeling close to one another. The rare exceptions include addressing each other with first names rather than formal forms of address; but even these are so few in number as to be notable (turns 3, 18, 19, 47). The group uses no special nicknames or in-group names. Though one sees the slurring of sounds that indicates social proximity, this impression is offset with a degree of formality in the words chosen. For example, in turn 2, Lance says "our purpose is to further converge on the features. . . . this is the next step in further refining that discussion." His use of the word "peripheral," the laughter it provokes, and his own redefinition of the word are also indications of an uncomfortable formality that exists among the team members.

This incident and the other uses of humor in this conversation are occasions for pointing out troubling differences, rather than the jokes that provide occasions for team bonding. Humor here invariably implies a negative evaluation of some team member. It is never leavened by expressions of admiration, liking, or gratitude, or claims of common membership. Finally, though there are occasional examples of peremptory behavior (for example, Pete's decision to copy his agenda), there is no use of the peremptory requests or demands that reflect social closeness.

David's language displays the most social closeness in turn 3, where he is addressing Lance. Since he and Lance had worked together previously on other teams, his language is probably reflecting that connection. Lance doesn't noticeably respond in kind, perhaps because he is typically responding to Pete's socially distant and powerful speech.

Conflict Management

Conflicts among members of the Tech I team are typically managed through the use of force or power, met with accommodation or avoidance, as the analysis above shows. There are several examples of this pattern. The first occurs when Pete insists on using his agenda (turn 8), and Lance makes no attempt to stop him or demand that the group use his. This way he avoids the conflict that would be likely to erupt if he responded to Pete forcefully. In the exchange of turns 31 and 32, Lance explicitly accommodates Pete's show of forcefulness: he appears to acknowledge that engineering is present at the meeting to hear what marketing wants them to do to fix the product design.

When Lisa begins to engage in the significant conflict between marketing and engineering about whether modules must be included in the design (turn 33), Lance interrupts her with an explicit attempt to avoid the conflict by trying to take back his words "That was a poor choice of words" (turn 34). He clearly does not want to "get hung up on that." Lance, as he has said, sees the modules as "peripheral," whereas Pete argues that these are "as important as the heart of the motor is" (turn 26) and Lisa says they are "central" (turn 35). All the team members have heard and recognized this conflict, but they do not deal with it in a confrontational or collaborative way.

The tone of this disagreement is negative and judgmental. Feelings get expressed in subtle ways, as when the group laughs at Lance's use of the word "peripheral" (turn 2) or when Lance tries to reduce his concerns to the level of mere words (turn 34). Lance is not encouraged to explain why he sees this differently from the marketers; indeed, as we have already seen, the marketers do not listen to Lance most of the time. There is no attempt to explore the reasons behind his characterization of the module as peripheral, or to examine the consequences of adopting his position. At the end of this excerpt, Lisa does appear to be trying to reframe this disagreement (turns 35, 37, 39), but neither she nor the team takes up the conflict in this way. In fact, they allow Pete to redirect them to the list of other parts needed (turn 40) and never come back to this conflict during this meeting.

Negotiation Process

The Tech I team members typically negotiated their differences, as we observe in this excerpt, through the use of power differences and a process that was more oriented to winning and losing than to finding win-win solutions. Rather than trying to identify the underlying interests of each party to find possible overlaps, this team negotiates through the exchange of adversarial positions. This can be seen most clearly in the dispute about modules. Though Lance has indicated his willingness to focus this meeting on the design of modules (turn 2), Pete and Lisa focus on his characterization of (or position on) the modules as peripheral (turns 26, 33, 35). Each offers his or her own position on the importance and centrality of the modules. Pete even takes a position on finding "the right point" to start the discussion (turn 26), and diverts considerable team attention to this issue.

In this excerpt, the team does not display a particularly strong inclination to think of these conflicts as winning and losing, though other data indicate that some team members perceived the team dynamics this way. However, the joke about buying lunch reveals an orientation to think in terms of distributing both credit and blame along functional lines (turns 11–17).

There is little evidence here that members of this team try to negotiate win-win solutions through recommended tactics such as identifying their own and the other parties' interests, finding objective criteria for resolving their differences, or trying to invent new options for meeting the interests of all parties.[2]

Assessing the Tech I Team

In these excerpts, the Tech I team's interaction shows that the primary identification of team members is with their functional groups, moderate interdependence, high power differentiation, distant social relationships, considerable use of forcing, accommodation, and avoidance to manage conflict, and a win-lose negotiation process. (Figure 4.3 depicts the Tech I team's placement on each key dimension of interaction.) The profile that emerges is of an adversarial group, in which individuals with the best of intentions execute their responsibilities to the organization by adhering loyally to their functional standards, despite the opposition

Figure 4.3 Assessment of the Tech I team's talk.

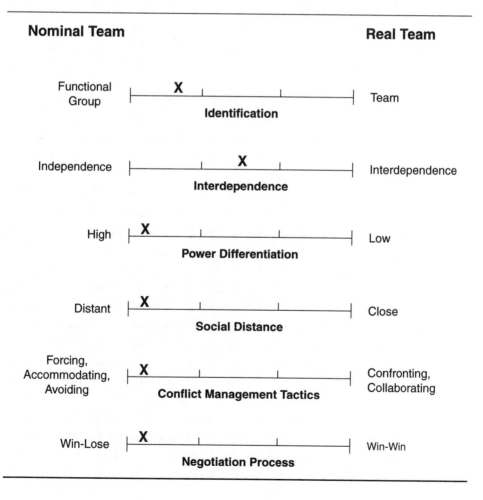

this creates within the team. They can also be seen making efforts to cooperate with one another, as explained below, but these appear to be superficial and strategic.

TEAM INTERACTION AND ORGANIZATIONAL CONTEXT

The talk of the Tech I team reflects several features of the organization in which it was embedded. (Table 4.2 summarizes the data on the organizational context and team design at the Building Controls Division.) Most of those structural features tended to push the team toward interacting near the left side of each dimension of figure 4.3. But several particulars of this project, at the time of this research, combined to make the team aware of their mutual interdependence to some degree.

The corporate pressure to maintain profitability was translated into divisional goals of cost containment and maintenance of share through quality. Though the general manager recognized the value of teams in achieving such goals, the division continued to rely on the functional hierarchy for the design of work, the hiring and managing of professional experts, and a cultural emphasis on individual accountability as a way of controlling costs. These factors preserved the corporate culture of strong identifications with functional groups and did little to foster team identification. See figure 4.4 for a depiction of the major forces shaping the dynamics of the Tech I team.

The Tech I project represented a very significant investment by the division—thus the stakes were very high. Because the project was nearing completion after almost five years in development, the day of ultimate team reckoning was relatively close at hand. The significance of the team work and the salience of its measurement had created a perception of team (horizontal) interdependence that the parallel development and team design had not affected. Because the engineers were evaluated on the basis of meeting their deadlines and budgets, while the marketers were measured by the quality of their products and their products' share, there had been little incentive for either to cooperate until now, when those abstractions were about to be translated into real, measurable, and multidimensional performance.

The division's senior managers were convinced that teams would provide the extra boost many of the professionals needed to overcome the demoralizing effects of recent downsizings and higher demands. Teams, they felt, would enhance the efficiency of human resources as

Table 4.2 Description of the Building Controls Division's organizational context.

Building Controls Division	
Feature	*Description*
Recent historical events	Loss, downsizing, and restructuring
Corporate identity	This is an autocracy
Precursors to teams	Business unit teams, simultaneous engineering
Divisional strategic goals	Cost and share
Initiator of teams	Former division manager
Expectations of teams	Speed, efficiency, collaboration
Nature of team task	Open-ended, near-term
Duration of team structure	3½ years
How teams were assembled	Skills-based assignment
Choice in assignments	No
Basis for team leadership	None
Size of teams	7
Multiple team assignments	Yes
Degree of dedication to team (percentage of team fully dedicated)	14%
Distribution of stakes	Formally variable
Mechanisms for assessing team performance	Formal monthly review, functional reporting
Hierarchical levels (from teams to top of divisions)	3–4
Role of functional managers	Unchanged
Liaison to managers	Program manager
Training	None

Figure 4.4 Major forces shaping the Tech I team's dynamics.

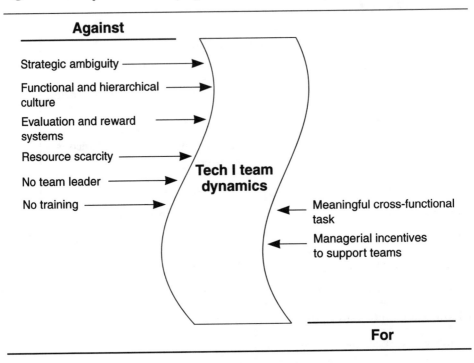

Against

Strategic ambiguity

Functional and hierarchical culture

Evaluation and reward systems

Resource scarcity

No team leader

No training

Tech I team dynamics

Meaningful cross-functional task

Managerial incentives to support teams

For

they created the motivation to collaborate across functional lines. To facilitate further the development of cross-functional cooperation, the organization had also recently created shared objectives for the functional managers.

The theory behind shared objectives was that if team members' functional managers felt interdependent, then those team members would feel less pressure to pursue their own functional goals at the expense of team goals. For example, each Tech I team member reported to one of three people who shared some of the same performance objectives, such as meeting the Tech I launch date. If these shared objectives were met, the functional managers would receive a larger bonus. To ensure that the objective was met, the managers had to encourage their direct reports to collaborate. They also needed to balance their own functional demands on their direct reports with the requirements of the team. However, it appears that this trade-off was either not so obvious to the functional managers or more difficult to implement than anticipated.

As we have seen, the interdependence among the functional managers created by shared objectives had little impact on the team members' perception of their *own* interdependence. This was primarily because the job descriptions of team members and their managers were still essentially functional in nature, and performance assessments were handled exclusively by each functional manager. In this context of extremely tight resources and high demands for short-term performance, team work did not count as much as did functional work. Thus team members were not held accountable for their team's performance because that might distract them from doing the things that would ensure the achievement of functional goals.

So, despite the creation of mechanisms (cross-functional teams and shared managerial objectives) to offset functional isolation and lack of cooperation, problems persisted. Furthermore, the teams created occasions and arenas for displays of functional distrust and competition. Team training in conflict management and negotiation might have helped this team manage the contradictory pressure they felt, but none had been provided for the Tech I team or any other team.

The strong identification with the functional groups combined with a perception of some interdependence explain the dynamics of power, social distance, conflict management and negotiation process observed in the team. Team members needed to, but did not, identify with one another. Though some of them were socially closer to each other than others, this lack of team identification but mounting sense of interdependence created social relations that were distant. Team members often exhibited a high degree of frustration, resentment, and distrust of one another. At the best of times, they were merely civil. Attempts to influence one another and manage the constant conflicts were based on the power differences among the functions.

Marketing had higher status in the organization than engineering, and the team members from marketing had higher stakes in the team project by virtue of two factors. More of their individual time was allocated to the project, and their functional manager was the only member of the team with primary profit and loss responsibility for the product, as well as bonus eligibility. This meant they had more power, which they tended to display. But it also meant they were more dependent as well, which led the others to resist that power on occasion. An example of this is Lance leaving the meeting before it was finished and refusing to answer seriously Pete's questions about that. The observed conflict management tactics of forcing, accommodation, and avoidance were consistent with the use of power differences.

Because there was no single appointed team leader and there had been no training in managing the inevitable team conflicts, there was no force arguing for a win-win negotiation of the disparate interests, and no capability for achieving it. As a result of all these factors, the team employed a win-lose process of negotiation, with an unspoken attitude of "I can't win this, but I can be sure I don't lose by making you look like the culprit." Overall, the character of the team talk was distinctly adversarial, which was not surprising in light of the organizational structure and corporate culture, but hardly desirable considering its strategic requirements.

LESSONS FROM THE TECH I TEAM

There are several lessons in the experience of BCD and the Tech I team. Some people at BCD felt that the major cause of the Tech I team's problems was the lack of leadership on the team, perhaps even higher in the organization. Indeed, there may be some basis for this argument, for the Tech I team certainly lacked the positive influence that the Alpha team had in the form of a competent, elected leader who willingly shared power. The team task here was certainly cross-functional and meaningful, as was the case for the Alpha team. If anything, the Tech I team's task was too cross-functional and significant, given the organization's cultural and structural emphasis on functional hierarchy and individual accountability. In contrast to the Alpha team's situation, in which its specific, focused, and time-limited task represented the first opportunity to demonstrate the members' decision-making ability, the Tech I team was at the end of a long, frustrating experience of trying to overcome the organizational barriers to working cross-functionally.

The *first* lesson of this case is that even though departments or divisions may become strategically more interdependent, the people in them do not automatically perceive themselves to be interdependent. The *second* lesson is that, in organizations like BCD, where the corporate culture and organizational systems have historically emphasized functional performance, the most salient interdependencies are in the vertical reporting relationships. Professional employees are far more dependent—for the things they care about, like interesting assignments, promotions, and raises—on their functional managers than they are on their team (the latter might be labeled "horizontal interdependency").

This division tried to use the vertical interdependencies to create perceptions of horizontal interdependency in their cross-functional teams by making adaptations in the performance review and reward system. They created a set of linked objectives in the performance plans for the functional managers to whom team members reported. Therefore, the managers of team members had an incentive to support the team, rather than having incentives that only pushed them—and their subordinates on that team—in the opposite directions. The managers thus were given an incentive to shape their direct reports' perceptions of interdependence.

The problem was that these common objectives represented small and different proportions of the managers' whole sets of responsibilities. Therefore, they were not strongly or equally motivated to act in ways that would give the teams priority over their functional responsibilities. In fact, given that the performance plans of these managers consisted primarily of functional work *and* that successful accomplishment of most of these objectives earned each a sizable bonus, these managers had a greater incentive to push their subordinates in the opposite direction. So when push came to shove, as it often does in the context of a very lean staff, team members and their managers alike knew "where they got their hits" and gave their functional responsibilities top priority. Clearly, the managerial incentives to support team work had little impact in a corporate culture that was so functionally and individually focused. The *third* lesson is that, when functional responsibilities are significantly greater than cross-functional responsibilities (and have higher payoffs), conflicting demands on a person's time will be resolved accordingly.

This situation presents another important lesson about the problems that individual accountability creates for team work. When individuals are to be held accountable for their contributions to a team, they do what can be seen or documented for their reviewers, even at the expense of team outcomes. They act on their teams to enhance the measures on which they are individually measured, like budget hours or market share.[3] Furthermore, when team members are held individually accountable for team outcomes, unproductive conflict is highly likely. The *fourth* lesson from the Tech I case is that individual accountability poses considerable problems for team work and that mechanisms for holding teams accountable for achieving the team task are preferable.

The *fifth* lesson from this case is that, in the context of strong functional identification and moderate interdependence, teams need the ability to manage conflicts effectively. The team system at BCD provided neither team training nor procedures to help these professionals manage their differences effectively.

The *sixth* and final lesson offered by this case is that team talk recreates the organizational barriers to team work. We saw again in this chapter, as in chapter 3, that the way team members talk to each can reflect organizational power differences. It also can reinforce organizational stereotypes, re-create or widen cultural chasms between groups, and prevent team members from identifying with one another. We have seen too how such team dynamics may have a significant impact on an organization, particularly if the organization has assigned a critical task to a team.

While this chapter provides some answers to the questions posed in chapter 3, it creates more questions about cross-functional teams: Would the existence of a formal team leader responsible for coordinating information and resolving conflict have prevented the problems that had paralyzed the Tech I team and brought them precariously close to disaster? Would giving the leader greater stakes in team outcomes give him or her the necessary incentive to act in ways that would make the team more productive and better able to determine what it needed to do its assigned task well? Would training have encouraged and enabled the program manager or another team member to make effective observations on the team's dysfunctional process? Why weren't team members being held accountable for the team's performance problems? In the next chapter, we will answer some of these questions.

CHAPTER 5

Leadership and Team Accountability

The Wayne Division and the Front-End Team

Thiis chapter describes a very carefully designed team system, six months after its introduction. The design includes features that previous chapters identified as potentially critical to effective team work: a designated team leader and a mechanism for team accountability. The Wayne Division of Heritage Manufacturing Corporation was already realizing substantial benefits from its cross-functional teams: the development cycle was shortened, and functional isolation and antagonism were being eliminated. Yet there was a pervasive sense that the teams were not really the locus of decision making and problem solving, as advertised. Listening in on the Front-End team of the Wayne Division, we hear people suspended in a precarious position: midway between commitment and doubt. Like the professionals at the Medical Products Division, the majority of Wayne employees were excited at the prospect of contributing to a better product, and they believed teams were an appropriate vehicle for achieving that goal.

HERITAGE MANUFACTURING CORPORATION

Heritage Manufacturing, a major player in the heavy equipment industry, had grown substantially through acquisition. Acquired companies were operated as separate divisions, a system that worked successfully until products proliferated. To simplify the engineering process, design tasks were then distributed among the divisions. In addition, Heritage established "project centers" to manage all product development. By the mid-1980s, however, sales faltered and competition from the Japanese increased.

The company began planning a major reorganization in May 1986, which eventually collapsed seven divisions into three product groups and consolidated engineering and manufacturing responsibilities. Heritage hoped that its reorganization would improve efficiency, encourage fresh ideas, and foster a greater sense of teamwork. Within these broader aims were three specific goals. First, it sought to improve its project-cycle timing, the time it takes for a product to go from concept to customer, so that new products could be launched faster. By consolidating operations and moving authority further down the hierarchy to those closer to the product and to the customers, Heritage intended to respond faster to market changes. Second, the company sought greater control of its costs. In contrast to the former arrangement under which each division had an assortment of staff and responsibilities, the reorganization created self-sufficient units capable of controlling costs. All functions, from engineering to sales, were consolidated from as many as seven separate staffs into just three. Third, Heritage hoped to improve the quality of its products, which had suffered from lack of divisional accountability and complicated lines of communication.

Two years after the reorganization, as Heritage Manufacturing continued to watch its market share decline while costs increased and competition intensified, the company took austerity measures. It changed cost-of-living raises to payments that would not increase the salary base, and it abandoned cash bonuses. As its most significant move, Heritage set out to dismiss 20 percent of its white-collar employees over a two-year period. The elimination of these people and its effect upon morale added to the chaos created from the reorganization. In the winter of 1988, tremors from the reorganization could still be felt throughout the company.

The Wayne Division

The last four years have been traumatic. We were fat, dumb, and happy here for a long time. (Middle manager, Wayne Division)

In October 1988, Heritage's corporate reorganization cascaded to the Wayne Division (WD), a large division of the Product B Group, one of the three operating groups. Formed during the 1986 reorganization of Heritage, the division operated four plants and employed 8,000 people.

In its first two years, WD was having trouble controlling costs, producing its products on time, and maintaining quality. With the arrival of a new division head, however, WD introduced its own form of restructuring to achieve several of the same goals the company had pursued three years earlier: achieve faster cycle times, control costs, promote teamwork, and move decision-making authority further down the organization. Under the system known as "cross-functional management," WD instituted teams comprising professional-level managers from different functional areas. Although the system had been evolving since 1986, and though talk of teamwork had always been prevalent, managerial employees at WD felt unprepared when they were suddenly thrust into the new team structure. Nonetheless, WD became the best-performing division in the Product B Group, and one of WD's plants led all Heritage plants in quality. Other divisions began visiting WD to learn from the simultaneous management system often credited for WD's rebound.

Cross-functional Management and Teams

WD described cross-functional management as:

> a method of reorganizing traditional phases of product development and implementation; through it product phases are not performed in a linear fashion with one staff completing a phase of development and "passing the baton" to the next, but it is a method that integrates functional staffs so that all staffs may participate in the earliest phases of product development and improvement.

(See figure 5.1 for a representation of the intended relationship between Wayne's teams and its strategic goals.)

From 1986 through 1988, the Wayne Division had studied ways to introduce simultaneous management. An experimental program unveiled during the summer of 1987 did not survive for more than a year, but its demise did teach the division several lessons. First, WD learned that all layers of management had to be part of the cross-functional management structure, or there would be resistance to the

Figure 5.1 The Wayne Division: teams and strategic goals.

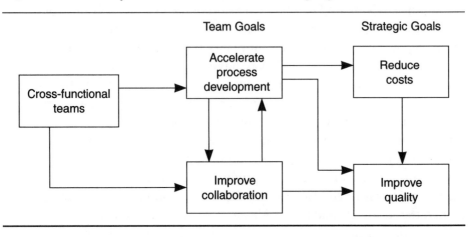

concept. Second, it realized that all functional areas had to be involved in planning the division's management strategy. With these lessons in mind, WD formally introduced cross-functional management in October 1988, but all features of the plan were not in place until April 1989. Although functional lines remained intact, to manage product development WD established teams that cut across functions. Every hierarchical level of management had a corresponding set of cross-functional teams, so teams reported to the teams above them (see figure 5.2).

Product improvement teams (PITs), which had existed prior to the reorganization as a mechanism for ad hoc problem solving, brought working-level engineers and their functional counterparts together to solve product and assembly problems. These PITs reported to Product teams (PTs), which coordinated all management efforts related to their piece of the product. For example, the Front-End team managed the front section of the product, and the Frame PIT reported to that product team. Countless PITs, many formed only when problems arose, reported to twenty-six PTs. In turn, these PTs reported to two cross-functional management teams (CMTs): one in charge of the exterior of all WD products, and one responsible for the interior and electrical aspects of products. The CMTs served as policy-setting bodies and were not designed to manage product development directly.

Between October 1988, when the plan was announced, and April 1989, when PTs assembled for the first time, WD also integrated product

Figure 5.2 Organizational chart for the Wayne Division and the Front-End team.

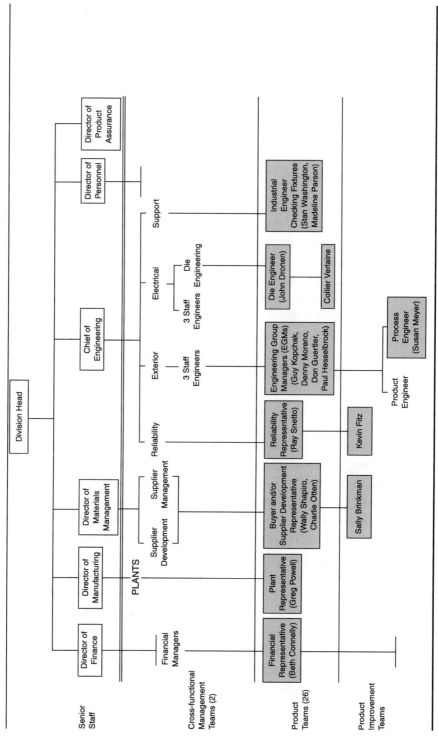

Note: Shaded boxes represent Front-End team members.

and process engineering. In January 1989, with no model to copy, WD put process and product engineers into one functional line. Product and process engineers worked together at the hierarchical level of PITs; they both reported to an engineering group manager (EGM). These EGMs were senior product or process engineers who had responsibility for a major section of the product. They and their functional counterparts formed the PTs.

Product Teams

Told to see themselves as small businesses managing one part of a product, product teams were made up first-level managers from as many as ten different functional areas. By design, team members came from the same level of the organization. However, in practice, direct reports of some team members became de facto members because they regularly represented traveling or otherwise engaged managers.

The EGMs, who were from the same organizational level as the other team members, were assigned as team leaders. The EGM was the only person fully dedicated to a given team, thus there were significantly higher stakes for him or her than for other team members. Promotion opportunities for the engineers who were successful team leaders were great, but so was the burden of team failure. To give teams some flexibility, WD had intentionally formed the teams without specifying concrete operating procedures. However, within a few months of team initiation, a task force convened to make recommendations for common reporting practices. After several months of experimentation and confusion, PTs began operating in fairly standard fashion during the summer of 1989.

Product teams met weekly, biweekly, or monthly. In accordance with a rotating schedule, EGMs presented quarterly reports to one of the cross-functional management teams. In these reports, they outlined their PTs' performance in ten areas called "imperatives": assembly time, piece cost, deproliferation (reduction in the number of parts), durability, investment, product performance, reliability, process cycle time, supplier performance, and buildability.

The imperatives reflected WD's aim in establishing PTs. With all functional groups coming together in a team to focus on ten specific areas affecting production and performance, each PT had the potential to make significant improvements in its piece of the product. PTs also opened channels of communication among functional areas and allowed all disciplines to get involved early in product development.

Wayne's teams, although created to administer a new process of product development, were *not* designed as or used for development per se—that was the province of the product engineer. To accomplish this task prior to the team structure, he or she frequently had called on specific knowledgeable professionals in the other functions; for the most part, these were the professionals who came to be assigned to that engineer's product team. The team itself was assigned to manage the product, but what exactly this meant was not clear. The teams were expected to commission ad hoc problem-solving teams and resolve interdisciplinary issues that arose in the process of developing the product to meet cross-functional objectives. By design, these teams "managed" the product. In practice, because the product engineer had disproportionately higher stakes than any other team members, he or she—rather than the team—both developed and managed the product.

During their first few months of operation, PTs had problems in team dynamics and encountered organizational obstacles. PT members identified several problems with the way the teams were set up. PTs were organized according to parts of the product, and though engineering group managers (EGMs) worked on only one part of the product, their functional counterparts were responsible for *more* than one part. Therefore, aside from the EGMs, PT members all served on more than one PT and thus felt frustrated as they watched every one of these PTs stumble through the process of settling procedures. The situation was exacerbated when PTs did not achieve levels of productivity as quickly as participants had expected. PT members became more impatient as they saw their efforts focusing more on delivering reports than on making and implementing decisions. People perceived, some earnestly and some cynically, that the PTs were simply reporting structures. PTs also suffered from fluctuating attendance and uneven participation.

Personal relationships within teams reflected many characteristics of Heritage's cultural history. PTs served as melting pots for the "refugees" from various Heritage divisions restructured during the 1986 reorganization. Engineers from one of the original Heritage divisions had the reputation of being "stubborn" and "unimaginative"; engineers who had originally been with one of the others were thought to be "elitist" and "undisciplined." At the same time, EGMs enjoyed a distinctive status, considerably above the other PT members. As one EGM realized, "All the other people in the PT are playing in engineering's ballpark." After years of seeing product engineering dominate the organization, other functional professionals were now excited about contributing equally. Nonetheless, they saw equal participation unfolding slowly. While building team cohesion, therefore, PTs also had to merge cultures and integrate functions. Since no history of mutual trust and confidence existed, fundamental personal relationships had to be formed from scratch.

Moreover, rather than replacing the old organizational structure, simultaneous management seemed to have created a system of dual structures. A strong functional organization not only persisted, but continued to direct people's efforts and attract most of their attention. Issues pertaining to a single functional group continued to be addressed by upper management (those in the two levels above PT members) in separate meetings and reports. Meetings abounded, from those engaged in cross-functional management to those focusing on single-function issues such as piece cost, design, and reliability. It was unclear whether all these meetings were necessary, and not only did PT members not understand the purpose of each meeting, but they felt overburdened by the reports they had to deliver to the various meeting bodies.

WD also lacked support systems for PTs. In the area of operations, PTs began asking for information systems to track imperatives. Although WD could provide overall figures for some imperatives, such as piece cost and investment, it could not yet provide actual figures broken down by PT. WD hoped to implement an evaluation system that reinforced team participation, but no system was yet in place. Heritage employees were accustomed to evaluations that focused on individual performance in the functional area and promised rapid promotion within that function.

Thus, although PT participants were enthusiastic about the gains cross-functional teams promised, after the first few months of operation, they had mixed assessments of the PTs. Here are some of their comments:

"PTs are a glorified way to work on programs the way we've always worked on them."

"It's no longer 'your problem' but 'our problem.'"

"People think this is another phase we're going through. There's been so much rapid change that people can't get excited anymore."

"One of the goals of the PT was to bring the different disciplines together with the same focus. That focus was generated by product engineering."

"You have got to be comfortable with conflict and with people issues in order to direct activities. So some of the EGMs—don't take this as being a slap to engineers—but their education and their job-related work has not forced them into dealing with specific conflict issues and people issues."

"From where we were two years ago, we're really coming around."

"It has to be perceived that there's a commitment by upper management that this is a system we want to stick by and support. Or is this the program of the week?"

"You need to feel confident enough in the person that you report to, that you have full responsibility for what you do."

"People are opening up, saying, 'I understand.' "

"We spend entirely too much time in this organization meeting with people and then sending them letters about what we spoke about."

"We're going into a new building in about a year and a half, and the building is labeled 'Engineering.' It seems like a small thing, but under the cross-functional management process, it's everybody working together."

"Oh, the change is for the better."

THE FRONT-END TEAM

The Front-End product team met every second Friday from 9:30 until 11:30. Because so many of its members also served on three other related PTs, the four PTs held a joint meeting. Each of the four PTs controlled $10 million in investment. The members of the Front-End PT were:

Guy Kopchak—Engineering Group Manager (EGM) in charge of the Front-End PT. He was a process engineer with an MBA who had been in Wayne Division for a year and had previously worked in advanced design. He felt excitement about the PTs and the opportunity they offered to run a small business.

Susan Meyer—Design engineer serving under Guy. He had asked her to become facilitator of the PT, and she had accepted. Before coming to WD, she had worked as a plant engineer.

Madeline Parson—Industrial engineer. She had worked as a production supervisor before coming to WD.

Beth Connelly—Financial representative. She had been with Heritage since 1973. Prior to her current assignment, she had been in charge of investment management for a new product designed by a special team.

John Dronen—Die engineer. John was considered one of the most knowledgeable die engineers in the organization.

Greg Powell—Plant representative. Greg had worked his way up to become the superintendent of a plant and served in that capacity since 1973.

Charlie Otten—Supplier Development (quality control of supplies). He had come to WD in the past year after working as a quality director at a fabrication plant where he had thirty years of experience. Charlie was responsible for WD's initiative to improve the standard of its sheet metal.

Stan Washington—Checking Fixtures group (quality control in manufacturing). He had begun working for Heritage in 1948 on an assembly line, and was about to announce his retirement.

Wally Shapiro—Materials Management. Wally had been with Heritage since 1969, his sophomore year in college. He had spent his entire career in materials management and worked his way up the hierarchy.

In addition to the three engineering group managers—*Denny Moreno, Don Guertler, and Paul Hesselbrock*—whose PTs met jointly with Guy's, several other people regularly attended the Front-End PT meetings, either to represent an absent team member or to stay informed of the team's decisions:

Sally Brinkman—A direct report of Wally's.

Collier Verlaine—Financial representative from die engineering. Attended only when PT needed his assistance.

Ray Snetto—Reliability and testing.

Kevin Fitz—A direct report of Roy's.

THE FRONT-END TEAM'S TALK

The excerpts of conversation that follow were taken from the third Front-End team meeting observed. It was held approximately eight months after the team was first assembled. The following members attended this meeting, though not all participate in these excerpts: Susan Meyer, Guy Kopchak, Denny Moreno, Don Guertler, Beth Connelly, John Dronen, Sally Brinkman, Charlie Otten, Greg Powell, Ray Snetto, and Madeline Parson. Prior to this part of the conversation, there had been several presentations. The first, made by the team facilitator, Susan, was about a new format for guiding the team work; she had developed this format from a recent task force report. She reminded the team of its purposes, then presented a matrix that mapped each of the team imperatives, its quantified target, ownership, and comments. She proposed that the team members structure their meetings to update one another on their progress. There was general consensus to do so. Following this discussion were three lengthy presentations by team

---

It is important to note that people do not speak the way they write. They repeat themselves, they leave things out, and they don't always speak in grammatically correct sentences. Sometimes these "mistakes" are meaningless and irrelevant to the conversation. Often, we don't even notice them. Frequently, these behaviors are meaningful and they provide the attentive listener with clues for interpretation. For the purposes of this transcription and the interpretation, I have faithfully recorded what the speakers actually *said,* using the following conventions:

****	where utterances have been deleted
//	overlapping talk or interruption
. . .	a pause of one second or less
(3.2)	a pause of more than one second, length indicated in seconds
[ ]	an explanatory insertion
.	a falling intonation marking end of assertion, even if it is not a grammatically complete sentence
?	a rising intonation marking question form
italics	emphasis

members, each one either addressing or responding to a question from an earlier meeting about procedures, such as how supplier quality was to be assured, how funds were to be requested, and how a particular engineering request affected the work of another function. Then came time for open discussion, a representative excerpt of which is presented and analyzed below.

1 Susan: Next, we have EGMs go over their items, and then any discussion you have. Want to volunteer for going first?

2 Guy: Yah, me. Beth, we have a project that I'm not sure how to handle moneywise. We're working with the Advanced Design Group. We want to implement mig-welding in certain locations in our plant where we have . . . bad conditions. We own one of these kinds of robots which is over in the process development center where we practice to make sure that it was really a viable thing, that it would work. And we've got to the point where we think it will work. Now we want to put it in the assembly plant and see if it works under assembly plant conditions, and then if it works in that assembly plant we'll probably want to put it in the other assembly plant. We need $280,000 to put it in the first assembly plant. And, ah, there's been . . . I guess my understanding is that normally the plant would put in the facilities request for $280,000, but in this case//

3 Beth: And write a project, just like hardware.

4 Guy: What we want to start out with is, we want to get the stuff and put it in there and prove that it works under an experimental basis or have a manufacturing process development project, and if it does work, then they'll buy them from us after, or they'll pay for them later. I guess what I'm trying to figure out is, you know, can I take $280,000 out of my or my boss's budget, buy them, put them in there, and then have them pay me back?

5 Beth: No.

6 Guy: No . . . well, we've got, we got money that we use for engineering projects, now we've got simultaneous engineering, we've got engineering and manufacturing together, this is a manufacturing development project.

7 Beth: Brad talked to Tom a little bit about it. I wasn't part of that discussion, so I don't know what the detail was. Tom told Brad to pull some more information together on it. . . . Normally I see that

. . . you're saying, you know, you're saying you really kind of want an improvement.

8 Guy: Well, it's been proven in the laboratory.

9 Beth: Okay, that's your research and development money.

10 Guy: Well, but, but //

11 Beth: I know //

12 Guy: That's only partly been proven then.

13 Beth: I agree.

14 Guy: If you can make it work in the lab, whether it can work on the line is a different story. If [the plant] doesn't want to spend the money and try it for a couple of months and find out that in the plant it really doesn't work//

15 Beth: Let me check and see what Tom investigated. Tom was supposed to look into that . . . I know what you're talking about. I'll have to get back to you. You're talking theoretically a million dollars. The question is do we go to [inaudible word] group, or pre-plans, do a basic quotation, do we do minor.

16 Guy: Tim has been involved in this one too. Maybe Tom can talk to Tim and between the two of them figure out what's appropriate. We don't want to rush out and buy them for all the plants until we know if it works in one plant.

17 Beth: Yeah, and what you learn in one plant you might want to change if you're going to buy it, or modify it or something. Let me //

18 Guy: Okay.

19 Susan: Any others?

20 Guy: And the other thing is, Sally, we're still talking about some nontraditional metal parts that might come from [inaudible word], like extruded roof rails and roll-form rockers. . . . At what point do we move out of just us engineers talking about it and upstairs doing more things about figuring out who might really supply them and become involved in early sourcing?

21 Susan: I thought Wally said he was going to take the lead on this.

22 Guy: But I want to know what that means . . . Also, you know, John's here, we need to figure out what the role of die engineering is in that same situation, you know, nonstamped parts that might still come from Heritage sources.

23   John: I don't know whether you're aware of it or not, but labor relations has already had some calls in there, and they had a call from Chuck, and the union is already concerned about the B-1000, that there was word out that there's stuff, possibly to be put on the outside, and I've already got calls on that already, and I told them.

24   Denny: Put stuff through like plastic handles?

25   John: Yeah, and they've already talked about the clips that you got in Dixon [plant]. All right. They know about it. Hey, you can't hide a thing.

26   Denny: We didn't plan to, really//

27   John: These type a things, these type items they have to go through our department and we work with them, and if they do not have the facility to design them. You see, what the union is saying is that say you come up//

28   Guy: Slow down a little bit. The parts I'm talking about I think there's a plant, there's a Heritage plant that would like to make them, and I'd like them to make them, so what do I do?

29   John: Okay, do you have the parts, something we can work with?

30   Guy: Sure.

31   John: Okay, I need that and then I'll go out and make sure that we supply, make the parts. You process them and get something that we can work with and then I'll go and make the parts, make sure that we have facility if I have to go up to Product A Group or wherever to get them designed. The same way with the plastic ends. I've got the direction already. Now, see, what they're saying is that if this is a new way of doing business and we're going to build a product like that, that if that's a new way of doing business they want to be trained in order to do that function. We can't go outside. That's where the problem is.

32   Sally: As far as the B-1000 program goes, if we identify those items that have the potential for becoming plastic from steel or a major metal, then a "potential for outsourcing" form needs to be, an outsourcing application, needs to be submitted.

33 John: See, that's where the tool guys' strategy, and I'm already getting calls on that so I know.

34 Sally: Right, but I guess the position should be that there's a break and if you want to go to a different technology or a different processing for that product, I guess I wouldn't support not doing it in plastic, because if that plant can't produce a part or one of our own subsidiaries which currently, today they've reviewed two subsidiaries that can produce plastic panels and neither one was chosen to put business into. I don't think that's a rationale for stopping going to plastic products, but I think it would make us look at other items that those fab plants could have a potential contribution.

35 John: But, I need the parts, what they look like and then I will see what I can do, and if I can place them in, hey, like you say, Guy, if you have to go to Product A Group, I'll go to Product A Group, or if you go wherever to make the parts. I need the product intent and then I'll go.

36 Sally: Maybe we should have a meeting, a separate meeting so we know exactly what we're looking at . . . [inaudible: Sally and Guy arrange a meeting]

37 John: Go ahead.

38 Denny: I was going to say *my* understanding of the ninety-day letter is that whenever outsourcing is being contemplated that you need to write one.

39 Sally: Yah, but you're at phase zero, really.

40 Denny: Don't need one on the B-1000?

41 Sally: No, I mean, as you say, as we start to pick, like that we might mainstream B-1000 //

42 Denny: It doesn't say that, though. It says whenever it's contemplated replacing a current metal part with something new, then we should write a ninety-day letter. Maybe we ought to clarify with Fred when we need to write these letters.

43 Sally: Okay, 'cause I wasn't around //

44 Denny: We went through that with Hal, that's something we were considering going outsourcing on. We read the letter of the law, which was handed out to us, which says whenever you're contemplating replacing //

45 Sally: Well, I've never put that for every single part, panels, borders //

46 Denny: Fred and I and Hal had some go-arounds, and Fred told us "Aw, write 'em anyway." We're certainly contemplating that right now.

47 Susan: Any other items? Don? Paul?

48 For Paul [one of his direct reports representing him]: I only have a couple of items I'll forward from Paul. One of them is the structuring of the meeting we talked about in the beginning. He's concerned about, if the format of the meeting is a decision-making type format then it ought to be more structured.

49 Susan: He talked to me Wednesday. I don't know if anybody has any other suggestions on what to do for the meeting. If the four EGMs want to get together and talk about it, you know, if you four PTs want to have separate meetings to talk about what should happen in these meetings, or is today's format okay, or does anybody else have any suggestions?

50 Guy: Today's format was okay with me.

51 Denny: I'd like to concentrate on the product and process as much as we could. If we start to do that more . . . I think we're getting there.

LINGUISTIC ANALYSIS OF THE EXCERPTS

This interaction is remarkable for the amount of the discussion devoted to the exchange of information about procedures. Members of this product team were conscientiously using their time to fill the numerous communication gaps that challenged their ability to do critical work on the product. After Susan notes that they had reached the point in the agenda for the team leaders (the EGMs) to make their contributions, there are *four* consecutive exchanges about procedure (turns 2–17, 20–28, 31–46, 48–51).

The analysis of the team's talk is guided by the team talk audit. See table 5.1 for a summary of the analysis.

Identification

The Front-End team is clearly a group of experienced and competent people who identify strongly with their work and organization. Their

Table 5.1 Audit of the Front-End team.

Dimensions	Samples of Team Talk	Your Interpretation	Score
Identification	"We want to . . . we need . . . to" (1) "that's your Research and Development Money" (9) "through our department and we work with them" (27) "If we start to do that more" (51)	Virtually all the plural pronouns used here refer to the functional groups. One exception is Sally (32, 36, 41) although she too uses "you" occasionally to mark a functional boundary between herself and others (39). Another exception is Denny (turn 51).	Functional
Interdependence	"what I'm trying to figure out" (4) "Let me check . . . I'll have to get back to you" (15) "I need that and then I'll go. . . . You process them and get something that we can work with and then I'll go and make the parts" (31) "I wouldn't support not doing it" (34)	Overall, these team members act as if they were independent of one another. Though one of the team leaders (Guy) expresses needs explicitly (2) and team members express some willingness to fulfill those needs, the interaction sounds like a trade between independent agents, especially in the absence of acknowledgments of mutual interests and needs.	Independence
Power Differentiation	Questions seek information (4, 20, 28) but only team leader asks "No." (5) Interruptions (3, 10, 11, 18, 26, 41–46) Topic changed by facilitator after seeking permission (19, 47)	There is some power differentiation here but not much (virtually everyone interrupts at some point). The team facilitator and leaders show their slight power edge by asking most of the questions. However, the power of the financial analysts can be seen in Beth's monosyllabic, negative response to one of the leaders' question about his budgetary discretion (4–5).	Moderately low
Social Distance	"Beth, we have . . ." (2) "My understanding . . ." (38) "I wasn't part of that discussion" (7) No joking, no slang, no reference to feelings	A general lack of personal connection and a moderate formality on everyone's part indicate that these people don't feel close to one another socially.	Moderately distant

Table 5.1 Continued

Dimensions	Samples of Team Talk	Your Interpretation	Score
Conflict Management Tactics	"You're saying you really . . . want" (7) "what you learn you might want to change" (17) "Let me check" (15) "you can't hide a thing" (25) "I wouldn't support not doing it" (34) "Maybe we should have a separate meeting" (36)	Empathizing with others' interests, needs. Taking a conflict to a higher-level manager. Postponing a decision. Judgment.	Avoiding
Negotiation Process	"the position should be that" (34)	Arguing from positions (34). Very little real negotiation occurring.	No Answer

frequent use of "we" indicates that they feel a part of a group working toward a shared goal; however, virtually every use of "we," "our," and "us" refers to the functional departments of the team member speaking. In the fifty-two uses of these three words, only eight (turns 1, 32, 36, 51) referred clearly to the team. Interestingly, only three of these were expressed by a formal team member (Denny in turn 51). The others were voiced by junior representatives to the team and by the appointed team facilitator. Three other uses of "we" are ambiguous. In turn 15, Beth uses "we" when she ponders how to help Guy solve a problem. However, it is not clear whether she is identifying with Tom (her manager) or with Guy. Some support for the latter interpretation can be found in her implicit identification with Guy in earlier turns (7, 11, and 13) when she empathizes with his experience. Guy's own use of "we" is similarly ambiguous in his question when "do we move out of just us engineers" (turn 20). Up to this point, he has used numerous plural pronouns to identify himself with the engineers he works with, and his "us engineers" explicitly shows his identification with them. However, here Guy is speculating about the transition to a team form of decision making, and his "we" might refer to the team, the company, or again, to the engineers. Finally, five of the uses of the plural first person pronouns refer to the company (turns 31 and 34), as indicated in the first instance by John's reference to union-company disputes and agreements, and in Sally's reference to the ownership of the subsidiaries. Otherwise, the plural pronouns in this transcript reflect identifications with the functional departments of each speaker. In turn 20, Guy uses three first person plural pronouns.

The team's identification with their functional groups rather than with one another is also signalled throughout by the use of singular pronouns that draw attention to the boundaries that separated team members from one another. For example, John's repeated use of "I" and "you" in turn 35 also displays an identification with his functional group rather than with the team. It points out the boundary that separates him from Guy rather than the one that encircles them both. It connotes a clear distribution of responsibility, without explicit or implicit acknowledgment of their interdependence. Denny's defensive reaction in turn 26 indicates that he has interpreted John's "you can't hide a thing" as a personal accusation of the engineering managers rather than a generic observation about life with unions, thus corroborating this interpretation of John's behavior as a way to distinguish himself from the engineers and perhaps to assert his independence from them.

Interdependence

When these team members talk, one gets the impression that they are essentially independent actors meeting in good faith to exchange information and assistance. There are no explicit or implicit acknowledgments of mutual interest or need, and only one proposal for joint action (turn 36). A minimal interdependence is implied in that individual needs are voiced, advice is sought, information is given, and a willingness to help is expressed by several team members. Yet even in the context of such interdependence, team members talk about themselves in the singular and assert their intentions to take independent actions. Three examples illustrate this. When Beth says, "Let me check. . . . I'll have to get back to you" (turn 15), linguistically she is asking for permission to take independent action, thus reflecting some dependency. Though socially, this meaning is a much weaker, the wording still shows some sense of interdependence. John explicitly characterizes the dependency relationship as an exchange: "I need that and then I'll go out and make sure" and "You process them and get something that we can work with and then I'll go and make the parts" (turn 31). Sally's version of this independence-interdependence relationship is more interesting linguistically. When she says, "I guess I wouldn't support not doing it in plastic" (turn 34), she expresses independence of others on the team (who want her to purchase a metal part) but signals a perception of her dependence on others by substantially reducing the force of her assertion. She uses three different linguistic forms to accomplish this: "I guess," the "would," which in contrast to "will" implies "with your permission," and the use of the double negatives, which is grammatically more complex and therefore less bold a denial.

Beth's language in this excerpt is perhaps the most variable along this and other dimensions of team talk. Sometimes she adopts an interdependent and collaborative stance, as manifested in turns 7, 11, and 13 when she expresses agreement and empathy with Guy, and in turn 9 where she offers to help. However, her other behavior conveys more independence and greater power. In turn 5, for example, her abrupt and unelaborated negative response to Guy's request (which, in a sense, is for both information and permission) seems quite harsh and uncooperative. Even though she gives him the information he seeks and the permission may not be hers to give, Beth could have chosen other linguistic forms to convey that content while also signalling solidarity with him. In other snippets of conversation among these team members, the tension of being somewhat interdependent can also be seen in their use of power differences.

Power Differentiation

Overall, this team shows only moderate power differentiation, though there are differences in the organizational power of these team members. With the exception of Susan, Sally, and Kevin, all are from the same job level in the organization. However, Guy, Denny, and Don (and Paul, who is absent from this meeting) are the team leaders and will get most of the credit for the team's successful performance. Theoretically, in this new design, they should also get more of the blame as well, making them more dependent on the other team members; but, since this is the first iteration of this design, no one quite knows what to expect in terms of accountability. This uncertainty is observable in the interactions of the team leaders with Beth and John. Beth, as the representative from a powerful finance department, has lots of control over the team leaders' actions, though the new team design presumably makes her accountable to them. This ambiguity in their status can be observed in Beth's linguistic behavior. As discussed above, Beth expresses a willingness to help the team leader, but she behaves like a person with equal or greater power, interrupting the formal leaders, asking them questions, and asserting her independence.

John is from die engineering, a department that in the old sequential product development process had less power than any department or group, with the possible exception of the plants. However, in the new team process, he should have greater input into the decisions of the product designers. Much of his language in this excerpt displays this sense of having equal power with the other team members. Yet in turn 28, Guy appears to be countering John's independence and distance by using a rare—especially for him—display of power difference. He does this by using the imperative verb form, "Slow down." This show of power, though, is mitigated by his subsequent request for advice from John.

Another interesting power struggle can be seen in the conversation between Denny and Sally (turns 38–43), which is analyzed below as the unique incident of conflict in this excerpt. It follows the snippet of conversation (turn 34) discussed above in which Sally uses independent and powerful speech with mitigation, by asserting her power as buyer to resist an engineer's proposal for use of a material other than plastic, but mitigates its force, as described. Also, by using the verb "support" (as opposed to "agree" or "accept" or "approve") she minimizes the differences between herself as buyer and the engineers. She is also identifying with the materials group (with the phrase "not doing it in plastic," which refers to the materials group's new policy of plastic as the default material). Though it is not unambiguous, her use of "us" here seems to refer to the materials management group rather than the team because the semantic context is materials management's initiative to make sourcing decisions that balance best value with effective utilization of subsidiary plants.

Despite these incidents of equivocal power, the team's typical pattern of interaction displays low power differentiation. There is not a dominance of the floor by those members with greater organizational power. Everyone interrupts and is interrupted (turns 3, 10, 11, 18, 41–46). Though the team leaders and the facilitator ask most of the questions (1, 4, 19, 20, 24, 28, 40), the fact that the questioners wait for answers and listen to them suggests that these questions are actually seeking information and not being used to display a right to interrogate. Also, the team leaders answer questions of others (turns 29–30) and allow others to change the subject (turns 19, 47).

Social Distance

This team uses very few of the distinctive linguistic markers of social distance. Team members do not use formal forms of address or nicknames. They neither use excessive politeness nor make the kind of peremptory demands that people make of friends and family members. Their forms of speech are not particularly formal or informal. Their talk indicates that socially they are neither distant nor close. Taken together with the data on power differences, these data suggest that these are people of relatively equal power who may draw closer socially over time.

Conflict Management and Negotiation Process

This interaction is typical for this team in that, although latent conflicts can be detected, the conflicts rarely are engaged and the team members do not negotiate their differences. Although there were clearly differences of skill, expertise, and experience among these people, the negotiation and integration of these differences and the resolution of conflicts they create was not being handled *by the team itself*. The typical tactic for managing conflict here is avoidance by postponing discussion (turn 36) or by referring the conflict to higher managers for resolution (turns 15 and 42). One could even interpret the extensive discussions of procedure as avoidance of conflict through reference to policy and procedure.

The only overt disagreement in the interaction occurs in the segment of interaction between Sally and Denny (turns 38–46) in which they are debating about the requirements for outsourcing documentation. In the segment, Denny repeatedly uses linguistic behavior that displays a sense of his having greater power than Sally. He starts (turn 38) by asserting his understanding of the policy. Though this is not an explicit disagreement, denial, or contradiction of Sally's proposal (turn 36) that they meet at a separate time to discuss particulars, his assertion in effect negates her suggestion by keeping the topic in discussion. Sally's disagreement (turn 39) with his interpretation is expressed through her use of "but," which signals negation. Her negation manifests a sense of power parity, but by reengaging in the discussion, she allows Denny to shape the conversation. In her three subsequent turns (41, 43, 45), she acquiesces to interruption by Denny, a common pattern of mutually recognized power differentials.[1]

Yet Sally tries other strategies that could conceivably minimize the distance between herself and Denny. For example, in turn 41, her use of the plural first person in reference to a task and a decision that has traditionally been the design engineer's—mainstreaming a new design feature into the existing model—suggests shared responsibility, which would in effect mean that there was less power difference between them than was traditional. She also displays empathy and an interest in integration with her attempt to use his own words, as signalled by her "as you say" in that same turn.

The coup de grace is Denny's mention of two men in Sally's department who are more senior. In one case, he implies that Sally does not have the power to establish the procedure by proposing that they go to Fred, who is two levels higher than Sally, for clarification (turn 42). In turn 43, Sally appears to concede, but as she tries to save face, Denny again interrupts her. This time (turn 44), in addition to reference to the written policy, he adds another more senior manager's point of view to his argument. Though Sally interrupts him in a final bid for credibility and equal power (turn 45), his third interruption with reference to Fred and Hal carries the day, at least with the other team members. Sally does not try again and Susan brings the discussion to a close (turn 47).

Some part of this power differentiation may be warranted by the difference between Denny and Sally in terms of their hierarchical positions within the company, or by the fact that even within the team structure, Sally—being the subordinate of one of the team members—is not a formal member in her own right. However, she does attend many meetings and is clearly trying to act within and on behalf of the team (turns 32, 36, and 41). Denny's linguistic behavior in the meeting as well as his going outside of the team for resolution of cross-functional problems indicate a perception of independence, an unwillingness to negotiate differences within the team, and a lack of identification with the other team members.

As mentioned above, there is no negotiation in this excerpt. The only behavior that even reflects a win-lose or win-win orientation is

Sally's reference to what "the position [of materials management or possibly the company] should be" (turn 34), which is offset by Beth's effort to reframe Guy's interest, possibly so that it would not conflict with policy (turn 7). In fact, in all of the team meetings I observed, there was only one real attempt at negotiation of differences. Interestingly, it occurred not among team members, but between two of the members' functional managers who happened to be present. However, even that negotiation was not resolved within the team setting. This indicates that this team did not meet one of the central criteria for being a team: members did not integrate their differences.

Perhaps the most interesting display of independence, social distance, and lack of identification in this team interaction appears in turn 48, in which a subordinate of one of the team members expresses the member's dissatisfaction ("He's concerned") with the way the team is doing its work. Even if Paul had a compelling reason for not attending this meeting, his deputizing someone else to bring this negative assessment for him suggests a lack of personal concern for the feelings of other team members; one of our cultural norms is that criticism should be delivered face to face. Many people would probably feel criticized and experience some degree of resentment about not being able to question him about this opinion or dispute it. Furthermore, this action on his part also could be interpreted as a lack of commitment to participating with the team in fixing its problems.

Interestingly, this criticism seems to cause Denny, after his earlier self-distancing from the team, to identify with the team. In his turn 51, in response to Paul's critique, Denny uses the first person plural "we" three times in reference to the team, and the gist of his comment is supportive of the team.

This snippet of team talk is characterized by cordial, if not socially close, linguistic forms and few displays of power. Though team members seem inclined to help one another and disinclined to battle over the distribution of work, blame, or credit, they display only minimal identification with the team and minimal recognition of being interdependent with one another. Though there is disagreement and expression of differences in this team, this analysis of a typical excerpt from the team's interaction indicates that members do not negotiate or integrate these differences. They are essentially a team in name only. (See figure 5.3 for an assessment of the team's talk along the key dimensions of team interaction.)

Figure 5.3 Assessment of the Front-End team's talk.

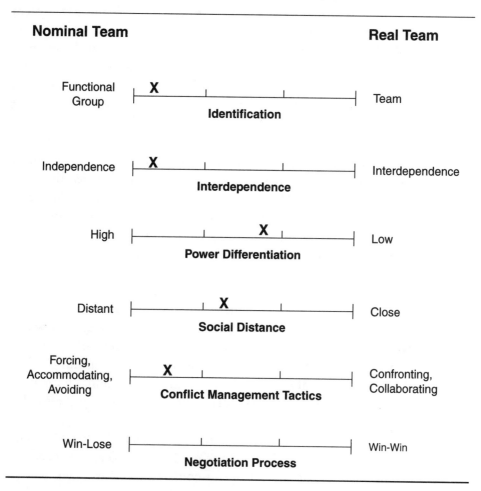

TEAM INTERACTION AND ORGANIZATIONAL CONTEXT

Why do we observe this pattern of interaction? The absence of negotiation and integrative activity in this interaction is important in itself and also accounts for the other aspects of the conversation. The generic team tasks of negotiating and integrating the knowledge distributed among team members were not being done here *because* they were being done elsewhere—by the team leaders, or if there was conflict, by managers. Three types of evidence support this conclusion. First, there was no negotiating and integrating in any of the meetings observed. Second, there *was* negotiation of differences by the teams of functional managers to whom the product teams made their periodic reports. (Indeed, as mentioned above, the description of the team system at Wayne indicated that one purpose of the managerial teams was to resolve differences that the teams could not.) The third source of corroborating evidence was comments in interviews with many team members to the effect that "teams do not make decisions; decisions continue to be made by the functions or by managers fighting it out."

Revisiting the contextual features of this organization (see table 5.2) explains why integration occurred outside of the team. The sheer size of the corporation created coordination contingencies that had been long and well served by structure, systems, and standard operating procedures. As a result, much of the work of the organization involved designing, communicating, assessing, and modifying the organization. This interpretive activity occupied much of the time and energy of the managerial work force. When the loss of market share led to downsizing and restructuring, the design activities became even more salient. In the context of fewer resources, higher demands, and new work arrangements, it was imperative to know what work was being done where and who had what expertise and what responsibilities. Interpretation of the structure and systems was no longer merely a cultural routine, it had become a critical *prerequisite* for getting professional-level work done. Teams provided a natural forum for accomplishing the needed exchange and interpretation of information.

The corporate pressure to regain market share led to divisional goals of reducing costs and improving quality. As had always been the case, each function of the enterprise contributed in its own way to these ends and therefore had its own set of subgoals against which it was measured. These were then further subdivided within each of the functional hierarchies so that every individual could be evaluated on the basis of how well each had performed against the assigned functional subgoals. This functional work assignment and evaluation procedure was not altered with the introduction of teams. Team members were assigned to slots on teams *as part of their functional responsibilities.* Employees continued to report to their functional managers, who conducted their performance evaluations and made promotion and salary decisions. Thus, the functional hierarchy of goals and performance evaluation preserved the interdependence between functional managers and their professional employees who served on teams. (See figure 5.4

Table 5.2 Description of the Wayne Division's organizational context.

Wayne Division	
Feature	*Description*
Recent historical events	Market share drops; downsizing and restructuring
Corporate identity	We are the structure
Precursors to teams	Early attempts at teams, simultaneous engineering
Divisional strategic goals	Cost and quality
Initiator of teams	Middle manager
Expectations of teams	Speed, efficiency, collaboration
Nature of team task	Open-ended, long-term
Duration of team structure	8 months
How teams were assembled	Position-based assignment
Choice in assignments	No
Basis for team leadership	Lead function
Size of teams	10
Multiple team assignments	Yes
Degree of dedication to team (percentage of team fully dedicated)	10%
Distribution of stakes	Formally variable
Mechanisms for assessing team performance	Formal quarterly report, functional reporting
Hierarchical levels (from teams to top of divisions)	5
Role of functional managers	Unchanged
Liaison to managers	Team leader to team hierarchy
Training	None

Figure 5.4 Major forces shaping the Front-End team's dynamics.

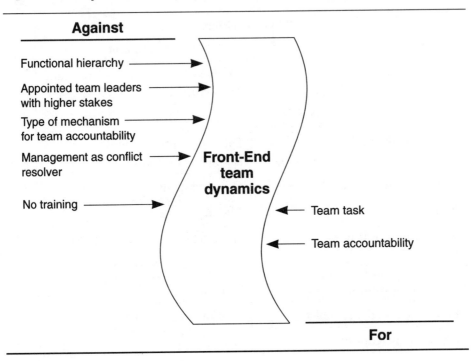

for a depiction of all the major forces shaping team dynamics at Wayne Division).

Wayne's hierarchy of cross-functional teams was designed to manage the reintegration of these subgoals. But the existence of the hierarchy with the explicit expectation that each level would resolve conflicts that could not be addressed on the level below, together with the functional interdependence, virtually ensured that conflicts created by functional differences would be pushed up for negotiation. Because teams weren't required to resolve the conflicts that arose as they sought to integrate their differences, they tended not to.

Two other features of the team system also encouraged teams to push integration responsibility upward. The first was the mechanism for team accountability, which was the quarterly report of the team's progress to the team of managers. This provided the channel for pushing up differences. Furthermore, in practice, this was not actually a mechanism of *team accountability* because team members were not required to be present. The only people who were required to participate and "account for" the team were the team leaders. Feedback on team performance would be handled by either the functional manager or the team leaders. However, the functional manager could choose not to, and the team leaders had no formal means for holding team members accountable.

The second feature of Wayne's team system that motivated teams to avoid negotiation of their differences was the differential in the stakes that team members had in team outcomes. The team leaders had significantly higher stakes than other members not only because they alone had to present the team's report to the management teams but because they were the only members assigned to a single team. Because they had more time to devote to the team task, they tended to do whatever integration could be done. Thus their performance was more dependent on other team members than the reverse, and there was little interdependence among team members as a set.

Because teams did not have to negotiate their differences, team members were not interdependent. Because they were not interdependent, there was little need to use power. Also, because there was no need to integrate, there was no need to develop social closeness and less opportunity since so much of the work was done outside of teams. This also minimized the motivation to identify with the team, particularly if this identification implied distance from or conflict with the functional area, from which rewards were derived.

LESSONS FROM THE FRONT-END TEAM

In chapter 4 we learned that even assignment of a critical interdependent task and creation of managerial incentives for encouragement of cross-functional collaboration were insufficient to offset the functional loyalties and cross-functional antagonisms that can seriously impede team work. We hypothesized that designating a team leader and creating a mechanism for team accountability could create a positive sense of interdependence and motivate resolution of the numerous conflicts that hobbled the Tech I team. In this chapter, we learned that although these design features may be necessary, they are not sufficient to create a perception of interdependence among team members that will motivate them to negotiate their differences.

By virtue of having high stakes in the team performance, the team leaders at the Wayne Division were motivated to do the coordination tasks that groups or teams require. However, this individual account-ability did not guarantee that they would be able to "drive the other team members" to make the necessary contributions to the team task and to negotiate their differences in an integrative fashion. Even the existence of explicit team goals ("imperatives") and the existence of a mechanism for holding teams accountable for their performance (the quarterly reports) did not create a perception of interdependence among team members. The result here was mixed. The Front-End team was not immobilized by unresolved conflict. Its interaction was not marked by power displays, social distance, distributive behavior, or forcing. On the other hand, the team members were not integrating their differ-ences to accomplish the task. The functional hierarchy was still the principal locus of cross-functional decision making. This occurred because, despite the quarterly reports, team members were still held accountable individually for the functional work, a part of which was their participation on the team. Thus, team members remained far more vertically dependent on their functional managers than they felt horizontally dependent on one another.

This case describes a very thorough, yet not particularly effective, team system design. It leads to several very important hypotheses con-cerning professional team work: Do the typical hierarchical and func-tional organizational structure and individually based evaluation and reward system as a whole act as major impediments to professional team work? Are there any mechanisms that can, in the context of functional hierarchies and individual accountability, create perceived interdependence on the part of team members and integration of their differences? Is there any solution to the problems observed in these cases?

In the next chapter, we see a marked contrast to the three cases we have just examined—in terms of both the team talk and the organiza-tional context. A comparison of this case with the others will help us answer these questions that remain unresolved.

CHAPTER 6

Personal Commitment and Organizational Accommodation

The Occupational Health and Environmental Safety Division and the Eurous Team

This chapter tells a most unusual story of an organization that committed itself to teams; of teams that, by all accounts, realized everyone's hopes; and of the Eurous team, which typifies this remarkable relationship. In one sense, it is a story about speed and how to get it. However, the moral of this tale is that it takes a long time to create the kind of teams that can accelerate product development while achieving other strategic goals. As we listen in on the Eurous team, we get a palpable sense of what team work could and should be. And from an analysis that juxtaposes this interaction with its unusual organizational context, we understand at last what it takes to get real cross-functional team work.

THE OCCUPATIONAL HEALTH AND ENVIRONMENTAL SAFETY DIVISION

The Occupational Health and Environmental Safety Division (OH& ESD) was one of 3M's forty-two divisions. 3M had gained a reputation as one of the United States' most innovative companies,[1] and its $10.5

billion in annual sales (1988) came from products as diverse as office supplies and surgical preparation solutions. 3M boasted over 100 core technologies, R&D spending nearly double the average rate for the fifty largest U.S. companies, and more than $3 billion in sales from products introduced in the past five years. 3M employed 83,000 people throughout the world, and international sales reached $4.4 billion in 1988.[2] The company took pride in having developed a successful two-track career system, which allowed scientists to climb the corporate ranks alongside managers without leaving research and development.

OH&ESD was quickly becoming one of 3M's most progressive divisions. Once a sleepy unit, OH&ESD had transformed itself into a highly innovative division in a company whose reputation rode on innovation. OH&ESD manufactured products to help in workplace health and safety. Respirators (face masks) worn by workers handling gas, vapor, and particles—as in oil drilling and car painting—formed the largest share of the division's products, but more recent products included insulating materials used in clothing and clean-room suits. The division recorded over $100 million in sales for 1989, but people were proudest of the way their division continued to generate 25 percent of sales from products introduced within the past five years.

The History of OH&ESD

In 1982 Robert Hershock returned to St. Paul, Minnesota, from Switzerland, where he had been head of 3M's European operations, to become head of OH&ESD. When Hershock became general manager, OH&ESD was relying primarily on two products. One respirator had been introduced in 1961, the other in 1973, and together they accounted for a major portion of the division's sales. OH&ESD was a 3M aberration: it suffered from a low technology base. It had few products in development and was in what people at the division referred to as a "harvest mode," in which profits were taken but little or no investment occurred. The climate at OH&ESD reflected its lackluster performance. Most senior managers had either taken early retirement or transferred to other divisions.

The organization had been run autocratically, with the general manager issuing orders on a weekly basis. Directors of all the functional areas kept the strategy to themselves, and employees were given little responsibility. Barriers erected between functions were impregnable, and people were not encouraged to take risks. Morale remained low throughout OH&ESD. By 1985, the division generated only 12 percent of its sales from products introduced in the past five years. Bob Hershock knew the division had to make dramatic changes.

The Move to Teams

"We fell into teams out of necessity," Hershock recounted, "and fear." The necessity included 3M's insistence that each division adhere to the 25 percent rule, especially after the company's rough financial performance in the early 1980s. The fear? "My own," stated Hershock.

Hershock had been reading a lot about teams, and he witnessed how futile 3M's traditional approach to teams (business development units, or BDUs) was at OH&ESD. Those teams were intended to chart new opportunities and new products within a particular area of the division's business, but they left most people with a similar impression: thirty-five people gathered in a room, doing nothing but arranging their next meeting. Hershock wanted to capture the same orientation toward innovation that BDUs were intended to foster, but he sought to create a system agile enough to inspire risk taking and personal involvement. Together with the laboratory director (who oversaw research and development, product engineering) and a single consultant, Hershock designed OH&ESD's action teams.

"To set up the teams," Hershock later recounted in an article highlighting the division's efforts for a 3M audience, "we had to do a tremendous amount of restructuring. This created opposition from those people who were very structured and focused on their specific job responsibilities." (See figure 6.1 for an organization chart with one action team.) The major opposition came from middle managers, who felt that teams infringed on their authority and on the control they had over their direct reports. Teams threw the managers' responsibility into question, and managers saw a conflict between their goals and the goals of teams. Hershock discussed the painful transformation the division undertook, and he underscored a fundamental principle that would anchor action teams:

> Change like this is an evolutionary process, and there are a lot of problems to deal with. You can't expect to move from one system to another without some complications . . . and without some people

Figure 6.1 Simplified organization chart for the Occupational Health and Environmental Safety Division and the Eurous team.

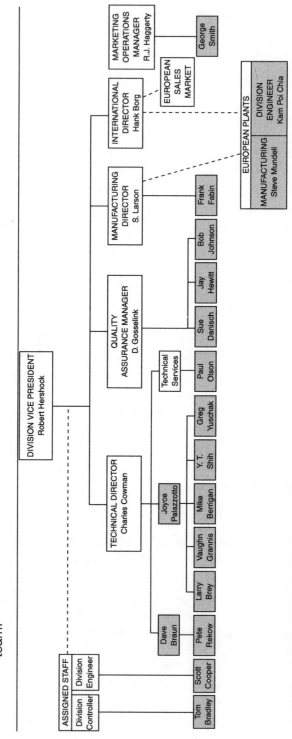

Note: Shaded boxes represent Eurous team members.

not buying in. I had to deal with a lot of fence guarding and parochialism . . . people saying, "This isn't my job; it's *their* job."

My major irritation is people who put walls around a job description. What I'll say is, "Hey, your job isn't process engineering manager or whatever; your job is to use your skill to do whatever is necessary to get the business moving in the right direction."[3]

Even after extensive training, not everyone felt comfortable with teams, and some people left the division. But action teams revived OH&ESD and inspired an additional organizational change. Laboratory, process engineering, and quality assurance were all placed in one building and united under one line of management.

THE INTRODUCTION OF ACTION TEAMS

Robert Hershock introduced teams to develop new products and to do so quickly. The traditional, serial approach to product development would not suffice. Hershock also set an ambitious goal for action teams: cut new product development time in half. With an emphasis on the timely introduction of new products, action teams were expected to accomplish several other objectives as well. By cutting across functions, teams would promote interdisciplinary cooperation and understanding. By focusing on new products with high potential, teams would create an innovative atmosphere at OH&ESD and increase the level of risk taking. Teams would be formed around products with significant potential for growth, products that could boost the division's technology base and expand its array of new products (rather than product modifications or line extensions). Teams would rally people around a project, allow them to identify with a product, thereby instilling a sense of ownership, and, as a result, inspire heightened commitment to quality. Teams would enable OH&ESD to respond to changing customer needs. (See figure 6.2 for a diagram of the relationship between teams and strategic goals.)

The Plan

Together with Charlie Cowman, director of the laboratory, and Doug Peters, a local consultant, Bob Hershock tried to think through the obstacles teams might encounter, and they tried to anticipate the support

Figure 6.2 The Occupational Health and Environmental Safety Division: teams and strategic goals.

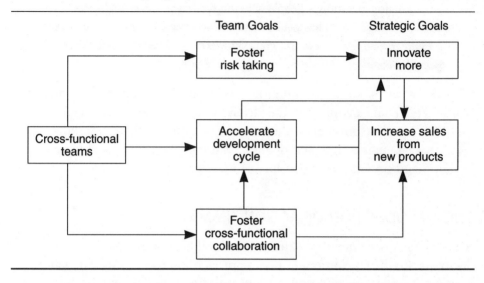

the division would need to provide if it were to accommodate teams. To transform itself from a complacent, risk-averse, autocratic organization into an innovative, flexible, and daring one required forethought—and risk on Hershock's part. Hershock decided to introduce teams alongside the existing organizational structure, which would be left intact. Teams would take their ideas to the operating committee—Bob Hershock and the functional directors—who would designate resources to be provided by the functional managers. By maintaining the existing structure while introducing teams, senior management sought to balance control with risk. Instead of swinging back and forth between the two extremes, Hershock and his cohorts hoped to create an ongoing mixture.

For teams to be successfully introduced, people had to be taught to operate within this new format without relying on practices indigenous to the traditional structure. People had to feel comfortable working together before they could approach projects with the risk-taking attitude Hershock sought to foster, an attitude of "Why not try? What do we have to lose?" OH&ESD focused its training on the personal and interpersonal foundations of becoming a team member, rather than on the formal group aspects usually emphasized. Instead of teaching people the steps in producing a team's mission, goals, and strategies, OH&

ESD helped people understand the personal and interpersonal impediments to teamwork: concerns about acceptance and respect, stereotypes of other functional areas, and work style. Training taught people to become team members, empowering them to believe they could—and should—do whatever had to be done for the project, regardless of background, position, or function.

Features of the Action Team System

The team system at OH&ESD had several salient characteristics that ensured practical success. Although the division had as many as forty development projects ongoing, it established teams around a limited number of those projects (eleven at the beginning). Teams formed around only those products that had significant potential for growth. This allowed the division to focus its energy on the most promising projects and to support those teams properly. The first set of teams concentrated on projects previously identified, and it took some coaxing to appoint team leaders. However, the second generation of team projects, such as the Eurous, conformed to Hershock's intentions. To create a team, the person developing the product idea had to convince senior management that the product warranted a team. The product had to be worthy of the resources it would get, and it had to elicit participation from the professional ranks. Voluntary participation proved vital to OH&ESD's team system, as did the central figure, or champion. The champion was the team leader, the person with undying belief in the project who had to recruit team members to participate.

Membership on a team did not exempt an employee from doing his or her regular job—teams existed over and above normal responsibilities—so people would volunteer, would only share in the commitment and risk, only if they felt that the project was worthwhile. Individuals represented themselves on the teams, and part of team training focused on how members should represent themselves rather than their disciplines. If they volunteered for the team, they were to do whatever was necessary for the project, and specifically not serve as sentinels for their functional area. Even though OH&ESD maintained its existing structure, when it came to teams, team members were to help solve problems, not represent their functions. In the words of Hershock, Cowman, and Peters, team members "were turned loose in the organization to make a contribution."

Bob Hershock made sure that once a team was assembled, it received all the support from upper management it needed. Providing adequate support paradoxically required accurate information but limited reporting. Hershock believed that if the reporting became too formal, it distracted from the real work, and the information became less accurate as presenters strove to look better to those who would evaluate their performance. He also believed that managers, when faced with formal reviews, tended to meddle; and the overall atmosphere became political and less trusting. To counter these tendencies, action teams reported progress quarterly, at an informal lunch meeting for all team champions with Bob Hershock and other senior managers. The lunch meetings fostered trust and encouraged champions to share good and bad news. It produced trust between teams and senior managers, and it convinced teams to approach managers whenever they encountered serious obstacles.

That had been reinforced already through the role of sponsor. A person from Bob Hershock's senior management team was assigned to each action team, not to monitor but to provide support. The sponsor did not run the team and did not monitor it on behalf of Hershock. Rather, the sponsor served as an advisor, mentor, and troubleshooter; most important, he or she could run interference and obtain resources the team was having trouble securing. The sponsor's attention reinforced the senior managers' commitment to teams, particularly in the eyes of team members, and it opened a channel of communication to the senior managers.

Results

OH&ESD has introduced twenty new products to the market since 1986. According to Charlie Cowman, the division's success rate with action teams is 90 percent; that is, nine out of ten products developed by the action teams were on the market on time, with significant market potential. In 1992, 30 percent of the division's sales came from products developed in the past five years. The division reported that teams had in fact cut product development time in half. The estimated time to market for new products ranged from four months for products using an existing process to twenty-four months for a product with an entirely new process and new equipment. One team member, however, disputed the division's claims.

We haven't set any records on product development. It's been six years. I know we'll find a way to say it's three and a half just to make Hershock happy.

To the surprise and initial shock of division management, teams spent far more money in the initial months of a project than under the traditional development procedure. Anxiety disappeared when senior managers realized that teams were only using funds sooner, while total expenditures for the duration of the development remained the same as before. The division benefitted, however, because products were getting to market sooner and generating sales earlier than they would have under the traditional process. OH&ESD had found a way to accelerate its growth.

THE BEGINNINGS OF THE EUROUS TEAM

Jazz is spontaneous. . . . Everybody is reacting to what others in the band are doing, and that's it. What you're doing is it. (Dave Braun, jazz cornetist and Eurous team leader)

Dave Braun began research on Eurous in 1985, and soon afterward he hired Pete Rekow to work with him. Together they developed the core technologies for a new type of respirator, creating handmade prototypes along the way, and presenting their idea to others at OH& ESD. Initially few people other than the two thought a viable product could be developed, but as one chemist explained in 1989, "I've seen a 1 percent chance for success rise to 50 percent."

Steve Mundell, a manufacturing expert and process engineering director at 3M's plant in Aycliffe, England, first learned about the Eurous project when Braun visited Europe in 1985. As the product idea developed, Mundell wanted Aycliffe to get the product. The two core technologies, Mundell felt, could make Aycliffe an important plant. When Eurous ran out of money in 1987, Aycliffe provided some funding to advance the project. Eurous gained momentum, but in 1988 the team experienced its greatest disappointment. Instead of developing two new gas and vapor respirators simultaneously, OH&ESD chose to focus effort on one at a time. The directors disbanded the Eurous team and dedicated people and resources to the other respirator under development. Hank Borg, international director at OH&ESD and Eurous team sponsor, explained the directors' decision:

It was a strategic decision. We saw that the other respirator could get to market faster, and we saw Eurous as better long-term. Eurous might replace the other. Since that one will be easy for competitors to copy, the Eurous is our trump card. When we put the other one out, we stun competitors, and just when they're getting their copies on the market, we'll introduce Eurous and knock them out. We spoke about this at length with Bob Hershock.

By all accounts it was a difficult, disheartening decision that Bob Hershock and his staff did not make easily. A senior manager remembered the day the decision was made:

We had thirteen action teams two years ago, but we didn't have the resources to support them all. So the division took some people from Eurous and put them on the other to get it back on track.

I still remember Dave's reaction. Dave went in to see [Bob] Hershock and [Charlie] Cowman and the other directors who were meeting. He said he had faith that they would choose the 3M product, the one with seven patents and new technology, not the me-too product. Dave said, "You let me down. You lied to me. You disappointed me. I guess I was wrong [to have had faith in you]." Dave felt Eurous had greater potential for success than the other respirator. Hershock responded that it was just a matter of priorities at the time. Dave was still angry.

I went to see Dave, to comfort him and tell him I thought highly of him for saying what he felt to the directors. I told him that at least the other respirator would surprise competitors and draw the fire, and the Eurous could come in and hit them broadside. Dave said, "Baloney. The directors are just copping out."

Braun and Rekow continued to work on Eurous, and as the other respirator moved to the market, the Eurous team began to re-form. (See table 6.1 for Eurous team roster.) By January 1989 the team had coalesced, and in May the team became fully staffed, getting two members from 3M Europe, a full-time person from division engineering, and a plastics engineer. By the late summer and fall of 1989, the team was completing the "lab" stage of development—product and process design—and preparing its request for final funding. The effort had been cross-functional from the beginning, and the team would now have to convince division management and the next level of authority, group

Table 6.1 Eurous action team roster, August 1989.

Name	Affiliation	Time Dedicated to Eurous Team
Mike Berrigan	Product Engineering	100%
Tom Bratley	Controller's Office	5%
Dave Braun (team leader)	R&D	100%
Larry Brey	R&D	25%
Kam Poi Chia	Division Eng. (& Ayecliffe Plant)	75%
Scott Cooper	Division Engineering	75%
Sue Danisch	Product Engineering	10%
Frank Fabin	Manufacturing	5%
Vaughn Grannis	Process Engineering	100%
Jay Hewitt	Quality Assurance	20%
Bob Johnson	Process Engineering	25%
Steve Mundell	Manufacturing (Aycliffe Plant)	25%
Paul Olson	Tech Services	5%
Joyce Palazzotto	Management (Lab)	50%
Pete Rekow	Product Engineering	100%
Y. T. Shih	R&D	100%
George Smith	Marketing	5%
Greg Yuschak	Product Engineering	100%

Note: Process and product engineers, R&D, and technical services were all grouped under one line of management, referred to as Lab, which reported to the Technical Director, Charles Cowman.

management, that Eurous merited $8 million for manufacturing equipment and scale-up.

As it began to form, the Eurous team experienced some of the classic tensions inherent in any product development. Joyce Palazzotto, lab manager, described how tension with the technical people manifested itself on Eurous:

> The manager has typically done what Dave Braun does. Both of us were frustrated early on. He wanted control of the technical and management resources. I wanted to get involved. He wouldn't let me; I didn't give him the resources. The turning point was a meeting in 1988. Some higher-ups from the U.K. were in, and Dave had a meeting with them. I went to Dave and asked about the meeting. He said, "You weren't invited, so you can't come, and it's not my meeting anyway, so I can't invite you." I was really upset. I went to the meeting anyway. That was a turning point. Dave saw my support. He saw I was willing to butt in even when I was turned away. Dave saw how interested I was.
>
> Dave also went to team training, and that seemed to create a change. Right when he got back, he seemed to be more open. It was not just him, though. I had to learn to work with him too.

Getting manufacturing engineers (from division engineering) to work on the project resembled many of the classic tales of cross-functional tension; one process engineer referred to it as a "tug of war." The team felt that it needed input from a division engineer to create a viable product. Meanwhile division engineering insisted that, with such a strain on resources, when the team got a viable product, division engineers would devote the necessary time and effort. But the team worked through tensions and obstacles, coalescing around Eurous itself. As the team member from division engineering commented, "People need a purpose, a mission, a goal. That's what Eurous gives us."

THE EUROUS TEAM IN FULL SWING

At any one time, there were between fifteen and twenty people formally listed as members of the Eurous team. By May 1989, a core of approximately seven people spent most of their time on the Eurous project. But even those who spent as little as 10 percent of their time on Eurous were considered integral members of the team. Braun felt that the degree of commitment to the team did not reflect the percentage of time a person spent on the project. He cited the example of Sue Danisch, a product engineer. "Although she spends only 5 to 10 percent of her time on the respirator, she made a strong commitment to the team and wants to work on the product." The team had a formal meeting once a month to review information and progress, discuss and solve special problems, and anticipate upcoming steps. Team members, however, interacted almost every day, and smaller subsections of the team met all the time to get things done.

There was a tremendous amount of finger pointing: finger pointing at the source of team members' commitment. While many team members credited Dave Braun with inspiring their commitment, Braun and others felt that the product itself elicited their effort and energy. The product, mutual commitment among team members, and Braun's relentless faith in the team and the product all contributed to their success.

The Team Leader

"Dave Braun is one of the few inventors of his kind left in America, one of the true dreamers who can make the dream come true. He is one of the great creative thinkers." Those were the words of a senior marketing manager, but they could have expressed the impression Braun had made on most people at OH&ESD. He had already achieved great success within the company, having risen to the second highest level in the technical ladder of 3M's dual hierarchy. By his own admission, his most unlikely accomplishment, though, was his success as a team leader. His skill as a team champion, however, was not in doubt. "Dave's sincerity inspires me," said one team member. "You just don't want to let the guy down. He doesn't pressure. It would be like letting down your parents."

An accomplished jazz cornet player, Dave Braun seemed as nimble guiding the Eurous team in the improvisational effort that created a unique team and product as he did playing with the legendary Butch Thompson. His dedication to the product was infectious, and his humor relieved the inevitable tensions arising from team work. Through his actions (and inactions), Braun emphasized the team structure. Through carefully designed agendas, expert meeting facilitation, and attentive follow-up, Braun provided the coordination that would ensure the team members' commitment to one another and belief that their contributions would have an impact. For example, after every team meeting, he drafted extensive minutes, describing progress and infusing further encouragement:

> The day started with a capital forecast that had little chance for success in the U.K. Through careful study, led by Chia, of the filter making and carbon handling and by Mundell's suggestion that we look at an introduction based on intermediate level filter makers, we were able to begin to see possibilities. Cooper then visualized a way to make two filters per pallet, thereby increasing output of the larger production filter maker.

This precise language delineated the nature of the problem, "a capital forecast that had little chance for success," without laying blame, yet without dodging the issue. The minutes exuded the spirit of effort, anticipation, and realistic confidence embodied in the actions themselves: "we were able to begin to see possibilities." When Steve Mundell and Kam Poi Chia first joined the team for meetings in May, Braun provided them with a loose-leaf binder full of snapshots of each team member, his or her phone and fax numbers, and functional affiliation.

Braun could recognize personal problems between team members and tried always to address them quickly. When Kam Poi Chia and Scott Cooper first began working together, they clashed. Both strong-willed manufacturing engineers, they were stationed in different countries and held different positions on certain issues. As Braun noted, "There are egos there." As they continued to "buck up against each other," he got them together in a meeting and had them work out their differences. By routinely soliciting others' opinions and contributions, Dave fostered a team culture in which team membership was as important as team leadership. In effect, by letting others talk, he was restraining himself; like an expert jazz performer, he was contributing just what the team needed to produce a novel but well-integrated product. Braun made a concerted effort to *maintain* nourishing conditions for the team.

Team members' admiration for Braun also illuminated his leadership. Steve Mundell recounted this story:

> He's fifty but still wants to learn. He comes across a new idea and wants to explore it. When he visited Aycliffe and heard about Just-In-Time, he wanted to learn about it. He wanted to see a cell at the plant.

Another team member tied Braun's ability as a team leader to his technical expertise:

The team works well together. There haven't been any significant personality problems. Very few squabbles. I attribute that to Dave. Someone as technically knowledgeable as he is gains the respect of all the technical people.

He's willing to listen, and he argues on the merits. Dave will sometimes argue as forcefully as anyone, but we'll argue back. He's fair.

Many team members admired Braun for his inspirational ability:

Dave Braun is a spark plug. You need someone like that to get a new project off the ground. He never gets discouraged. I'd like to be like that.

Braun's reputation and dedication impressed those outside the team, which further aided the team. One team member commented, "He's not just a technical foot soldier who developed a new respirator. He has a lot of clout." It was clout he had gained from his position in the technical hierarchy, but it was also clout he and the team had gained from demonstrating the viability of Eurous.

The Member

Pete Rekow demonstrated what it meant to be a team *member*. He described the predominant attitude among Eurous team members, an attitude he epitomized:

We want a successful product. People look at the end result rather than protecting their narrow interest. No one *really* cares about the marketing forecast [as an entity in itself]. None of us succeeds unless the product succeeds. . . . Bottom line has to be, What are we trying to do here? Make a product.

Rekow's candor enabled him to voice whatever concerns he had regarding the team, whether related to the product or to team dynamics. His knowledge of the product and faith in it made him an informed contributor, one who created a comfortable climate for other team members to follow his lead. Braun underscored that value:

Pete's been living with this thing for four years, so he brings emotion to it. He says what he feels when he feels strongly about something.

That sets a good example for the others. It's commitment to the product.

Like Hershock, senior managers, sponsors, and team champions, Rekow showed a degree of insight uncommon at other organizations as he assessed what he had to do to make teams work:

> My approach to making people comfortable with exchanging information is to do it yourself. Put up your data and let people take shots at it. You do it by example.

But Rekow refused to paint himself the hero, readily acknowledging the difficulty of actually sharing your information and submitting yourself to criticism. "My ego gets involved. My job is to come up with ideas. I've had my feelings hurt." Rekow also served as a role model in numerous ways, as one team member observed after the team members had rehearsed their presentations for the laboratory approval meeting:

> Pete's presentation was the best. He's so cool and confident up there.
> He's been working on this for five years, so he knows the product well.
> His attitude is, "Go ahead, ask me questions. I know the answers."

Team members got along well, and many would have agreed with Palazzotto about the intrinsic reward of participating: "It's more fun the more you get involved." Even with Braun's inspirational leadership, team members were largely self-directed. "Dave is a good leader," commented one team member, "but people on the team get together in subgroups to get things done, so they're leaders too." Braun himself concurred:

> The mark of a good team is one that can function without the leader.
> It's getting to the point where I could just leave these people alone.
> They're self-motivated, and they're working hard. I don't need to do
> the old management technique of going to everybody and saying,
> "Well, how are you doing on that?"

During the first week of September 1989, the team gathered for a week of meetings to resolve central problems in preparation for approval of final funding. Mundell reviewed the day's accomplishments later that evening:

At today's meeting, we took the lap-top to a conference room, questioned all the assumptions that have gone into our [Mundell and Chia's] figures, and ran them through Lotus. At the end of the day, the figures are not ours, they're the team's. There should be no surprise when it goes for approval. It should belong to everybody.

The Eurous team had an inner circle of people who had been working on the project longer and for whom Eurous continued to occupy most of their time. Although this intimidated some of the newer team members, the team remained careful to avoid groupthink and peer pressure. Braun noted how Mundell had compiled cost figures with up to 20 percent contingency included. "We could have coaxed Steve to reduce the estimates, 'Steve, you can do it, can't you?' But it's not good to do that. We want Steve to support whatever he submits."

As a mechanism for coordinating effort across functions, the team depended upon effective exchange of information. The degree of knowledge shared among Eurous team members proved how pervasive was the candid discussion Pete Rekow preached. Pete, a product engineer, discussed his relationship with Vaughn Grannis:

Vaughn is a process engineer. In six months, I expect Vaughn to know everything I know about the product. I'll do process work. Vaughn will do lab work. I just can't imagine any place being successful without lab people doing that. You just know so much about the product.

Grannis shared Rekow's analysis. "The blur between Pete and myself, and what we're doing, there's a very definite crossover." Their collaboration, however, was not limited to product and process engineering. In one notable instance, they jointly drafted a specification document for a piece of manufacturing equipment. Design and process engineers had seldom worked together prior to action teams, and specification of equipment traditionally came under the sole domain of manufacturing engineers. But the manufacturing engineer, Scott Cooper, was tied up when the team's schedule and budget needed specifications to be drafted, so Rekow and Grannis drew on the knowledge they had accumulated from working on the team. Rekow continued the story:

We recognized a need to get a start on this. We felt our capital spending was too high, largely because we didn't get to the vendor with a specific enough idea for a machine. We had to show the vendor that we knew what we were doing. Vaughn and I sat down and wrote the draft specification to get us off dead center with that issue. Now Scott Cooper will polish it and go out with it to vendors.

It's somewhat unprecedented for a lab person to write a draft specification for a $1 million piece of equipment, but the most important thing is the exchange of information. It's not that people aren't doing their work. It's just a by-product of an open exchange of information. The key is being free and open with information.

Turned loose in the organization to make a contribution, Eurous team members had almost literally fulfilled Bob Hershock's hopes, described earlier: they were using their "skill to do whatever is necessary to get the business moving in the right direction."[4] As one team member explained, Eurous was introducing people to the very real challenge of approaching work differently:

> To some extent, the team is helping people understand group responsi-
> bility, but the [U.S.] culture is so deep that people have the individualis-
> tic urge. . . . People approach the team with the attitude of, This is
> going to be a successful product and I want to be part of it—that's
> in their heart.

Members were not infallible, of course. One acknowledged his lack of preparedness during the first rehearsal for the team's approval meeting. But the shared sense of responsibility to the team and project motivated him to compensate for this:

> I wasn't prepared on Monday and basically got up and begged for
> forgiveness for being unprepared. I pulled some stuff together and
> wrote a draft on Tuesday . . . I practiced the speech into a tape
> recorder this morning. I went back every few sentences and listened
> to myself. I didn't like the diction, so I'd do it again, and then listen
> to myself.

Like everyone at OH&ESD, the Eurous team was still learning to do team work. Team members also clung to individualistic concerns, so central to organizational life in the United States, but even a troublesome issue like reward elicited uncommon insight, exchange, and self-aware-ness. While teams at other organizations still tried to sort out how they should operate as a team, and while some argued about what they should be doing in team meetings, the Eurous team discussed a serious issue for teams in general, rewards. Their conversation was the most candid, thoughtful analysis of team reward and its complications I heard at any organization, even in individual interviews on the topic. How, in an organization designed to reward and compensate individuals, do you deliver rewards to the team? Dave Braun posed the issue at one team meeting:

> I don't know whether you realize it or not, but I think management is very pleased with the work of the Eurous team. We're so close, and we're struggling, and we're working hard, and we're doing things. But the way they look at it, they saw us stay on schedule, they saw us deliver for the field tests. They get all these reports back from Europe, and I think they're very, very pleased, and they want to reward us.
>
> So what we then have to think about is, how can we do that, something we want to do, and avoid—a lot of times when you do that, any team does that, you get a lot of . . . there've been people that are not on the team right now that contributed early. You can't take everyone, you just can't. And so we have to live with that. We have to think about it, and we're going to have to live with that. So the lower profile thing you do, the least that [danger] is. I mean, if you go on a trip, that's pretty high profile. Everyone knows about it.
>
> You see what I'm driving at here? There's been people on the team earlier, that they made some good contributions too. . . . I for one just do not like to leave bad feelings with that kind of thing. Does anybody have any comments? How do you feel?

The team members discussed the dangers of excluding past team members who had done extensive work but moved to other projects. If you include everyone ever associated with a team, the reward for really pulling it off becomes meaningless. If you exclude certain people who contributed earlier, you risk undermining the team system. How do you assess the individual contribution of each member? The team concurred with one team member who concluded: "I don't even think this group should concern itself with what the reward is. I think this group should just decide who all contributed, give it to management, and go from there. . . . We decide the bodies, they decide the dollars."

Pressures and Problems

As the Eurous team prepared for approval meetings and debated rewards, many team members were contemplating the challenge of shifting from a development phase to a manufacturing one. The challenges would be twofold. First, the team would have to draw more heavily now from different expertise than had transformed a technical impossibility into a viable product. Inherent in this shift lurked a deeper challenge. Dave Braun and Pete Rekow would have to relinquish control, a necessity driven in large part by the fact that production and marketing for the Eurous respirator were in Europe. They would have to let the team focus increasingly on manufacturing and marketing concerns, and allow the team to refocus itself around members with expertise in those areas. Some team members expressed anxiety about operating without Dave Braun's leadership. Dave insisted that the team would function perfectly well without him, but team members would also have to build confidence in themselves to confront the next stages when Dave moved on to a new project.

Another dilemma, unrelated to the stages of product development and affecting action teams in general, had been created by the organization's philosophy and practice of accommodating the organization to the team process for developing new products. One of the accommodations made to the centrality of teams and the resultant discomfort of middle managers to being "out of the loop" and "out of the action" was to allow managers to join teams. The political concession ensured support for the teams, but as a deviation from the team recruitment practice, it created some difficulties. Five of the team members of the Eurous team were Joyce Palazzotto's direct reports. While some of them felt that they would act differently if she were not a member of the team—that she inhibited candor and prevented them from doing what was best rather than what pleased her—others did not feel at all inhibited and felt that her contributions were crucial. Only by being on the team, they believed, could she truly understand the value of the work they were doing.

Despite these pressures and concerns, many of which were symptomatic of OH&ESD's evolutionary development of a team-oriented organization, the Eurous team retained its commitment to the product and kept its focus on the team's own goals and schedules. Members' team work, accomplished through their team talk, reflected the organization's commitment and accommodation to team work. More importantly, the team interaction—that is, the team work—affected the organization. As the following section demonstrates, the team interaction motivated and achieved cross-functional collaboration and controlled risk taking, realizing the development of a new product as quickly as is feasible, given the strategic goal of increasing new product revenues. To understand how this was accomplished, we turn now to observe the team at work.

THE EUROUS TEAM'S TALK

At the time of these observations, the Eurous team had almost completed the product design phase. Although numerous design tasks remained, the primary team activities at the time of these observations involved preparing final documentation for the managerial reviews that would initiate full-scale production. The excerpt that follows was taken from one of the team's regular meetings. Attending this meeting were: Dave Braun, Pete Rekow, Y. T. Shih, Greg Yuschak, Jay Hewitt, Bob Johnson, Scott Cooper, Mike Berrigan, Sue Danisch, Vaughn Grannis, Joyce Palazzotto, Tom Bratley, and Ron Hagkull, a special guest from Division Engineering.

It is important to note that people do not speak the way they write. They repeat themselves, they leave things out, and they don't always speak in grammatically correct sentences. Sometimes these "mistakes" are meaningless and irrelevant to the conversation. Often, we don't even notice them. Frequently, these behaviors are meaningful and they provide the attentive listener with clues for interpretation. For the purposes of this transcription and the interpretation, I have faithfully recorded what the speakers actually *said,* using the following conventions:

****	where utterances have been deleted
//	overlapping talk or interruption
. . .	a pause of one second or less
(3.2)	a pause of more than one second, length indicated in seconds
[ ]	an explanatory insertion
.	a falling intonation marking end of assertion, even if it is not a grammatically complete sentence
?	a rising intonation marking question form
italics	emphasis

In this excerpt, Pete Rekow (a product engineer) presses the team to consider whether the market research that has been done is adequate. The team is slow to be persuaded. Dave Braun is resistant to Pete's view that more research should be done. The team's motivation to take the results at face value comes from a recognition that more tests would create delays, negatively affecting the team's projected schedule. Just prior to this excerpt, Joyce has been reporting on upcoming field tests, which Pete interrupts (turn 1) to express his negative opinion about the design of that marketing research. Though there is no European marketing representative on the team, Joyce is the primary liaison between the team and marketing, and in effect, Pete might be interpreted as challenging her judgment.

1 Pete: Um, I'm still real concerned about this spray guard thing. I mean, so much of what's new in the product relates to the construction environment, i.e., the spray guard and so on and . . . I understand the concern about getting into the auto trade, or whatever to not let too many people know about it, but . . . boy, one small . . . it's like, *that*'s our, that's our product. That's what we're reviewing, essentially is this spray guard. I guess if the powers that be are *com*fortable with that, who am I to say anything *but* it's not like we're just making a standard spray guard //

2 Dave: Well, certainly//

3 Pete: On this thing, it's a that's a different you know in every other respect, this product works as any respirator, not that there's that many. But I mean, *yes*, the materials are different but it's still a respirator like any other product. But the way you actually *use* it's //

4 Dave: Especially the spray guard.

5 Pete: // different, is different. // And I guess that //

6 Dave: How big is //

7 Pete: I don't know, it's just is a concern that we get into those, I know that they're thinking about that and aware of that but it seems me that to save * * * *

8 Dave: It increases//

9 Joyce: It's a concern I think that we all share but . . . and they haven't been able to//

10 Pete: Are all of these sites our sites?

11 Joyce: No no. About half //

12 Pete: So that //

13 Joyce: of them are, half aren't. As I understood it, the reluctance to go into the construction trades market, which is a really completely different distribution network, with a different sales force and so forth. They may, he, we were talking today and they may end up having to go to some different accounts but they wanted to get the feedback on these first before they did that. So I, I agree //

14 Pete: Well, I would just say that//

15 Joyce: if I were them

16 Pete: we should emphasize that //

17 Joyce: if I were them, I would want to get more construction feedback because that's what I'm shelling out my millions of //

18 Pete: Hey, it's fifty percent of the market. Period. The construction market, that's where the market is. I mean, people dropping chemicals, that's not . . . I mean, I think it gives us a lot of good feedback. I mean I'm *happy* to hear that they found it comfortable and so on. But then there's also the issue that we're testing a product with a heavier pressure drop against all of these other respirators, so there's also gonna be somewhat of a bias that way which isn't . . . I mean//

19 Jay: How big a study is that in Germany?

20 Joyce: They're all very small studies, on the order of a week. I mean we only sent 200 **** . . . they're probably using ten per account.

21 Jay: But you will be at the one in Germany?

22 Joyce: Yeah, I will be at the one in Germany.
   [Silence (3 seconds)]

23 Pete: I mean . . . do we feel good about it? If six people wear this in Germany, wear this respirator [slight laugh] product, is that enough? I don't know. I mean, how do *you* feel about it?

24 Dave: I feel like it increases the risk, I always have, but I think we have to . . . you know, it's their product and we have to trust them. There's an element of trust there. I mean, like you say they're happy with it, I guess we have to accept that, I mean we //

25 Pete: *I* don't know that we have to *accept* it. I mean if the, I think we have some input on where things are at, we have some influence if . . . *I* don't know. It's just a concern *I* have.

****

33 Dave: Hopefully that will be true, we wouldn't have to do any more work on it. But if we may have to be prepared for some feedback that says "okay, we gotta to make that a little better," we might find that feedback.

34 Joyce: I think that Pete's point is very well taken. I think we need to have further discussions with Keith again, expressing that we need more construction feedback. I think that we can get some too, we're talking about a month down the road. I don't know that that really changes anything about the decision points that we've got. It may change some fine-tuning of the spray guard or something like that but uh . . . I mean . . . your . . .

35 Pete: Yeah, just . . . 'cause, I don't know, 'cause.

36 Dave: All right, anybody else?

LINGUISTIC ANALYSIS OF THE EXCERPTS

As we have done in previous cases, we will use the team talk audit to guide our analysis of this excerpt from the Eurous team's talk, listening for the forms and functions critical to team work. The summary of this analysis is presented in table 6.2.

Identification

In his first turn, we can readily see that Pete identifies with the team; his use of "we" and "our" here and throughout the conversation invariably refers to the team. Dave and Joyce also reflect their identification with the team through their use of "we" (turns 9, 20, 24, 33). This pattern of speech is typical not only of Eurous team members, but of team members throughout this organization. The strength of this team's identification with one another is also indicated by the absence of other identifications. Pete never uses "we" to refer to his functional department or to any other group. Though both Dave and Joyce are also members of the management group, they never use "we" to identify

Table 6.2 Audit of the Eurous team.

Dimensions	Samples of Team Talk	Your Interpretation	Score
Identification	"that's our product" (1) "it's not like we're just making a standard" (1) "do we feel good about it?" (23) "we need to have further discussions with Keith" (34)	"We" and "our" refer only to team. Pete implies that the team can say how he feels. Joyce identifies so much with the team that she talks as if the whole group will talk with Keith, not just she.	Team
Interdependence	"we may have to be prepared . . . we gotta make that a little better" (33) "a concern . . . we all share" (9)	Each of the team members who participate in this conversation expresses a perception of common dependence and shared obligation.	High interdependence
Power Differentiation	Interruptions of Joyce and Dave plus dominance of the conversation by Pete	Power differences do not limit this team. Pete, who has a lower position in the organization than Dave or Joyce, interrupts them, and they allow it.	Low power differentiation
	"*I* don't know that we have to *accept* it." (25)	Explicit disagreement with higher-level manager.	
Social Distance	"*I* don't know that we have to" (25)	Affrontery of explicit disagreement is reduced by expressing an opinion in the negative form.	Social closeness
Conflict Management Techniques	"I'm still real concerned" (1)	Expression of need, disagreement.	Collaborative confrontation
	"How do *you* feel about it?" (23)	Exploring perspective of other.	
	"we may have to be prepared for some feedback" (33)	Exploring consequences of other's interest.	
Negotiation Process	"Are all of these sites our sites?" (10) "How big a study is that . . . ?" (19)	Use of objective criteria.	Win-Win
	"Pete's point is very well taken. I think we need . . . more construction feedback." (34)	Integration of perspectives.	

themselves with any group other than the team. In fact, the only use of "we" to refer to anyone other than the team is Joyce's "we" (turn 13) in a report about an actual event.

One other interesting linguistic construction shows the strength of Pete's identification with the team. In turn 23, Pete asks the other team members whether "we feel good" about the research plan. By using "we" here, Pete implies that the team is a single entity capable of telling him what he feels. If he had used "you" in this question, he would be separating himself from the other team members. His probably implicit linguistic choice binds the others to him as his dissenting view threatens to pull him away. Indeed, Pete's identification with the team and his perceived interdependence with other team members needs constant reinforcement as the conversation proceeds, because he continues to assert his independent judgment on this matter and speaks in powerful (but interdependent) terms to bring others to his way of thinking.

It is clear from these linguistic data that there is strong identification with the team among virtually all the team members. This assessment puts the Eurous team at the team endpoint on the identification dimension (see figure 6.3).

Interdependence

Pete, for all his assertions of independent *thought* here, never expresses an intent to take independent *action*. His use of the "I" always refers to thinking, such as, "I mean," "I understand," and "I guess" (all in turn 1). The sense one gets of Pete's independent thinking is tempered by his frequent explicit references to the team's interdependence: "our product" that "we're . . . making" (turn 1). Other team members also express a similar degree of perceived interdependence. Dave's four repetitions of "we" in turn 33 remind the team that the consequence of adopting Pete's views will be a burden or a boon that the whole team will share. Joyce also acknowledges the team's interdependence with her explicit reference in turn 9 to a "concern . . . we all share" and her repetitions of "we need" (turn 34). In addition, much of this team's interdependence is implicitly acknowledged in its treatment of power differences. The team clearly belongs at the interdependence endpoint of that dimension of team talk (see figure 6.3).

Figure 6.3 Assessment of the Eurous team's talk.

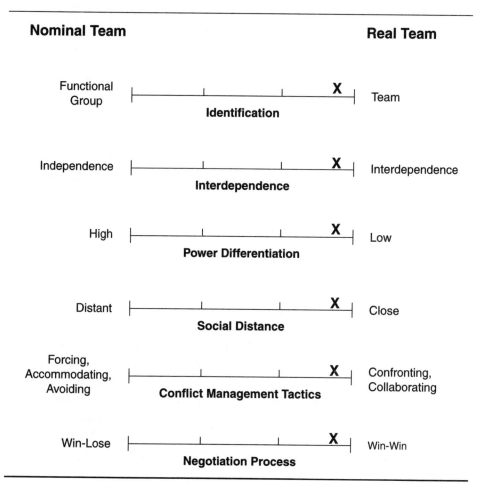

Power Differentiation

This team routinely minimizes the differences in organizational power among its members. Dave, as the team leader and one of the corporation's distinguished scientists, and Joyce, as a functional manager, have considerably greater organizational power than the other team members. However, listening in on the team, one is amazed by the equality of influence this team displays most of the time. This excerpt is typical in that, in a variety of linguistic forms, a team member speaks as if he has equal or greater power than the two more senior members.

Furthermore, we also observe here how both Dave and Joyce actively minimize the power differences by granting this power to Pete and by refraining from exercising the linguistic prerogatives that the power differential gives them. Pete repeatedly interrupts Joyce (turns 1, 10, and 18) and Dave (turns 3, 7, 25), and in most instances, he is given the floor. Pete and Jay question Joyce (turns 10, 19, and 21) and receive answers to each of their questions.

In turn 9, Joyce displays her own tolerant interpretation of Pete's behavior as well as her closeness to him by echoing his language, acknowledging and sharing his point of view ("a concern . . . we all share"). She allows him to interrupt her again (turns 9–10), and where she might have claimed some independence by refusing to answer his powerful questioning, she instead tacitly acknowledges their interdependence by giving him the information he demands (turns 10 and 11). However, she resists his bid to retake the floor (turn 12), continuing on in turn 13 to both explain the decision and agree with his point. She may also be identifying an opportunity to address Pete's concern ("they may end up having to go to some different accounts"), but she is interrupted by Pete.

In turn 23, Pete follows his question to the team with a direct question seeking Dave's feelings on the matter. Dave, like Joyce, answers the question. In so doing, he ratifies Pete's right as a team member to act in this way that subordinates organizational power differences to the interests of effective team interaction and work. Perhaps the most explicit evidence that power differences are minimized by this team is Pete's immediate disagreement with an opinion that Dave, the formal team leader, has just voiced (turns 24 and 25).

Indeed, Dave's triple repetition of "we have to" (turn 24) appears to assert a leadership decision, though his "I think" and "I guess" before two of these assertions mitigate the strength of that conviction. In light of these assertions and despite the signals of indecision, Pete's clear disagreement is surprising. It is uncommon for anyone,[5] much less someone of lesser status, to express disagreement immediately following the statement of an opinion. Pete does so here and is not interrupted, chastised, or challenged to explain his dissent. This may be due in part to the tentative clauses that he uses to surround his disagreement: "I don't know that" and "I don't know. It's just a concern. . . ." These constructions soften the force of the negation and thus minimize the threat to Dave's face. Nevertheless, Pete's and Dave's linguistic behavior indicate that organizational power differences do not need to be acknowledged in the confines of this team. This could be because such differences are dysfunctional for a team, or because these people feel close to each other socially and therefore it is inappropriate to call attention to the differences in their organizational positions.

Social Distance

In the Eurous team's interaction, one typically observes few of the linguistic forms that reflect social distance. This episode is something of an exception. Here, because Pete is taking such a strong, independent stand (especially relative to the more senior members of the team), he uses several linguistic forms for showing deference, which is usually a sign of social distance. In turn 1, he says "who am I to say anything," and in turns 7 and 25, he undercuts his opinion with the words, "I don't know."

The rationale for interpreting Pete's hedging behavior as an exception required by the content of this particular conversation is that, throughout the rest of the excerpt, we can hear many of the linguistic forms that reflect social closeness. Everyone is on a first-name basis; colloquialisms (like "Hey" in turn 18) are used; sounds get slurred and words are left out (turns 18, 33); common points of view are taken (turns 1, 9, 18, 33); and team members echo each others' language (Joyce in turn 9 "It's a concern . . . we all share" echoes Pete's words in turn 7: "it's just a concern"). Overall, one gets the sense that this is a socially close team that knows how to express and manage conflict effectively.

Conflict Management Tactics

The Eurous team members manage this conflict as they manage most, by confronting the disagreement collaboratively. As pointed out earlier, organizational power differences are not used to suppress or resolve the conflict. Rather, Pete is given the floor to express his dissenting views, and indeed he dominates this part of the conversation. His team members listen to him with very few interruptions and respond to his questions. Other team members ask questions to explore his perspective (Jay, turns 19 and 21). Pete and Dave both test likely consequences of the current plan (turn 23, 24, 33, 34). The overall tone of this conflict is nonthreatening. Though some of the discussion is descriptive and factual, Pete also tries emotional appeals (1, 23) to move his teammates. This, however, is not the emotional conflict that one sees when problems have been personalized.

Negotiation Process

The negotiation of this conflict is clearly governed by a win-win mentality. Those with organizational power do not use it defensively. (For example, Joyce might have used power to suppress Pete's views at the beginning, or Dave might have refused to answer Pete's questions and thus won the battle to leave the field testing to market research.) Joyce and Dave, and other members, might have taken the position that to reopen this issue would just put the team at risk of not meeting their self-set schedule. Instead, they explored Pete's concern, giving it time for consideration.

Pete uses win-win negotiation tactics when he probes the potentially objective criteria of how many test sites would be used (turn 10) and how many tests would be run (turn 23). In turn 23, he makes a very explicit bid for integrating perspectives on the issue. His linguistic choices in making this bid remind his colleagues of their interdependence, shared identity and proximity—"do we feel good about it?" (turn 23)—through the "we" and the question itself, which presumes such closeness that one member could answer for the collective.

Ultimately and explicitly in turn 34, Joyce integrates her knowledge of the field test process and of her relationships to the marketing group with Pete's thoughts on the product. In so doing, she identifies an action that accomplishes this integration. She also acts collaboratively by analyzing the consequences that requesting new information will have on marketing's schedule and on the team's progress toward its goals: "we can get some . . . a month down the road. I don't know that that really changes anything about the decision points that we've got." Though Joyce does not promise to act on Pete's suggestion, her words "we need to have further discussions with Keith again, expressing that we need more construction feedback" can be interpreted to mean that, in light of her liaison role. Dave's solicitation of other views (turn 36) and the absence of any additional dissenting behavior on his part suggest an acquiescence to this integrative outcome.

Summary

Throughout this excerpt of team interaction, we observed recurring patterns of team identification, interdependence, low power differentiation, close social distance, a confrontive-collaborative style of conflict resolution, and a win-win negotiation process. This assessment places the Eurous team at the far right of each key dimension of being a real team (see figure 6.3). These people acknowledge their differences and negotiate them collaboratively. Through their linguistic patterns, they are able to realize the value-creation potential of integrative negotiation. We might in fact say that this team approximates the ideal of team work. What accounts for this? As we have in earlier analyses, we turn now to the organizational context to answer this question.

TEAM INTERACTION AND ORGANIZATIONAL CONTEXT

Clearly, the team members' shared sense of interdependence and their common identification with the team are factors leading them to prefer social closeness to power differentiation as an influence strategy. Their team identification and perceived interdependence also explain the collaborative conflict management tactics and win-win negotiations. How are this perceived interdependence and team identification generated? An analysis of the descriptive detail on the organizational context and team design, summarized in table 6.3, provides answers.

Several aspects of the team design contributed to the identification with the team. The basis on which teams were assembled was individual skill, and the process was recruitment. This approach made team participation a matter of personal choice. Teams sought members on the basis of their personal knowledge and expertise, and members had the autonomy to choose which teams they would join, rather than being assigned to them by their functions. In joining a team, they were identifying with the team and voluntarily entering into, and committing personally to, an interdependent relationship.

The interdependence was enhanced through the process of setting team goals, schedules, and budgets. Unlike the other organizations studied, 3M did not have these targets handed down to the team by senior managers or to team members by their functional managers. Thus, the OH&ESD team members' vertical interdependencies tended not to interfere with the development of horizontal interdependency.

Table 6.3 Description of the Occupational Health and Environmental Safety Division's organizational context.

Occupational Health and Environmental Safety Division	
Feature	*Description*
Recent historical events	Sluggish growth
Corporate identity	We are innovators
Precursors to teams	Early attempt at business unit teams
Divisional strategic goals	Sales and innovation
Initiator of teams	Division manager
Expectations of teams	Speed, collaboration
Nature of team task	Open-ended, near-term
Duration of team structure	4 years
How teams were assembled	Skills-based recruitment, voluntary participation
Choice in assignments	Yes
Basis for team leadership	Commitment to product
Size of teams	15–20
Multiple team assignments	Yes
Degree of dedication to team (percentage of team fully dedicated)	20%–50%
Distribution of stakes	Informally variable
Mechanisms for assessing team performance	Informal quarterly lunch meeting, team-set goals and schedules
Hierarchical levels (from teams to top of divisions)	3–4
Role of functional managers	Changing to supplier
Liaison to managers	Senior manager sponsor
Training	Everyone

Rather, because they created their own targets together, the action teams created their own interdependencies. The informality of periodic reviews provided little or no managerial control over, or direction to, the teams. The absence of such a force signalled to teams that they were responsible for managing their own progress toward the goals they had set.

The changing role of the functional managers also contributed to the sense of interdependence and team identification. As they shifted from controlling the work of their professional employees to supplying resources to the teams, managers oriented to the teams rather than to the individual employees and relinquished some of the attention they had commanded from them. Thus the vertical interdependencies within the functions lessened and horizontal interdependencies could develop undeterred.

Finally, the training about team work conducted throughout the professional and organizational ranks served to orient managerial attention to teams. This diluted the attention given to functions and allowed for identification with the team. Furthermore, through training, the team members at OH&ESD not only developed the motivation to integrate their differences, they also developed their ability to manage their conflicts and negotiations. This type of training also made it easier and more reasonable for the competent team leaders, chosen for their product focus, to share power with the team members. It created effective team membership.

The forces affecting the Eurous team's dynamics are depicted in figure 6.4. Figure 6.5 depicts the links between design features, team process, and outcomes.

LESSONS FROM THE EUROUS TEAM

The case of the Occupational Health and Environmental Safety Division and the Eurous team provides two major lessons and numerous compelling insights about team work. First, it demonstrates that personal commitment to the team can be an extremely powerful factor in shaping team identification and the *perception* of interdependence, which in turn influence the talk and actions of the team. Second, it demonstrates that organizational accommodation to the requirements of real team work has power to create teams that achieve strategic goals. Specifically, this case shows that it is possible to create a context that fosters personal

Figure 6.4 Major forces shaping the Eurous team's dynamics.

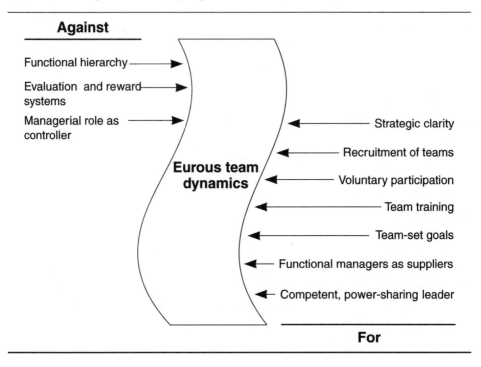

Figure 6.5 Team design features, team work, and outcomes.

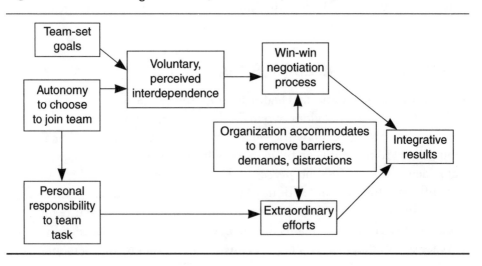

commitment and mutual interdependence among team members. Furthermore, it shows that this is possible *without* some of the features that theorists[6] identify as critical to effective teams but that managers find highly impractical to implement—for example, total dedication of a person's time to a given team, team accountability, and clear, consistent strategic direction.

The support for these claims comes from the comparison of the data from all four of the research sites. In OH&ESD, we finally encountered an organization in which the consensus view of teams was very positive. There we also encountered a team characterized by features of team identification, interdependence, low use of power, social closeness, collaborative conflict management, and win-win negotiation; thus it deserved to be considered a real team. The other teams we observed varied along the six key dimensions of team talk, but taken together, their interaction suggested that the three were closer to being nominal teams than real ones (see figure 6.6).

The organizational context at OH&ESD was also markedly different from the others studied. This qualitative correlation between the team interaction and features of the organization is enough to suggest that some relationship exists. But, as anthropologist Bateson[7] would ask, what are the differences that make a difference? Table 6.4 summarizes all the descriptive data on the four organizational contexts. Appendix A describes the research methodology.

The organizational variables that distinguish OH&ESD from the other organizations are highlighted in table 6.4. Two types of variation are depicted. Framing is used for features where there is significant variation between OH&ESD and the other three organizations, all of which were very similar on that dimension. Shading is used for features that OH&ESD shared to some extent with one or more of the other organizations.

The five contextual features that distinguished OH&ESD in significant ways from the other three organizations form a unique team design: skill-based recruitment of members, voluntary participation, team-set goals as mechanisms of team accountability, the supplier role for functional managers, and training in team work. As discussed earlier, the power of these features stems from their effect on team members' personal commitment to the team and its work. This commitment led individuals on the OH&ESD action teams to identify with the team and willingly take responsibility for creating and achieving the team

Figure 6.6 Assessment of four teams' talk.

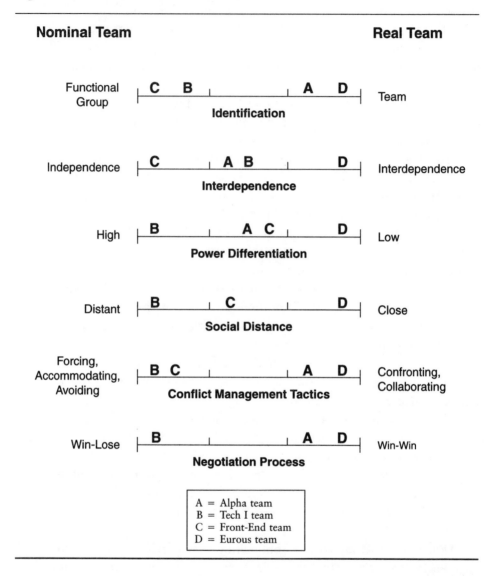

Nominal Team		Real Team

Identification
Functional Group → Team

Interdependence
Independence → Interdependence

Power Differentiation
High → Low

Social Distance
Distant → Close

Conflict Management Tactics
Forcing, Accommodating, Avoiding → Confronting, Collaborating

Negotiation Process
Win-Lose → Win-Win

A = Alpha team
B = Tech I team
C = Front-End team
D = Eurous team

goals that fit with the division's strategic goals, as summarized in figure 6.5.

If the first four features of the team system at OH&ESD (recruitment, voluntary participation, team-set goals, and a new role for functional managers) created a *willingess to do the difficult, personally demanding, and often conflictual task of integrating* one's expertise

Table 6.4 Descriptive comparisons of research sites.

Feature	Medical Products Division	Building Controls Division	Wayne Division	Occupational Health and Environmental Safety Division
Recent historical events	Downsizing	Loss, downsizing and restructuring	Market share drops; downsizing and restructuring	Sluggish growth
Corporate identity	We *were* family. Now?	This is an autocracy	We are the structure	We are innovators
Precursors to Teams	Early attempts at teams, human resource consulting	Business unit teams, simultaneous engineering	Early attempts at teams, simultaneous engineering	Early attempt at business unit teams
Divisional strategic goals	Cost and share	Cost and share	Cost and quality	Sales and innovation
Initiator of teams	consultants	Former division manager	Middle manager	Division manager
Expectations of teams	Efficiency, delegation coordination	Speed, efficiency, collaboration	Speed, efficiency, collaboration	Speed, collaboration
Nature of team task	Closed, near-term	Open-ended, near-term	Open-ended, long-term	Open-ended, near-term
Duration of team structure	6 months	3½ years	8 months	4 years
How teams were assembled	Position-based assignment	Skills-based assignment	Position-based assignment	Skill-based recruitment, voluntary participation
Choice in assignments	No	No	No	Yes
Basis for team leadership	Lead function	None	Lead function	Commitment to product
Size of teams	7	7	10	15
Multiple team assignments	Yes	Yes	Yes	Yes
Degree of dedication to team (percentage of team fully dedicated)	14%	14%	10%	20–50%
Distribution of stakes	Formally variable	Formally variable	Formally variable	Informally variable
Mechanisms for assessing team performance	Formal periodic report, functional reporting	Formal monthly review, functional reporting	Formal quarterly report, functional reporting	Informal quarterly lunch meeting, team-set goals and schedules
Hierarchical levels (from teams to top of divisions)	4	3–4	5	3–4
Role of functional managers	Unchanged	Unchanged	Unchanged	Changing to supplier
Liaison to managers	Senior manager coach	Program manager	Team leader to team hierarchy	Senior manager sponsor
Training	None	None	None	Everyone

with that of other professionals, then the training on cross-functional team work gave team members the *ability to manage those challenges*. The training at OH&ESD prepared team members for the tough realities they would face in shifting from individual performer to team member. It provided them with alternative explanations for the behavior they might observe in one another, as well as strategies for managing the realities and the pressures on each of them that could negatively affect team process and performance.

Perhaps the most distinctive lesson that OH&ESD offers is that organizations needing teams must be prepared to learn from teams what accommodations they require in order to be effective. Bob Hershock understood at the outset that organizations must be prepared to identify and remove all the barriers to effective team work, but several important accommodations became obvious only over time. One of the earliest accommodations that OH&ESD made to its teams' needs was to introduce team training for middle managers whose professionals served on the teams. Another was the adaptation in the functional managers' role vis-à-vis the team. When it became clear that the functional managers' efforts to control their human resources (that is, to do their job) were having a negative impact on team members' contributions, the managers were advised that their role was to supply the action teams with the human resources they needed. An additional and important accommodation that put force behind this rhetoric was a reduction in the pressure on functional managers to control costs, resulting in a substantial investment of resources in maintaining the organization's ongoing work while developing and supporting teams.

The Eurous team itself offers insight into one of the questions posed in chapter 3 about team leadership. It supports the theory that a team leader who is viewed as highly competent and who shares power can help foster a commitment to a team task. However, insofar as the team leadership here is buttressed by significant organizational support for team work, the case is inconclusive about the relative contributions of organizational features and leadership. It is also not clear whether these characteristics in a leader are necessary, or merely desirable, for fostering team commitment to interdependence. One interesting question that this case poses is whether such team leadership is effective because it inspires *responsible membership*—the contribution of whatever the team requires. The next chapter elaborates on the concept of responsible and effective team membership and provides advice on how to make effective interventions to reshape team dynamics.

Overall, the case of OH&ESD and the Eurous team illuminates an intricate relationship among individual motivations, organizational culture and design, team talk, and team work. Juxtaposed onto the questions and lessons from earlier chapters, this case develops our perspective on the many organizational pressures compounding the problems that individual paradoxes pose for teams. Chapter 8 makes these insights explicit, identifying the organizational contradictions that affect cross-functional teams, explaining how these pressures converge with and magnify the force of individual preferences on teams, and recommending managerial actions to create effective team dynamics.

PART III

Team Possibilities

The preceding chapters have documented the realities of team work in four organizations and have thrown into high relief the numerous challenges of working in and managing teams. They demonstrate how significant differences in the organizational contexts of cross-functional teams relate to differences in the linguistic patterns through which team work is accomplished. They show how the contexts in three of the four companies—despite the pervasive conviction that team work was critical to organizational performance—simply did not provide key conditions[1] required for team effectiveness.

This disparity between intention and action was largely unrecognized by the managers of these divisions. They didn't choose to deprive their teams of the requisite supports for effective performance. Nor was the lack of support a simple matter of financial constraint.

As discussed in chapter 1, the most succinct explanation for the organizational impediments to team work that I observed is that the team *form* of work is inherently paradoxical. That is, it entails a constant struggle with apparently opposing values.[2] The tensions posed by team work occur at three levels: within individuals, within teams, and within organizations. The sheer volume of paradox and contradiction can easily crush team work into a flatter, simpler, hardier form of existence. Indeed, most of the teams observed in this research had adapted themselves well to their environments. *They became the kinds of teams that their organizations allowed to exist.*

However, this need not happen. There are other possibilities. Although organizations play the most influential role in shaping team dynamics, the relationship between organizations and their teams is not necessarily deterministic or unidirectional. Just as organizational forces push teams, teams can push back on an organization if they recognize and use the power of language to create new social structures. Teams can create new possibilities for individuals, teams, and organizations.

Chapter 7 offers advice to teams about creating new possibilities. It presents a methodology for auditing team talk, a set of team profiles for diagnosing team problems, and linguistic strategies for intervening to reshape team dynamics. The chapter concludes with the sobering recognition that even if teams can re-create themselves, their potential will always be subject to organizational constraints.

Chapter 8 identifies these constraints, which teams experience as a set of contradictory pressures. Fortunately, contradictions, unlike paradoxes, can be eliminated or resolved. For, as we have seen, team work is inherently paradoxical for individuals and teams; thus tensions or contradictions in the organizational context that exacerbate the condition of struggling with oppositions must be minimized in order for teams to accomplish their goals. This chapter distills the lessons for managers that come from listening to teams as they grapple with these pressures. It describes the organizational possibilities for creating the environment teams need to thrive.

CHAPTER 7

The Power of Language

Advice to Teams

n the last chapter, responsible team membership was identified as
a factor shaping the collaborative and effective team dynamics
observed in the Eurous team. Responsible membership is defined
as the contribution of whatever the team requires. This concept, though
consistent with the team ideal of sacrificing individual interests to ensure
the meeting of team goals, runs contrary to two conventional ideas
about team work in organizations. The first is the theory that the
roles and responsibilities of team members must be clearly defined,[1]
presumably so that every task is covered, every team member knows
what is expected of him or her, and there is no wasted motion. Defining
responsible membership as the contribution of whatever the team
requires deliberately blurs the lines of responsibility to ensure that team
members do not get distracted from contributing to the team's goals
by focusing on their own part of the team task.

The second convention that this definition of responsible team members challenges is the unspoken rule that the leader has the right and
responsibility to monitor the team and intervene when appropriate.
The implied corollary of this rule is that team members do not have

such rights and responsibilities and should follow (or wait for) the leader's directions. Unfortunately, this corollary is enacted with great frequency. Despite feelings of frustration, boredom, and even complete disagreement, team members all too often sit quietly and defer to their leader. There are many troubling consequences of such deferential behavior: team members' time, energy, and talent are wasted,[2] they become disillusioned with team work and do not contribute fully, the total intelligence of the team may not be employed, and the leader may not even realize the latter.

The concept of responsible membership presumes that team members, like team leaders, have rights and responsibilities as a function of their membership in a team. They have a right not to have their time and talent wasted, a right to speak their mind, a right to be heard, and a right to lobby to have their perspective considered in the team deliberations. A team member also has the responsibility to contribute what he or she believes the team needs to achieve its common goal, regardless of the specific role or responsibilities assigned and regardless of his or her own position relative to others in the group.

Responsible team members monitor their team's dynamics and *speak up* when they feel that the team is not on course to achieve team goals. In the remainder of this chapter, we will explore what "speaking up" literally entails. Advice is offered for teams on how to use the power of language to shape and change team dynamics. However, before considering team talk as a tool for change, it is important to recognize the limits of its effectiveness.

Many people assume that the characteristics of team members—their motives, personalities, or abilities—are the primary influence on team dynamics. This is not the case. Organizational forces, as we observed in each of the four preceding chapters, are the most potent shaper of team dynamics. Factors like a functional culture, performance systems that emphasize individual performance, the functional manager's role, and the way teams are assembled had a profound effect on the teams we observed. We have seen how these forces place limits on what teams can be and do. However, we have also seen that the internal dynamics of teams are shaped by team members' actions, specifically, by the way teams talk to each other. Precisely for this reason, talk can be used as a tool to reshape team dynamics, and even to mobilize a team to push organizations for the support they require.

TEAM TALK: TOOL FOR CHANGE

In previous chapters, we have seen how language can be used as an analytical tool for assessing team dynamics in terms of critical features of team work. Now we will look at how to collect and interpret data from your own team. Next we will look at how to use talk to intervene and shape team dynamics.

Using the Team Talk Audit

The process of analyzing your team's talk requires that you employ two kinds of knowledge: your expertise as a fluent speaker of the language and member of your team, and the knowledge about language that you have learned here. In the process, you are becoming a lay sociolinguist: collecting data, observing linguistic forms and social functions, and making interpretations about what these data mean.

You will want to start by reviewing table 2.1 and table 2.2 to familiarize yourself with the kinds of language that reflect and create meanings of different types. Next, prepare yourself for making the audit by first observing your team talking. Use the questions in the audit to guide your observation. When you feel comfortable with what to listen for, you are almost ready to collect the linguistic data. However, before you collect data, you will need to explain to your teammates what you are doing. This is especially important if you are planning to tape meetings, in which case you will want to ask their permission to tape. Even if you plan simply to take verbatim notes during team meetings, you will want to prevent anyone from feeling under surveillance by explaining what you are doing and why. Be sure to use the language of real teams to express yourself! For example, you might express your own needs and concerns, relate them to the team's needs, and signal identification with the team and your sense of interdependence by saying:

> I have been feeling concern that our team dynamics are preventing us from achieving our team goals. I recently read a book about teams and language that might help us improve, and would like to see whether its approach would be useful to us. This step involves auditing our team talk. Would it be okay with all of you if I tape-record some of our meetings? I will be happy to let you know what I discover.

Ideally, you should record the team's talk on audiotape. Taped conversation provides a far superior record of what happened than memory or field notes, allows others to make their own observations and analyses of the same data, and allows you to review your observations and analyses. You will undoubtedly see some effect of recording on the team's behavior, at least initially. Generally, after thirty to sixty minutes of being taped and shortly after you have changed or turned a tape, people will resume focus on the work at hand and behave without self-consciousness.

If you feel that it would be too disruptive to the team dynamics to tape team meetings, or even to ask permission to do so, you can collect decent data by taking extensive notes during parts of multiple meetings. Collecting these data may be noticed and may cause some ill will among team members, so be sure to consider what your trade-offs are. However, in terms of data, what you lose in fullness of the record, you may partially offset through multiple samples of data. You might consider focusing on one dimension at a time, such as with what group team members identify themselves.

Episodes of conflict and conversations in which decisions are being made offer the most productive data for analysis. As you are recording your data, you will want to note where these occur in the conversation. After you have identified rich samples of data, you can use the team talk audit form (table 7.1) to describe that interaction.

Some caveats are in order before you begin to interpret the data collected. First, there is the question of stylistic versus meaningful differences; second is the question of how to summarize the data across team members to create a single team score; and third is the question of ambiguity.

Interpretation is complicated by the fact that people develop distinctive conversational styles,[3] largely from the cultures—national and corporate—in which they live. However, people tend not to recognize stylistic differences but rather use their own style to interpret others' actions and intentions. Consider, for example, two new team members, a marketer from New York and an engineer from Indianapolis, visiting a New Jersey customer together for the first time. The marketer is aghast when the engineer takes a full minute pause before answering the customer's questions and then launches into a very lengthy, highly technical response. She attributes this behavior to insecurity, narrow perspective, and possibly even incompetence. The engineer, for his part,

Table 7.1 Team talk audit form.

Dimensions	Samples of Team Talk	Your Interpretation	Score
Identification			
Interdependence			
Power Differentiation			
Social Distance			
Conflict Management Tactics			
Negotiation Process			

is appalled by the marketer's superficial understanding of the product, irritated by her frequent interruptions, and puzzled by the amount of time she has devoted to small talk. He feels she has wasted time that could have been spent persuading the customer of the product's technical superiority. He decides she is just another lightweight who knows nothing about the product or the customer and is merely marking time until she can get promoted. Ironically, the customer leaves this conversation with the greatest satisfaction. In the marketer, he feels he has someone he can really communicate with, someone who understands his business needs and who responds quickly. In the engineer, he sees a thoughtful technical expert. The team members leave with feelings of mutual suspicion and dislike, traceable largely to differences in style rather than substance. Overcoming these negative feelings in order to achieve a challenging goal for developing a new product will not be easy, but talking about those observations and interpretations is the key.

It is clear that small, seemingly insignificant behaviors can have big consequences. The engineer formed his negative impressions about the marketer on the basis of her repeated interruptions; the marketer's negative impressions of the engineer were based on his long pauses before answering questions. Chances are, neither person is aware of those behaviors, and if each listened to a tape of himself or herself, each would probably have a different and reasonable explanation for the behavior, if asked. The marketer might say she was just trying to focus the conversation more on the customer's needs; the engineer might say he was trying to think of everyday language to explain a technical situation. Unfortunately, most of us never examine our conversations or explore the effects they have, and such first impressions go on to shape subsequent actions and conversations. These team members are likely to treat each other as if their first impressions were accurate until and unless other data prove them wrong.

As you describe and interpret the linguistic behavior of your teammates, try to flag for subsequent analysis data that you think may reflect stylistic rather than substantive variations on the dimensions of team talk. For example, your colleagues from New York City may interrupt others more frequently than those from the Midwest, but their intentions may not be to grab the floor; they may merely wish to show solidarity, a regional style difference noted by researchers.[4]

Resolving the interpretation may occur through an examination of other linguistic forms of the same type (such as power differentiation) or may require checking your interpretation with the speaker and others.

The next question you will face is how to summarize the data across team members. First of all, it is important to observe the behavior of every team member on each dimension. You will need to note whether some team members consistently use a particular type of language. For example, to assess the degree of power differentiation in the team, you will need to determine whether it is always the same people who surrender the floor and answer the questions. Such linguistic differences may be revealing. However, after noting recurring patterns, it is possible to make a rough summary of team members' language along each dimension. Because language is so versatile and ambiguous, it is not possible or useful to make fine distinctions. Rather, it is enough, for the purposes of diagnosis and intervention, to assess your team as being at one of three points on each dimension.

The ambiguity of language creates significant problems in everyday life, not to mention in the diagnosis of team dynamics. One way of dealing with ambiguous behavior is to note the possible interpretations and look for other data that support or rule these out. For example, you might be uncertain about whether a question is intended to elicit new information, discredit a colleague by showing that he or she lacks information, or to reopen a subject for discussion. To resolve this uncertainty, you could observe the questioner's subsequent behavior to determine what he or she does with the response to the question. Another effective way of resolving ambiguity is to ask what the speaker means, either during the conversation or after. There is no reason to keep your analysis to yourself. In fact, several of the intervention strategies described below begin with all the members of the team analyzing their team talk and discussing their interpretations.

As you assign scores to your team's talk, keep in mind that these only are rough assessments and starting points for further interpretation of the team's talk. You can't make a mistake, although you might be perceiving only part of the linguistic behavior of a team member or be misinterpreting that behavior. Misunderstandings like these can be cleared up in conversations guided by the audit, which will be described later. Once you have assessed your team along each of the key dimensions, you are ready to profile your team.

TEAM PROFILES

The assessments of a team along the key dimensions of team talk permit an observer to diagnose the problems that are constraining the team work. Such diagnoses allow you to profile a team and plan appropriate interventions to change team dynamics. One way of profiling a team was explained in chapter 2: a team can be real or nominal. Another way of categorizing teams on the basis of these dimensions is described here.

For the purpose of diagnosis, the six dimensions of team talk are hierarchical. This means that two of the dimensions tell most of the story about the degree of "teamness" that a group of people exhibit. The other four dimensions help refine the diagnosis and lead to alternative avenues for constructive intervention. Figure 7.1 is a simplified depiction of this hierarchy. It shows only the more common combinations of the team dimensions.

Team scores on the dimensions of identification and interdependence are the most revealing of attitudes and predictive of other critical team behaviors. In combination, they indicate the degree of commitment that team members feel toward one another and their task, and they usually predict how a team will treat power differences, social distance, conflict, and negotiation.

A team's score on identification shows how much team members perceive themselves to be one with others on the team. A strong sense of oneness with the team makes it likely that team members will feel some degree of interdependence, regardless of organizational forces[5] working against it. A common pattern for teams with strong team identification is a high score for interdependence, even if performance assessments still formally reside with the functional management. At 3M, for example, where team members voluntarily joined teams and where teams created their own goals, these organizational factors shaped high team identification, which created voluntary interdependence. The Eurous team fit this assessment and represents the profile we'll call the *collaborative team*.

A pattern of team identification but independence is less likely. If found, it would probably indicate that the organization is divided into teams rather than functions. Thus, team members identify with the team as their formal organizational group. The absence of interdependence suggests that the organization has not created mechanisms for making

Figure 7.1 A hierarchy of team talk dimensions.

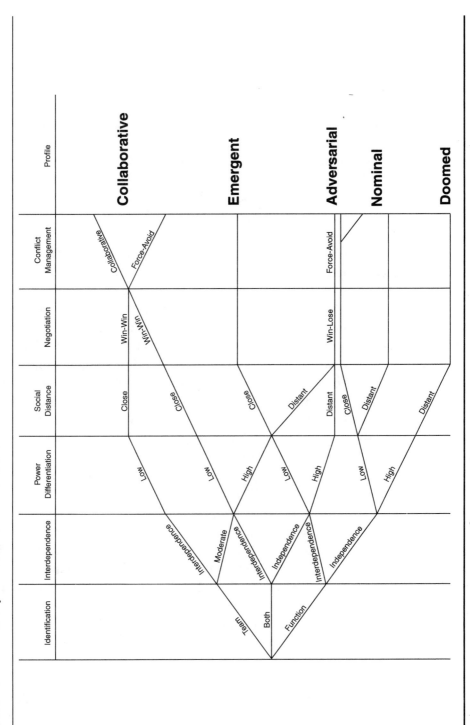

team members feel mutually accountable for their team's performance. Such teams may not be required to set specific goals; team performance is probably not measured, while individual performance is probably well monitored, measured, and rewarded.

A team with strong team identification but only moderate interdependence is a team in a precarious state. It could become a real team or revert to being just a group of individuals. Such teams probably experience ambivalence about the team assignment: organizational systems probably push toward functional identifications and create strong functional interdependencies, yet there is an attraction (whether due to organizational enticements or task appeal) toward working as a team. Organizational response to team initiatives will probably be a critical determinant of subsequent teamness. The Alpha team at the Medical Products Division fits this profile of an *emergent team.*

Teams that identify both with the team and with their functional groups are common in organizations that are assigning critical tasks to teams. This score would be expected in a matrix structure. However, unless the team members perceive themselves to be interdependent and act as if they were (i.e., by minimizing power differentiation and social distance, and managing conflict collaboratively), such teams are unlikely to accomplish those tasks effectively. Teams that feel interdependent but exhibit high power differentiation are vulnerable when conflicts emerge. The predictable tendency will be to use the power-related conflict management tactics of forcing, accommodating, and avoiding, and to negotiate in ways that ensures winning even if the other team members lose. This is the pattern of team talk we observed in the Tech I team, which is the profile of an *adversarial team.*

Social closeness may motivate members of teams with minimal team identification and little to moderate interdependence to resist the tendency to use power differences. This social alignment offers the potential for the team members to identify with one another and voluntarily assume interdependence, making it another type of emergent team. However, organizational forces and individual ability to manage conflict will determine how difficult a development this may be. The sections below discuss how a team member might proceed to draw on this potential.

Teams with minimal team identification or perceived interdependence whose talk is not characterized by high use of power differences are *nominal teams,* regardless of their degree of social closeness. In such teams, one often does not observe much conflict management or negotiation process, because the lack of shared identity or perceived interdependence means they don't have to engage in or resolve conflictual discussions. The Front-End team of Wayne Division is a team with this type of profile.

The combination of functional identification, independence, high power differentiation, and distant social relations is also possible, though this research did not involve any. Such dynamics are typically deadly, producing *doomed teams*. Intervention at the team level is highly unlikely to produce any change in team dynamics, except perhaps to cause the team to stop meeting.

THE INTERVENTION HIERARCHY

The hierarchy of talk dimensions described above relates to diagnosis. That is, if you want to know whether you are in a real, emergent, or nominal team, the team's position on the dimensions of identification and interdependence offer you the greatest insight on the team. The team's profile also indicates the appropriate order for organizational intervention to enhance team dynamics. Changes in organizational features like structure, reporting relationships, performance appraisal, and rewards will have a significant impact on interdependence and identification. Power differentiation and social distance are the social relationships that these organizational factors tend to produce, so changing interdependence and identification should create changes in the power distribution and dynamics. Over time, changes in these dimensions are likely to create new social relationships, thus creating the potential for altered social closeness.

When it comes to intervention by a team member, the hierarchical order of these dimensions changes. Starting with conflict management tactics and negotiation makes sense for two reasons: first, because they are controllable by the individual, and second, because they have the potential to affect the behavior of others. Negotiation research shows that individual behavior can have a significant impact on the conflict behaviors of others in a negotiation;[6] that is, cooperative behavior produces cooperative behavior and competitive produces competitive behavior. Furthermore, the way a person negotiates can alter power differences, even when the person seeking to reduce these has the least power.[7] Negotiation behavior can also produce a keener sense of interdependence.[8] This reduction of power differentiation and an increased perception of interdependence can also produce stronger identification with the team, which will reinforce the use of more teamlike behaviors.

In other words, team members can use their own negotiation language to stimulate a reconstruction of the team's perceptions of power, interdependence, and identification. If a team can and will construct a shared understanding of the relative costs and benefits (for individuals, teams, and organizations) of their current degree of "teamness," they have a basis for negotiating with one another about becoming more teamlike. In the process of negotiating, they may become a real team (even if for a limited team purpose) and in that capacity, they may decide to act jointly to influence organizational factors that work against their teamness.

For example, Lisa in the Tech I case might have stopped using tactics of forcing and power differentiation; started expressing her own needs, feelings, and interests; started to elicit and articulate the interests of the engineers (and the organization); and tried to find objective criteria for resolving conflicts and to invent new options. This significant change in her behavior, especially over time and with repetition, might have persuaded other team members to participate in a joint diagnosis of the team's problems, which could have formed the basis for a team presentation to upper management in which they identified organizational factors that impeded their progress and requested the resources required for effective team performance. The resources might have included more engineering assistance. Such an initiative coming from a team is likely to be more effective than coming from an individual. It also keeps everyone honest by eliminating the opportunity and temptation, when behind closed doors, to point the finger at individual team members.

If team members can talk their teammates into greater team identification and interdependence, they can in effect talk them into team work, at least temporarily. Recall the precarious position of the Alpha team, whose members were excited by their accomplishments as a team and eager to continue, but doubtful that they could sustain these feelings without changes in the organization and in management practices. The Front-End team too was teetering—not quite a team but also not quite certain about whether it could or should try to achieve that summit, because the organizational signals were so ambiguous. Because team dynamics are so vulnerable to organizational forces and team talk, we look now at the linguistic strategies and intervention tactics that teams can use both to alter their team dynamics and to push back on the organization to change features that limit their potential.

TALKING TEAMS INTO TEAM WORK

The following advice to teams about using language to change team dynamics as well as the organizational context in which the teams exist is organized by team profile. For each of these interventions, be sure to talk in the linguistic forms that reflect being part of a real team. The conflict management tactics and negotiation behaviors will be probably be among the first you'll need to employ, because the very act of intervening will probably create conflict. Be sure to review the linguistic audit to remind yourself of the most salient forms of team talk, and to prepare and rehearse a speech explaining team talk and the team talk audit like the example given above.

Collaborative Teams

Collaborative teams like the Eurous team are characterized by identification with the team, a shared perception of interdependence, low power differentiation, social closeness, collaborative conflict management tactics, and a win-win negotiation process. Such teams need not be talked into team work; rather, they require constant vigilance to avoid complacency that could lead to groupthink,[9] in which conflict is avoided in the interest of preserving goodwill. Collaborative teams may also go through periods in which high stress leads team members or leaders to manage conflicts through less collaborative tactics. When an audit of team dynamics finds that a team is talking this way, an appropriate intervention would be to:

1. Ask the team to do a team talk audit of its conflict management behaviors.
2. Ask the team to diagnose causes and consequences of this behavior.
3. Ask the team to devise a plan for altering the causes and reevaluating its conflict behavior at a later date.

The politically savvy team member will probably be wondering why the first step in this intervention, and the others, is not "talk to your team leader about team talk and suggest that he or she use the team talk audit." Indeed, managing power differences is critical to influencing team dynamics. However, because teams need all members to feel both free to and responsible for contributing whatever they can to achieve team goals, an approach to reshaping team dynamics must not emphasize power differences. Therefore, a team member who is interested in intervening in team dynamics needs to bring matters to the team, not the team leader. Although this may be somewhat risky, other actions can be taken to prevent the team leader from feeling that this action implies criticism of him or her. For example, you could give the leader prior notice of your intention to bring up this issue. However, this must be done in language that is respectful and reassuring without signalling a willingness to defer. If you appear to be asking permission, you may be given a negative response and then be forced to make a difficult decision. *Requesting* time on the agenda to share your "personal observations" about how the team is working together may be an effective linguistic strategy. Whether you give prior notice or not, another useful action is to talk with the leader after the discussion and reassure him or her that your comments were not directed at the leader but at the members.

Emergent Teams

Emergent teams are characterized by identification with the team and a moderate degree of interdependence, low to moderate power differences, moderate social distance, some use of collaborative tactics for managing conflicts, and win-win negotiating. The Alpha team at Medical Products was the example of such a team. Here's an intervention plan for changing these dynamics and reshaping an emergent team into a real one:

1. Ask the team to do a team talk audit. (Be prepared to present yours if asked.)
2. Explore the reasons for the assessments. (Be prepared to reinterpret team members' data with them.)
3. Ask the team to discuss the costs and benefits to the organization of the group reverting to nominal team status rather than pushing on to real team status.
4. Ask the team to discuss the long- and short-term costs and benefits to the individual team members of reverting to a nominal team or progressing to a real team.

5. Ask the team members to decide whether they are committed to becoming a real team.

6. If they are committed, decide what organizational support would be necessary to sustain the team and how to request it. If team members are not committed, decide how to manage nominal team status so that it is not detrimental to team members or the organization. For example, team members might decide they want to advise upper management that the team's charge cannot be met and recommend disbanding or making a change in the charge. Team members might decide to reallocate work assignments on the team so that individual interests—in minimizing team meeting time or gaining external visibility or meeting certain team goals— are achieved.

Adversarial Teams

Adversarial teams may vary in the combination of identification and interdependence, but they are distinctive in their high use of power differences, social distance, conflict management tactics that are not collaborative, and win-lose negotiation process. The Tech I team was this type of team. Here is a linguistic strategy that could reshape the team dynamics of an adversarial team:

1. Explain the concept of team talk and the team talk audit.

2. Ask the team to conduct a team talk audit. (Be prepared to present yours if asked.)

3. Discuss shared perceptions and the reasons for them. Be sure that the team considers organizational systems and pressures that have contributed to these feelings and behavior.

4. Ask the team to discuss the potential costs to the organization and themselves individually of not achieving team goals.

5. If these costs are high, ask the team to generate and evaluate scenarios for achieving the team's goals, including the resources and support required for each.

6. Ask the team to develop a plan for (a) advising management of project status and organizational reasons for this status,

(b) requesting needed resources, and (c) implementing the preferred scenario. (This will work best if there is team consensus and action by the team, rather than a representative member or subgroup.)

It is likely that the members of an adversarial team feel mistrustful of one another and will tend to view such initiatives with the suspicion that this is just another competitive tactic. To overcome this suspicion, it is important to employ the conflict management tactics and negotiation process behaviors of a real team, avoiding any use of power differences, and constantly signalling team identification and perceptions of high interdependence. It will also be useful to establish a win-win mind-set, to persuade the team to do joint analysis of the situation, with particular attention to the external forces bearing on team members. If relationships among some or all team members are particularly acrimonious, it is probably useful to have the most widely liked and respected team member propose and possibly lead this discussion. An outside facilitator may also be useful in getting the team unstuck,[10] although the sooner the team develops the capacity to manage its own process, the better.

It is also likely that members of such teams will feel pessimistic about the possibilities of (1) doing joint problem solving constructively and (2) acting effectively as a team to influence the organization. They will probably also feel that the costs of trying to get the team on track outweigh the individual benefits of either inaction or trying to deflect blame, at least in the short term. Therefore, it is important to focus first on the organizational causes of dysfunctional team dynamics; this will reduce some of the individual defensiveness. Following this with discussion of the organizational costs of failing to meet the team's goals gives the team a common viewpoint and possibly a common goal, which can create identification with the team.

Nominal Teams

Nominal teams are groups of people who are teams in name only. They are characterized by team talk reflecting functional identification, independence, low to moderate power differentiation, moderate social distance, and little evidence of conflict or negotiation. The Front-End team at Wayne Division was a team with this profile. Here is an intervention for such a team:

1. Ask the team to do a team talk audit. Be prepared to present yours.)

2. Discuss shared perceptions and the reasons for them. Be sure that the team considers organizational systems and pressures that have contributed to these feelings and behavior.

3. Request that team members explore together potential consequences (for the team, the organization, and individuals) of not achieving the assigned team goals. Often nominal teams are the result of the team goals being viewed by team members as either unimportant or less important than other more urgent goals or demands on their time.

4. Depending on the team's assessment of the team goals, ask the team to decide what to do. Unimportant team goals should lead the team to question senior management about the merits of consuming time and talent in team projects; important but less urgent team goals should lead to steps 5 and 6.

5. Propose that the team generate and evaluate scenarios for achieving the team's goals, including the resources and support required for each.

6. Suggest that the team develop a plan for (a) advising management of project status and organizational reasons for this status, (b) requesting needed resources, and (c) implementing the preferred scenario. (This will work best if there is team consensus and action by the team, rather than a representative member or subgroup.)

Doomed Teams

The worst profile of a nominal team is one characterized by functional identification, independence, high power differentiation, and social distance. Such teams are, in all likelihood, doomed to fail. In a situation where people feel no social closeness, no identification with one another, and no need to work together, the use of power differences to try to compel team work almost ensures that team members will defer to the more powerful. The result is typically little more than a set of meetings and decisions made not by a team but by the most powerful members of the team. The chances of a team member changing the dynamics of a doomed team are small. However, if the team goals are significant to the organization and the team member has courage, charisma, stamina, and linguistic skill, an intervention may be worth trying.

If you are among the more powerful team members, your most significant challenge will be to stop using your power and to control your own contributions to make space for the less powerful team members to step up to their responsibilities and claim their rights. If you have less power than other team members, your challenge will be to ignore that power and speak up. Once you have resolved the issue of power in your own mind and planned how you will talk in the future, the steps in the intervention are the same as the ones for a nominal team.

CONCLUSION

Many of the problems that teams face as they try to work together can be managed if the teams use the strategies described above for changing team dynamics and for exerting a positive force on the organization. These interventions are not easy, but in most cases they will be effective at least for a while. However, even if teams manage to alter their own dynamics through their talk and push themselves up a developmental trajectory, they are still boxed in by their organizations (figure 7.2). An organization's culture, reporting structures, performance evaluation and reward systems, and managerial roles will always shape its teams' performance. However much a team's dynamics may change, they will still bump into those features of the organization. This chapter has attempted to offer the kind of advice that will allow teams to shape their own dynamics so that they become a real team, capable of pushing through those constraints and acting as a positive force on the organization to raise the ceiling and open the space so that the team can deliver maximum benefit. If a team will take this challenge to reshape its own dynamics and push the organization to create conditions for high performance, its chances for success are better, because it's much harder for an organization to ignore or deny the demands of a team than the demands of individuals.

However, obtaining high-performance teams by changing teams and organizations from the inside out is hardly the most efficient and

Figure 7.2 Teams and organizational constraints.

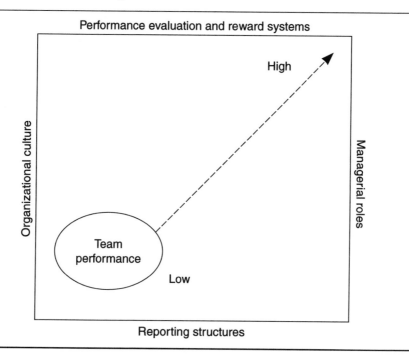

effective approach. Fortunately, there is much that organizations can and should do to change themselves so that they will enhance the possibilities of creating teams that will meet strategic goals. The concluding chapter explains the lesson for managers that come from listening to teams.

CHAPTER 8

Listening to Teams

Advice to Managers

Thisbook has argued that teams rarely measure up to our expectations and ideals for the very same reason that organizations fail
to provide teams with the requisite conditions for effective performance. Both phenomena derive from the struggle with the oppositions
that team work creates. This paradoxical nature makes team work
difficult to *do* precisely because it is so difficult to *comprehend*.

This chapter tries to untangle the perplexing knot of team work,
exposing the intricate interconnections among individuals, teams, and
organizations that have shaped the common experience. It explains
how team work's paradoxical requirements for both differentiation
and integration are severely threatened by both individual interests and
the bureaucratic assumptions embedded in organizational culture and
design. Both sets of pressures derive from deeply held cultural values,
making significant change in teams a challenging endeavor. Nevertheless, this chapter explains how changes in organizational design can
be introduced to help offset—and ultimately change—the individual
preferences that work against balance in teams. Specific strategies for
achieving that goal, based on the lessons from listening to teams, are
presented.

CONTRADICTIONS IN THE ORGANIZATIONAL CONTEXT OF TEAMS

Organizations have frequently been found to send contradictory messages to their members through numerous channels. However, the momentous changes in the competitive, economic, and technological environments of U.S. business over the past two decades have amplified this tendency dramatically. Initiatives to increase worker commitment through increased autonomy have clashed with efforts to standardize work methods in the interest of achieving process control.[1] Changes designed to streamline communication have produced information overload. In the case of cross-functional teams doing product development work, the attempts to achieve significant benefits have run into the wall of bureaucratic control. Yet, the need for both team work and control are so considerable that organizations and managers fail to recognize that these needs have produced numerous contradictions and, more importantly, numerous team casualties.

In the cases presented earlier in the book, several major contradictions in organizational strategy, structure, and systems were identified. They include contradictions regarding strategic goals, functional managers' roles, performance evaluation and reward systems, managers' orientation to control, and the focus of change.

Conflicting Strategic Goals

In three of the four companies in this research study, the divisional strategic goals were contradictory in that they created conflicting implications for action by teams. Teams were asked to make significant—and simultaneous—achievements on dimensions that are typically in tension with one another. For example, cost cutting was one of two primary goals at Wayne, Building Controls, and Medical Products. Another strategic goal was maintaining their market dominance through quality. A third divisional goal for teams, treated by managers as equal in importance, was the acceleration of the product development cycle.

This dilemma is not unique to teams; the old managerial saw, "I don't want it good, I want it Tuesday!" reminds us how common this contradiction is. The contradiction here was that a team cannot achieve all three goals simultaneously. Achieving and maintaining quality in such contexts is virtually impossible without some increase in costs, at least in the short term; and accelerating the development cycle can have consequences for quality and costs.[2] The consequences of these contradictory implications for teams was uncertainty and conflict about which goal should be used to resolve differences of opinion, to drive decisions, and to determine action. Team members, required to find solutions that maximized two or three criteria simultaneously, felt themselves to be in a double bind:

> I can take costs out of the product, but that will negatively affect its quality. I can do lots of things to improve quality, but they all add costs. What am I supposed to do?

Contradictory Expectations of Teams. The contradictory implications of strategic goals can create contradictory expectations of teams. In each of the four organizations I observed, there were multiple expectations of the product development teams, including various combinations of the following: fostering cross-functional collaboration, accelerating the development cycle, improving product quality, creating a more committed work force, getting more work from fewer people, and generating more risk taking.

The problem is that some of these expectations are mutually exclusive. For example, the double bind created by divisional goals of cost reduction and share retention through quality tightened when teams were expected to accelerate the product development cycle. Most of the team members interviewed recognized that earlier and better cross-functional collaboration could both create higher-quality solutions and accelerate the development cycle by preventing mistakes that were costly and time-consuming to fix. However, they also recognized more explicitly than their managers that the prior antagonisms had left walls that would need to be dismantled before a new collaborative structure of interaction could take their place and deliver the desired outcomes.

At Building Controls, teams were introduced as a means to accelerate the development process and foster cross-functional collaboration in the context of a corporate effort to cut costs without sacrificing share. These goals were translated into ambitious benchmarks and deadlines that, when missed, caused team members to fall into familiar patterns of interdisciplinary suspicion, antagonism, and finger pointing. Furthermore, earlier cost-cutting measures resulting in layoffs among professionals had deleterious effects on the commitment people felt toward the organization. This produced cynicism in many people and a self-defensive loyalty to the one who made firing and reward decisions—usually the functional manager—an attitude that inhibited the identification of professionals with the team.

This dilemma was further complicated by the fact that teams here served a compensatory or corrective function. Teams were introduced to offset the corporate cost cutting in the belief that team work motivates greater effort, enabling the organization to get more work done by fewer people. The division manager also felt that the peer pressure created by teams would force change on the bureaucratic engineering group that he could not accomplish.

The same phenomenon of introducing teams to compensate for other problems was observed in two of the other research sites as well: at Wayne to rebuild cross-functional relationships and at Medical Products to improve morale and improve the efficiency of the professional work force. Although teams were also created at these two organizations for the constructive purpose of developing better products faster, the contradictions among these expectations created organizational contexts that did not adequately support team work.

This is not to say that teams are incapable of managing the complexity of multiple goals. Indeed, the efforts I observed to achieve progress on multiple dimensions were most impressive. The problem was that, when teams were not advised as to the *priority among these strategic goals,* they were unable to accomplish the integration of their perspectives and the resolution of their conflicts, both of which were possible and desirable activities for a team. Without an objective criterion against which they could arbitrate their differences, they were forced either to struggle with an impossible task or to push the integration decision upward.

The contradiction between cost and quality also contributed to inadequate resources and ambivalent support from senior managers who wanted to develop the collaborative capacity and flexible organization that teams provided but were concerned about meeting short-term earnings targets.

Inadequate Resources. The contradictions described above were not widely recognized among the teams and managers I interviewed. The recognition of a third contradiction had an interesting distribution: team members discussed it frequently and vociferously, while managers rarely mentioned it. I refer here to the contradiction of assigning a task without providing the level of resources required to accomplish it.

At Wayne, Building Controls, and Medical Products, there was a widespread perception on the part of team members that although team work required more time and entailed higher expectations, they had too few resources to do the additional work. The scarcest resource was professionals' time. In all four of the organizations I studied, there was a feeling that some of the team members were stretched too thin, with assignments to multiple teams or too heavy a burden of functional responsibilities.

This perception of inadequate support was based largely on the uneven distribution of resources across the functions. While the lead functions of each company usually had sufficient staff to dedicate professionals to a single product or team, the supporting functions typically had too few professionals to make such unique assignments. Professionals from those functions had to distribute their contributions across several teams, thus preventing them from identifying personally with, or feeling personal responsibility toward, any one team. They had less at stake than dedicated members and were therefore less inclined to challenge functional priorities or hierarchical demands that might inhibit team performance.

Most managers I interviewed seemed to treat this uneven distribution as an unalterable given, even functional managers who seemed to recognize the problems this created for their direct reports. The solution to the limited contribution such team members could provide to any one team was generally believed to be found in training team leaders to run more efficient meetings.

Contradictions in the Functional Managers' Role

In this study, the organizational feature that applied the most pressure on team members to resolve their paradoxes in ways that impeded team work was the role of the functional manager (as created and reinforced through the functional reporting lines and evaluation and reward systems). Typically, this role was enacted as a controller of human resources. In these companies, as in many large U.S. organizations, the work was divided into functional specializations, and effort was motivated by the assignment of functionally relevant subgoals. Thus the role of functional managers was to allocate resources so as to achieve the assigned subgoals. The cross-functional team concept implies another, potentially contradictory, role for functional managers: the role of supplier of expertise to teams. Teams require functional expertise but lack the ability to assess, maintain, and supply that expertise; arguably, the best way to ensure that such resources are available is through a functional organization that has a supplier orientation to teams.

The contradiction for teams occurs when the functional organizations supplying team members control those resources *to optimize their functional subgoals,* and thus create suboptimal conditions for team work, which is designed to achieve cross-functional goals. For example, at Medical Products, professionals from the research and development department were assigned to serve on multiple teams, the result of functional efforts to manage its scarce resources efficiently while meeting organizational demands for representation on teams. This happened at Wayne also, where the result on the part of these team members was a lack of focus on the team's task, a lack of commitment to any one team, role conflict, and stress; and, on the team's part, a deep resentment and inability to achieve full integration. At Building Controls, the contradiction in the functional managers' role could be seen in the team members' unwillingness to accept trade-off decisions that would affect functional subgoals like engineering hours or revenues.

Contradictory Performance Evaluation and Reward Systems

The pressures that team members feel as a result of the functional managers' dual role is compounded by significant contradictions in the performance evaluation and reward systems. Two contradictions can be observed in these systems. First, although team members' primary work goals have become cross-functional in nature, evaluation and reward systems continued to direct professionals' efforts toward their functional responsibilities. The second contradiction is the unchanged focus on individual performance despite the recognition that team performance was critical to achieving divisional goals.

Functional Work versus Team Work.　All four of the organizations in this study continued to give functional managers the sole responsibility for evaluating and rewarding the performance of the professionals who served on teams. Their evaluation systems provided functional managers with little or no information on the contribution of the professional to the team effort. Thus functional managers tended to hold their direct reports accountable essentially for their functional work.

This functional definition of their jobs oriented professionals' attention and energy toward the functional hierarchy. It caused them to give priority to their functional tasks and, on occasion, to neglect their team responsibilities or to interact with the team in ways that protected their functional interests, even at the expense of team performance. The absence of mechanisms for holding the entire team accountable for its performance made this distraction from team responsibilities even likelier.

However, the team form of work seems to intensify the phenomenon in two ways. First, this form of work appears to increase the salience of the task demands by providing members with a broader perspective on their own work. With a more holistic sense of the work, team members are likely to see their efforts as more meaningful than was previously the case.[3] Therefore, team members are also likelier to want to see its potential realized—a goal worthy of challenging the boss's view. Second, teams provide members with a cohort for taking collective action to challenge managerial perspectives and/or commands that would have a negative impact on the team's performance of its task.

Several managers at Building Controls offered the following perspectives on this question: "The organization is more likely to take risks when [people] work in teams. . . . because [people] are empowered, or because they know more from being in teams." . . . "there's safety in numbers." . . . "It's easier to say 'we' think. It's harder to walk away from criticism given by a group."

Individual Accountability versus Team Accountability. The other contradiction in the evaluation and reward systems was the assumption of individual accountability in the context of interdependent task performance. The establishment of teams in these organizations was based—perhaps too implicitly—on the recognition that the requisite knowledge and experience to accomplish the work was distributed among individuals who could integrate it only through constant communication and mutual adjustment. Given this task requirement, individual accountability's concern with whose individual contribution yielded what portion of the final results was not only impractical, it was also *counterproductive to the integrative spirit of team work.*

When team members believe that such an algorithm is being applied to their work, they feel caught in the bind between doing whatever the task requires or employing strategies to ensure that their individual contribution stands out, even at the cost of achieving synergistic outcomes. At Building Controls and Wayne, where performance evaluation was based solely on the assessments of individual performance by the functional manager, team members resolved the contradiction by following their managers' directions and preferences, regardless of consequences for the team.

The situation at Medical Products provided an interesting illustration of this contradiction. There, team members expressed considerable consternation at the recent announcement that their performance on teams would be reviewed in their next evaluations. They were dubious about the process by which the data on their performance could be collected and fairly assessed: "Who's gonna do it? My manager doesn't know what I've been doing on the team. The team leader has her own goals, and she will want to make herself look like the most important person on the team." They were also concerned about the effects this process would have on the precarious camaraderie they had just begun to build: "We have finally begun to open up and trust each other. What happens if we start evaluating each other?"

At OH&ESD, the Eurous team members also were keenly aware of the potential for divisiveness that could be realized in the attempt to allocate credit for team outcomes to individuals. Their consensus view was that the only fair and effective solution was to distribute rewards equally. They were not concerned about the question of individual accountability. On their team, individuals were motivated by their commitment to the task and sense of responsibility to the team. Work assignments were allocated on the basis of what the team required and what team members could do. The team members felt interdependent and acted accordingly.

Despite a corporate review system based on individual and functional accountability, the members of the Eurous team managed this contradiction so that it did not impede the team. As discussed in chapter 6, the organizational features that allowed them to balance their individual interests with their commitment to the team included the recruitment process for assembling teams, the autonomy individuals had to choose team assignments, and the setting of goals by the teams themselves. These features led individuals to assume relationships of interdependence willingly. Because they had committed themselves to the team and its task, team members in the Occupational Health Division accomplished their individual goals in the context of the team task.

Managers' Orientation: Control versus Creativity

Another organizational contradiction faced by cross-functional teams derives from their being used to address significant problems for the organization. Teams are often introduced to handle the increasing complexity and higher stakes now present in the business world. Teams generate the type of integrative solutions required and can do so faster.[4] However, to achieve more creative solutions, teams appear to require some buffering from external constraints and demands.[5]

The higher the stakes, however, the more managers feel the need to monitor the team, and the more they tend to seek control over the project and the team.[6] This creates a dilemma of team autonomy. Tighter monitoring and control comforts managers and aids them (they assume) in ensuring the project's proper progress. This managerial urge to control thus impedes the very progress the organization has set out to gain.

The product teams at Wayne provide an interesting example of this tension. These teams were structured to accommodate the creative task of designing the product (the design engineers served as team leaders and were the only team members fully dedicated to a single team) and to facilitate creative solutions to the problems of improving quality, reducing costs, and accelerating development time. However, the teams observed devoted most of their energy to the structures of control. That is, they responded to managers' demands for quarterly progress on thirteen objectives by treating the production of that report as their task. As a result, few decisions were made, and initial outcome measures suggest that problems were not solved.

At Building Controls, despite a significant reduction in the control procedures employed in the product development process, the managerial culture of control was still so strong that professionals felt the need to make frequent symbolic gestures of submission to it. For example, one person said he kept a project chart prominently posted on his office wall to create the illusion of control. Another sent regular reports of his own time use to his senior colleagues in other areas "so they won't think I'm ignoring their projects and wasting my time." Several people there spoke of or alluded to a cycle of sanitizing the news as it made its way up the organization: "You can't break any bad news; that's dangerous."

The clear orientation in this organization was toward control. Creative problem solving was routinely sacrificed in the interests of "making the dates happen." Ironically, in this context where the sense of control was deemed so critical, there was less real control because accurate information was never passed on to management.

At OH&ESD, the senior managers gave up control when they chose to keep team reviews informal and verbal. But this surrender of apparent control provided them with more, accurate information as to what was really happening than the managers had at Building Controls.

Focus of Change: Managers, Team Members, or Everyone?

Before teams even encounter the contradiction between creativity and control in their interaction with functional and senior managers, they face a contradiction in their very definition. That is, teams are a change introduced by managers that ultimately changes the role of management.

Companies introduce teams to corral expertise at a lower level, a level more familiar with technology, products, and customers. By "pushing decision making down" to a lower level, organizations are exploiting the talent and skill that already exists, hoping thereby to create an agile organization capable of responding to internal and external demands more adeptly. But when managers create teams, they ostensibly divest themselves of certain authority, placing it in the hands of those more qualified to exercise it. In so doing, managers create the need for a new managerial role, the dimensions of which are difficult to decipher. If monitoring and control inhibit teams, how are managers to ensure that the right decisions are made? If teams have the ability to integrate information and make decisions, what do managers do? How does a manager hire, select, coach, and assess people whose work is done as team members?

The impact of teams on the managerial role was the least recognized of the organizational contradictions in this research. Though managers and team members in all four sites talked about problems that occurred in the relationship between teams and managers, especially regarding the limits of team authority, most spoke as if this was a team-level problem to be worked out or merely an issue of adopting a different, less directive managerial style. With the exception of OH&ESD, very few spoke of a need for managers to change. It was as if they assumed that their managerial roles were the givens within which teams and team members needed to operate.

OH&ESD, shortly after it had introduced teams, recognized that relationships between managers and teams were creating performance problems. It was quickly recognized that functional managers and even the operating committee would require training to learn how to enable rather than obstruct teams. Within a short period of time, the division developed training for managers and executives. Managers' roles shifted from controlling functional resources to supplying teams with resources, and executives' roles shifted from management of operations to performing strategic assessment and integration.

To the extent that the other organizations realized that team work was a major organizational change, most of the change was believed to be required of team members. Some managers in each organization appeared to feel the pressure that teams could apply to the organization. They acknowledged that teams create the potential for greater visibility, and therefore accountability, in managerial decision making. They also expressed concern, as I will discuss below, about what this implied for their own future. Most, however, continued to act as if the transition to teams was an intervention aimed primarily, if not exclusively, at the professionals on the teams. Ironically, this perspective was contradicted by the failure of managers in these three organizations to provide training in team work.

At Wayne and Building Controls, there was much discussion of the fact that the process of developing new products was being significantly altered from the old sequential approach. The new process of functions working simultaneously on a product was hailed as the solution to functional isolation and lack of cooperation, slow and costly development, and poor quality. Despite the acknowledged innovation in the technology for developing products, in those companies and at Medical Products, team members were expected to adapt quickly and easily to the new challenge of integrating their knowledge in group meetings. In contradiction to the expressed novelty and importance of this process, there was no training provided by these companies in the team technology.

By contrast, training was central to the OH&ESD transition to cross-functional teams. It not only served to reduce the contradictions and relieve some of the pressure from paradoxes that professionals and managers experienced, it also signalled to everyone that the organization was committed to the technology of teams. Through both the content of the training and the act of investing in the development of the team technology, the division acknowledged the challenges of team work and worked with its employees to identify and manage them. Such openness and commitment are critical in light of the daunting set of contradictions and paradoxes explored above. They become even more critical in light of the personal tensions that those create.

Ripples of Personal Tension

The contradictions just described amply explain the gap between our ideal of team work and its disappointing reality. As we consider how companies might organize differently to produce conditions more conducive to team work, it is also useful to take stock of a host of personal tensions that these issues precipitate. These tensions reverberate throughout the organization. Like the paradoxes that individual team members experience, senior managers and functional managers experienced ripples of tension produced by the introduction of teams.

Senior Managers.   For many division managers, the challenges of team work are enormous. Business problems are becoming increasingly complex and uncertain, requiring managers to risk high stakes on a form of work (cross-functional teams) that is not only problematic for the organization to accommodate but whose outcome is unproven. This becomes a very personal tension in times when high executive compensation serves as a constant reminder of individual responsibility.

Although executive compensation is beginning to place some importance on long-term outcomes as well as quarterly earnings, competitive pressure and threats of merger and acquisition have subjected many executives to the constant demand to maximize short-term returns. Teams can contribute substantially to the profitability of the organization, but initially they increase short-term costs. Executives determined to make teams work can, as a result, find themselves in the very difficult dilemma of having to decide whether to do what is in the interest of their own performance or what the team and task require.

Even when senior managers can ignore their own personal dilemmas resulting from the introduction of teams, they may also experience a tension about the psychological impact of giving teams the freedom to fail. Giving teams autonomy to make decisions builds trust, responsibility, and learning. However, an experience of failure may not, depending on the team, be so positive. Failure, or only moderate accomplishment, may prove counterproductive to team development.

Functional Managers. A personal tension very common to the functional managers I interviewed was the role conflict they experienced between two demands placed on them by senior managers. They were responsible for ensuring the quality of their area's specialized knowledge and for effective application of that expertise. To do so, they needed to monitor and control their resources. But the actions taken to accomplish this control were often antithetical to the latitude that effective cross-functional teams needed to do an uncertain job.

The functional managers (and the team members) faced a second dilemma that was rarely explicit but seemed to shape their behavior in and around teams: the demands that they attend to product quality and stay close to the customer, together with constant technological advancement, gave them greater motivation than ever to maintain and develop their special expertise. However, this specialization could limit their ability to integrate their knowledge with that from other specialists to make a marketable product.

A third tension to which functional managers were susceptible related to the degree to which their direct reports on the team gained expertise in other functions. As their direct reports gained broader business exposure, functional managers found themselves wondering, "How do I manage, if I don't know what's going on?" At both Wayne and Occupational Health, adjustments were made to the team system to include functional managers "in the loop."

If their role was not to control functional resources, and they were no longer expected to be the leading technical expert, and they knew too little about the cross-functional constraints on the product, many functional managers felt some consolation in believing that the critical task remaining to them was to resolve, with their counterparts in other functions, the inevitable disputes that would arise on the team. Indeed, one interpretation of hierarchy is as a conflict resolution mechanism, whereby each level of the hierarchy is responsible for resolving the conflicts of the level below. This perception, however, created considerable tension between functional managers and the teams that felt they could and should resolve their disputes themselves and reach an integrated solution. In some instances, it also pitted functional managers against senior managers, who insisted that teams be given responsibility for resolving their own conflicts. When this occurred at OH&ESD, the problem was addressed by placing functional managers on the team, a solution that was not without its critics.

PREFERRED RESOLUTIONS OF ORGANIZATIONAL CONTRADICTIONS

The contradictions that team work creates for individuals, teams, and organizations are not irresolvable. In fact, despite the rhetorical emphasis on balance along some of the dimensions discussed above (e.g., in strategic goals, in functional expertise and team performance), organizations often signal preferred resolutions of dilemmas like these. They indicate in often subtle ways how employees are expected to decode contradictory messages and act. Figure 8.1 depicts the "slants" that the organizations in this study gave (often unwittingly) to their conflicting communications and values about team work.

In three of the four organizations in this study, cost control was the most important strategic goal *as enacted by managers.* Though that may not have been their intention, the actions of managers vis-à-vis teams tilted toward cost control. Acceleration of the product cycle was a means to achieving that end. Though quality was rhetorically espoused, the actions and decisions of upper management (for example, in pressing for unrealistic deadlines or in deciding against team training) revealed a stronger preference for cost control.

Similarly, the preferred role of functional management was as controller of functional resources. The alternative role of supplier was implicitly recognized in the actions of identifying and assigning appropriate team members, but other behaviors that would reflect a perception of teams as customers were rarely seen in the three organizations. Instead functional managers allocated personnel sparingly to teams, and often dispatched these people to teams with the implicit demand that they protect their functional department from the incursions of other departments. Senior executives of the divisions, perhaps unintentionally, emphasized this preferred role for functional managers by continuing to hold them accountable for attainment of functional subgoals—without expressed concern for the impact of these on team work.

This preferred resolution of the contradiction in the role of the functional manager was reinforced by the evaluation and reward systems in these organizations. Despite talk of assessing team members for their contributions to teams, the unambiguous message of the evaluation and reward systems for team members and their functional managers was that they should, at all costs, act to achieve their individual

Figure 8.1 The pressure of organizational structure and culture on teams.

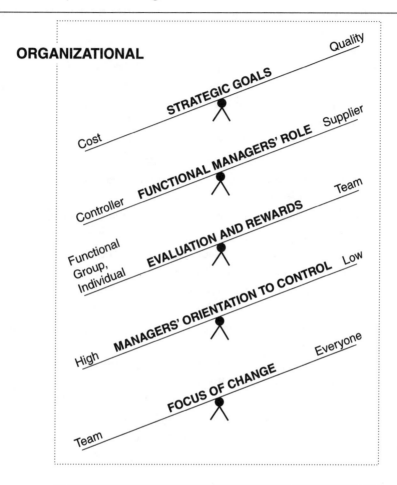

and functional objectives. This slant persisted also despite a broadly held belief that "good" team members sacrifice their personal interests for the good of the team.

The "tilt" toward individual and functional accountability and the executive tendency to treat functional managers as controllers contributed to middle managers expressing a higher orientation toward control rather than toward creativity. The stakes were high, both because of the nature of tasks teams were being given (such as Building Controls' Tech I team struggling to develop a product to replace the line producing 30 percent of the division's profit) and because of the unproven "technology" of cross-functional teams. Thus managers strove to maintain control, or at least a sense of control.

In light of these numerous contradictions and uncertainties, it is not surprising that the managers I interviewed tended to see teams as the primary focus of needed change. They recognized the need for change in order to achieve the benefits of cross-functional team work, but they rarely mentioned perceiving a need for significant change in themselves or in the organization as a whole. The solutions they offered for improving team work typically involved either training for teams or increased resources.

As figure 8.1 illustrates, these preferred resolutions to the organizational contradictions posed by team work all apply pressure to teams. In effect, they push team members to act in ways that differentiate themselves from their team, thus making it harder for the team to achieve the needed integration. Divisional demands for cost control are typically measured on a functional basis. With the performance review and reward systems relying heavily on individual and functional performance, these demands emphasize the controller role of functional management and heighten the orientation to control team members and the preference to see them as needing to change. Thus each team member is subject to a cascade of organizational pressures pushing him or her to act as an individual functional specialist *rather than as a team member.*

Figure 8.2 depicts the cascade of these organizational pressures with the individual preferences described in chapter 1, all bearing down on teams as they struggle to balance the paradoxical demands for differentiation and integration. As chapter 1 indicated, individual team members in this research experienced four paradoxes in their relationship to their teams: the paradoxes of individuality, identity, interde-

Figure 8.2 A cascade of paradox and contradiction.

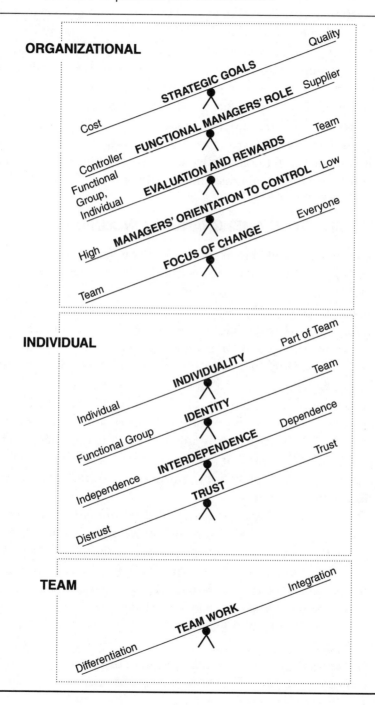

pendence, and trust. These paradoxes were experienced as a set of competing pressures to lean toward one's individual interests and needs or toward the team's. Like the organizational contradictions, these individual paradoxes tend to be resolved in typical ways. Our national culture, though it too comprises competing values, tends to tip the balance to some degree in the direction of the individual. Given this convergence of pressure, the weight in teams is likely to be tipped in the direction of differentiation, making the idealized notion of team work as balancing differentiation and integration seem virtually impossible to achieve. Yet competitive imperatives require some solution to the problems hobbling cross-functional teams.

LISTENING TO TEAMS, CHANGING INCLINATIONS

The implications of this explanation of the gap between the ideal of team work and the reality are considerable. It suggests that for teams to deliver on their potential, individual preferences must be either changed or tempered by organizational designs that restore the motivation for balance between differentiation and integration. The organizational changes required to achieve the appropriate balance in teams are enormous. However, when critical tasks require teams, such changes do prove both effective and efficient in the long run.

The senior management of the Occupational Health Division seemed to have an intuitive grasp of this set of interrelationships and trade-offs. They systematically attended to the team process and altered organizational systems that impeded team work. In effect, they changed the pivot of the organizational pressures on teams and created new demands for integration.

This research documents a set of dynamics affecting teams, some of which are widely recognized but most of which are inadequately addressed: when pressure for short-term earnings and limited human resources combine with the functional division of labor and a sequential interdependence in the work flow, a legacy of adversarial relations among functions develops that is unlikely to be overcome simply by creating cross-functional teams. Even a clear and engaging task like new product development is not enough to guarantee teamwork. The key ingredient to team work is a significant degree of perceived interdependence on the part of team members. The change in the task design that shifts the relations between functions from one of sequential interdependence to reciprocal interdependence does not translate directly into the shared perception of interdependence among cross-functional team members. By organizational design, most cross-functional team members are far less dependent on the other team members than they are on their functional managers, for functional managers control the commodities that the team members care about: their work assignments, performance evaluations, and rewards.

Certain common organizational approaches to creating and supporting interdependence are largely ineffective because they do not affect team members' perceptions of significant interdependence. For example, evaluation and reward systems that create pooled interdependence among top managers and functional heads do not translate directly into a perception of mutual interdependence among cross-functional team members. Holding team members individually accountable for accomplishment of the team task might work, but it doesn't seem to happen because team members usually have (too) many other functional responsibilities, which they perform well. This constraint applies even more strongly to the notion of holding teams as a whole accountable: how can you punish a whole team (and demotivate your direct report) if the reason the team did not achieve its goals was that several team members were focusing on their functional tasks? The strategy of giving the team leader a higher stake in the team outcomes is ineffective because it makes that person the integrator and removes the motivation for other team members to participate as fully in team deliberations as they could and should, especially in the face of numerous other demands on their time and attention.

This research suggests that, given the current state of development in most organizations, the critical capacity to make cross-functional teams work resides in team members themselves. This is because cross-functional team work is so inherently difficult, conflictual, and counter-cultural and because organizations and managers are still operating within a paradigm that impedes team work. Therefore, at least as a transitional step, organizational practice must be redesigned to motivate and enable team members (and their functional managers) to manage the personal and interpersonal conflicts involved in order to achieve the necessary balance between their differences and their integration. Such practices include recruiting (not assigning) team members and letting teams create their own goals and monitor their own progress. These approaches create a personal commitment on the part of each team member and the shared sense of interdependence that ensures each will act to manage well the inherent paradoxes, stress, and conflict of team work. These actions fall under the category of responsible membership. This research also suggests that team leaders who are competent and share power are effective because they inspire responsible membership. Training makes it possible for members to act effectively in this new role and this new form of work.

Another important lesson of this research is that team work requires the investment of adequate resources; otherwise it doesn't happen. Furthermore, we have seen here that team work takes more time at the front end than sequential work flows, but it can ultimately improve quality and innovation, save time and costs. Finally, we have seen that effective teams alter the role of managers, and if managers are not prepared for this or are if they are not encouraged to respond to this challenge, the organization risks having managers block or constrain teams.

For organizations whose tasks require team work, the meaning of this research is simple but profound. Those organizations, and their managers, must accommodate themselves to the requirements of team work. To assimilate teams into the existing categories of the bureaucratic organization (hierarchical prerogatives, functional divisions, individual accountability, and an orientation to control) is to gain little from a change that, even if minimally implemented, disturbs the status quo.

ACCOMMODATION, NOT ASSIMILATION

Most managers know they need to change the way work is done. They appear to recognize that teams are a way to do that, but for the most part, they seem unaware of how profound a change team work is and of the many subtleties involved in making a successful transition to teams. It is not surprising that the meaning of team work is so elusive.

American industry, which once progressed so slowly as to seem immutable, created structures that divided tasks into specialized functions and individual job descriptions. It also produced expectations of relative stability, gradual change, and automatic career advancement up a well-defined hierarchy. It is difficult for people with this mind-set to apprehend the rapidly shifting and changing stimuli that today's world presents. Past experience is no guide for the change.

The most natural inclination is to interpret new experiences in terms of what one already knows, that is, in terms of one's previous categories. Jean Piaget, the father of cognitive psychology, referred to this mental process as *assimilation*. He also identified another process of interpretation in which the mind adjusts its own structure of meaning to take in the new data. This process of creating a new structure, of adding and reordering categories, he called *accommodation*. This dichotomy is a useful metaphor for understanding differences in organizational change and is particularly relevant to the experiences that organizations have in interpreting and adjusting to the meaning of team work.

In three of the companies I studied, people interpreted the team concept through assimilation. That is, the starting point for creating teams was the accepted structure of bureaucratic principles of organizing. As depicted in figure 8.3, this structure's first principle is the preservation of owners' and managers' dominance in the hierarchy, which is achieved through control procedures including the division of labor

Figure 8.3 The organizing principles of bureaucracy.

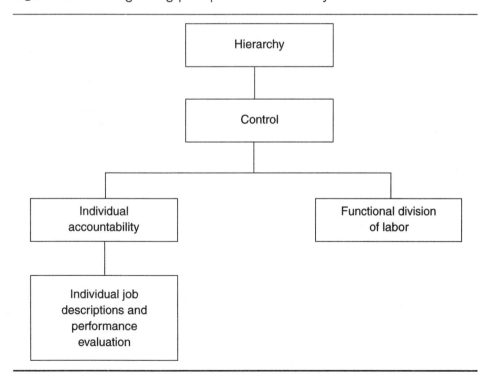

(typically by function) and individual accountability. Assimilating teams to this way of thinking amounted to two minor additions to that structure (see figure 8.4): adding "team participation" to individual job descriptions and assigning individuals in their functional capacity to teams. As three of the companies shifted from serial product development to concurrent development, they established teams in a manner that reflects a mental process of assimilation. For example, companies often refer to the new way of working as "parallel development," but just as parallel distinguishes it from the old serial method, parallel distinguishes the approach from an integrated one. By continuing to operate with divided functional responsibilities, the organization guided

Figure 8.4 Assimilating teams to the organization.

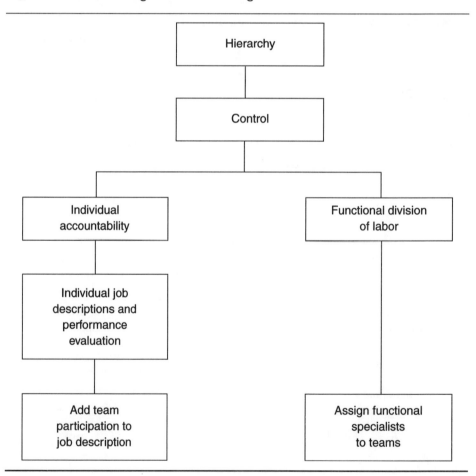

teams to work not on a single track but on separate, parallel tracks. The results produced by these teams were most disappointing.

Only one organization in this research study displayed the mental process of accommodation as it tried to make sense of teams as a new way of working and organizing. Occupational Health continually altered its structures, policies, and practices to meet the needs and demands of teams. Recall that the role of functional managers was altered in accordance with teams' assessments, training was expanded to alter those managers' perceptions of their roles and their hierarchical prerogatives, and the meaning and focus of control changed. The shift away from managerial control and a functional definition of professional work enhanced the personal responsibility professional employees felt and created a strong commitment to the team and the task. This provided the motivation for them to manage the conflictual, paradoxical task of integrating their differences.

Figure 8.5 depicts the new structure of organizational principles that the process of accommodation produced at Occupational Health.

Figure 8.5 Accommodating the organization to team work.

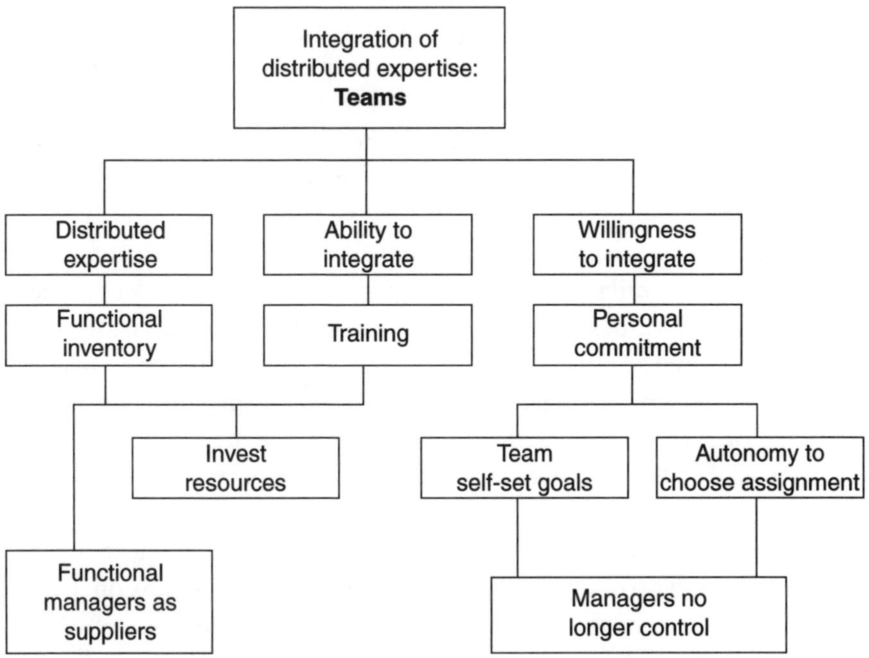

Starting with the principle that their strategic goals were to increase innovation and accelerate the speed of product development, Hershock and his advisors decided that to accomplish these goals, they needed teams capable of integrating the knowledge distributed throughout the organization. To achieve these kinds of teams, Hershock recognized that the teams needed three things: the requisite expertise, team members with the ability to integrate their different forms of expertise, and members with the willingness to do that difficult work. Additional organizational principles derived from this interpretation of the team phenomenon: to acquire the requisite expertise, to maintain the functional inventories of such expertise, would require an investment of more resources and a subtle shift in the role of functional managers from controllers of specialist human resources to suppliers of those resources to the teams. To provide team members with the ability to integrate while preserving their differential knowledge, training would be required. Finally, in order to ensure that team members would be willing to do the difficult balancing work of integration, Hershock realized that organizational control principles needed to be altered so as to foster personal commitment to the team and its task on the part of each team member. To foster this personal commitment, two new organizing principles were created: give professionals autonomy regarding their assignments to teams; and let the teams establish their own goals, budgets, and deadlines. One consequence of this last accommodation was that managers no longer controlled the product development process. Rather, the control was in the teams and in the team system.

The accommodation process amounts to a significant rethinking of what is important and how to achieve it. It also requires willingness to make the necessary organizational changes required to achieve those goals. The assimilation of teams depicted in figure 8.4 occurs when the bureaucratic values of hierarchy, control, functional division of labor, and individual accountability are treated as unalterable givens of organizational design. Fitting new organizational forms to the procrustean shape of these values, with little regard for the maneuverability that is being sacrificed, produces disappointing team performance and disillusionment—even cynicism—about the team concept.

At the OH&ESD, we observe accommodation in another sense as well. Though no one used the terminology of accommodation, paradox, or contradiction, the senior managers were in effect accommodating the organizational structure to both the paradoxical demands of team work itself and to individual preferences to resolve tensions in ways that emphasized their differences. The changes made at OH&ESD emphasized integration in teams. The organization thus provided a counter balance to deeply held individual values and preferences that training can only partially alter.

OH&ESD did not remove all the contradictions that team work creates, but it did change the direction of many of its organizational messages to teams and team members (see figure 8.5). By so doing, it achieved significant results from its teams. Thus it provides the inductive basis for this book's argument that to offset the pressure that culturally shaped inclinations of individuals—especially in the United States—bring to teams, the organization seeking team work must reduce the contradictions and alter the direction of influence it has on individuals and teams (see figure 8.6). Even the most entrenched individual preferences and habits can change direction with effective training, successful experiences with team work, and the constant reinforcement of integration through organizational structures and appropriate managerial roles. To accomplish this, organizations must accommodate teams.

Several strategies that organizations can take to accommodate to the requirements of team work have been suggested here, including:

1. Communicating the priority of strategic goals to teams.

2. Investing resources in teams, including training for teams, their managers, and senior executives.

3. Recruiting professionals for teams and giving them autonomy in choosing assignments.

4. Balancing the emphasis on team leadership *and* responsible membership.

5. Holding teams, not individual team members, accountable for team outcomes.

6. Changing the role of functional managers from controllers to suppliers.

Clarify Strategic Priorities

The reality of contemporary life is that individuals and teams have multiple goals and occasionally these goals will compete, each requiring

Figure 8.6 Accommodating the organization to teams.

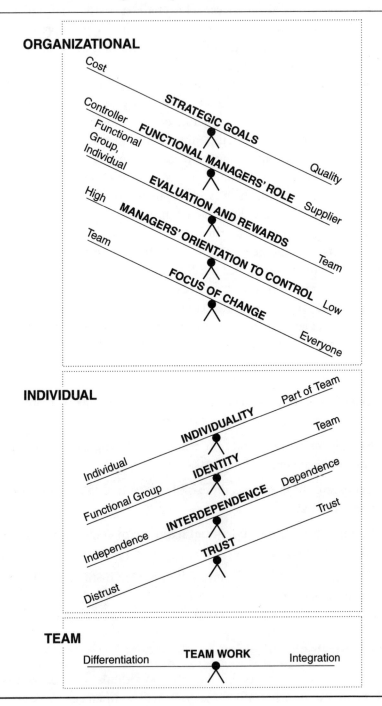

action contradictory to the other. There are essentially two solutions to such dilemmas: apply a predetermined priority among the goals to decide which action is taken, or discuss and decide the relative merits of each action and its effects on the goals. Each of these solutions has its advantages. The application of a predetermined priority saves time and prevents the exacerbation of negative feelings that can impede cooperation. The discussion and analysis of specific alternative actions, relative to the achievement of the multiple goals, allows for better control over unforeseen circumstances and therefore provides greater responsiveness.

These two solutions can be combined in team settings, if organizations are willing to accommodate. To realize the benefits afforded by teams as an integrative device capable of balancing and reconciling multiple subgoals, organizations need to communicate the priority of strategic goals to teams *and* give teams the authority and autonomy to resolve the conflicts and manage their progress towards these goals over time. Of course, taking this step in accommodating to team work requires that several others also be taken.

Invest Resources in Teams

For most professional employees, team work is a new technology, and as is generally the case with the introduction of new technology, there is likely to be an initial productivity decline. Given this reality, an organization that requires teams in order to achieve its strategic goals has no alternative but to make an investment of adequate resources in its teams. Teams need members with the appropriate expertise and the ability and willingness to integrate. As we have seen, this requires training and money—money for extensive training and money to hire enough people. Defining "enough people" is, of course, the biggest challenge. Two rules of thumb can be used. First, the proportion of people to tasks must be such that team members feel their ambitious goals are feasible; otherwise, team members will not be motivated to manage the numerous challenges of team work. If the majority of team members are expressing concerns or complaints about the work required, the prudent manager needs to listen, support efforts to adjust workloads, and, if necessary, invest in more people. Second, team members can and often will contribute well beyond their normal capacity when a team requires it. However, such stretches are difficult to sustain.

Creative combinations of additional training, rotations of assignments, and even sabbaticals can leverage fixed levels of human resources, but again, the prudent manager needs to consider carefully what level of investment is required in order to achieve the type of payoff the organization seeks.

Investing in teams entails recalibration of expectations as to how and when the team process will achieve strategic goals. The case of the OH&ESD illustrates this cognitive adaptation. The division executive recognized that he could accomplish his strategic goal of increasing revenues from new products through acceleration of the product development cycle. However, he also understood that an emphasis on speed could jeopardize product quality. Like many managers, he knew that collaboration across functions was the critical ingredient, and he identified cross-functional teams as the appropriate organizational structure for achieving collaboration.

Unlike many managers, he set his sights on collaboration as the intermediate goal, and he concentrated his efforts on establishing the kind of teams that would collaborate and the kind of organizational context that would produce and facilitate such teams. Only after these conditions were created was it reasonable to expect teams to deliver. Over the six years that his team system was developing, he recognized and accommodated his expectations to this reality. The payoff for him and the divisions was significant: new products proliferated, revenues from them exceeded all forecasts, product development times have been significantly reduced, and the division is now in the position of disseminating its methodology internally and externally.

Recruit Professionals and Give Them Autonomy

In typical project-oriented organizations, employees are assigned by their superiors a particular project or set of tasks. Within functional departments, such assignments are generally made on the basis of skills and experience. In general, this approach works well because it meets task requirements and provides organizational predictability and control of resources. Additionally, when the assigned task can be accomplished by an individual, the professional employee can derive a sense of satisfaction from the accomplishment of the task itself. On the other hand, when assigned to work on an interdependent task with a team, the professional employee is likely to feel concerned about two aspects of such an assignment. The first concern is whether the task will indeed be accomplished, and the second is how much credit or contribution one can claim for the achievement. Both concerns tend to be exaggerated in a system that measures and compensates performance on an individual basis.

Employees assigned to teams in such contexts can be expected to manage these concerns and uncertainties by assuming themselves to be responsible primarily for following their managers' directions. This transference of responsibility clarifies the implications of action and reduces anxiety. It enables team members to feel that they have acted responsibly and executed their assignments even if the team accomplishes nothing. The consequence of this interpretation of responsibility is a shortfall of personal commitment to the team and the task. Without this commitment, members will take every opportunity to avoid the challenges of confrontation, conflict, personal disclosure, and risk that team work inevitably entails. They can do this in good conscience—and without making a deliberate choice—by taking refuge in their responsibilities to do the team tasks assigned to them by their managers. That is, they "attend team meetings," "represent functional perspectives," "act as a liaison," or perform a host of other "team members' responsibilities" that are patently beside the point of accomplishing the team task.

Organizations can accommodate to this reality of team work by giving their professional employees the autonomy to choose team assignments. Team members who seek out such assignments or who are recruited to join teams are much likelier to feel personally committed to the team and the task. As a result, they will take responsibility for working through conflicts, making confrontations productive, and taking the necessary risks to make the team succeed.

Giving professionals autonomy in choosing their work assignments can create serious organizational problems, such as understaffed projects and underutilized personnel. However, these problems are not insurmountable and attending to them may create additional capacity within the organization. For example, personnel not recruited for teams may be asked to undertake self-assessment and developmental activities to enhance their capability to work on mission-critical tasks. Understaffed projects may be an indication of a need to reevaluate the projects' strategic fit within the organization. If found to be critical, such projects can be staffed through voluntary participation, working with professionals to identify career plans that fit both organizational and individual needs.

Train Teams and Managers

Even if organizations made all the changes described in this section, they would in all likelihood still not realize the full potential of team work. This is because these efforts do not address the individual attitudes, preferences, and behaviors that have been inculcated by culture. These can be addressed only through learning and the development of a new organizational culture that emphasizes cooperation and team work.[7] Learning and cultural change require not just structural adaptation but a commitment to training everyone who will be on a team, as well as the managers and executives who will interact with and seek to influence the teams.

Training Managers.   Managers need to learn how different teams are from the groups of individuals that they previously directed. They need to understand the new demands that teams will make of them and their direct reports. They will need to develop an understanding of their roles in a team-based organization and to practice enacting the new roles. Furthermore, because the managerial role has such a long history, the transition to a new set of practices will be challenging.

Participation in the training for team members would provide managers with vicarious learning about the new demands of teamwork. It could also signal to managers the commitment that the organization has to making teams work, thus mitigating some of the resistance that occurs when people are unconvinced that the new initiative will take hold. Also, it could reduce the resistance to change felt by those who have not participated in planning and shaping the change. To take part in training and provide feedback on it is to feel a part of the new initiative.

Data on the managerial transition[8] suggest that managers would benefit from ongoing seminars that allow them to share their experiences with other managers and develop strategies for performing their new roles and coping with the strains of the transition.

Training Teams.   The challenges that professionals face when participating on cross-functional teams are numerous. They must:

1. Learn to see their work as broader than the purely functional work they have done in the past.

2. Learn how to communicate with others who not only see the problem differently but have different terminology for the same phenomena.

3. Overcome their prejudices about people from other functions.

4. Figure out how to combine their various forms of expertise.

5. Decide how to resolve contradictions between what is good for themselves and their function and what is good for the team and the task.

These challenges are so difficult to manage because they encompass cognitive dimensions (How do I learn to think more broadly and communicate more effectively?) and dimensions that are more emotional or value-oriented. (Am I first and foremost an engineer or am I a member of the Product X team? Where do I owe my allegiance? How do I manage trade-offs between what's good from a marketing point of view and what's good from the team's point of view?)

To provide team members with the opportunity to learn these lessons, training for team work needs to develop both conceptual understanding about the phenomenon and mastery of a large set of skills. In the sections below, I discuss each of these categories of learning.

Conceptual Learning about Teams. I have argued in this book that team work is different from the kind of work that has been prevalent in the United States since large work organizations came into existence. It involves considerably more face-to-face communication, collective problem solving, and collective decision making. For these reasons, team work requires explicit accounting of one's judgments, negotiation of conflicting judgments, and mutual adjustment. Both because team work is a new technology and because it requires considerable mindfulness of several factors, teams need to develop new cognitive frameworks for understanding teams.

Several subject areas should be addressed. The first deals with the differences among individuals, groups, and teams, and the implications of these differences for managing and working in teams. The second critical subject for teams to learn about is the relationship among organizational context, teams, and outcomes. The third subject area deals with the paradoxes that individuals experience as they join teams. Fourth, since members of professional-level teams are typically functional specialists, they need to have some exposure to the distinctive ways in which the other functions look at the work. If members start with an appreciation for the contribution that others make, they will be less likely to attribute negative personal motives to others. Finally, teams need to understand the central concepts of interdependence and membership, how they relate to team work, and what implications they have for action and interaction.

Skills for Team Work. To be effective, teams need members able to observe, assess, and intervene in the process of interaction by which they do their work. Sharing accountability for the task gives each member the right and responsibility to express opinions and suggest improvements in the team process.

Team members need strong communication skills. In addition to being able to express their opinions succinctly and to provide compelling rationales for their judgments, they also must be able to listen well and to express their own views in ways that take the other members' views into consideration. They will need to be able to express dissenting opinions forcefully even in the face of opposition, and to provide support for the role of dissent.

Team work involves mutually acknowledged interdependence and an influence style that minimizes power differences by minimizing social distance. This suggests that the task demands of teams are intertwined with the relationship requirements. To be able to manage this complex set of interconnections so that the task is accomplished and relationships are preserved for future collaboration requires the ability to sense and respond to the feelings of others. It is also helpful for team members to be able to distinguish stylistic diversity (as was the case in chapter 7) from substantive differences. Mastery of various influence strategies should also contribute to effective decision making in groups.

The set of skills associated with conflict management are also critical for team members to develop. Among those most relevant are diagnosis of underlying conflict, distinguishing substantive from emotional conflict, recognition of the situational factors influencing the conflict, mediation, and win-win negotiation.

Teams also need skill in developing appropriate performance strategies. This requires that they be able to identify specific objectives, then develop and compare alternative approaches. Training in brainstorming and action planning is useful in this regard. Teams also need to manage their environment, which requires the ability to interact with executives, clients, and other teams. Developing the ability to plan with versatility and empathy proves helpful in accomplishing this aspect of the team work.

Balance Leadership with Membership

Effective teams require the personal commitment of all team members to contribute whatever the team requires, which, as stated earlier, I have called responsible membership. Designs that give disproportionate attention to the team leader role encourage team members to defer to the leader in decision making and conflict resolution. Furthermore, this kind of deferral is quite natural and easy for team members to do because it conforms to the hierarchical design that accords greater responsibility and discretion to the leader, and because they can justify their own inaction in some arenas by their action in others, as discussed earlier. When membership is not accorded equal importance and attention in a team design, it suggests that the team is merely another hierarchy in which the leader will perform the integration task. This, of course, suggests too that the organization is assimilating teams rather than accommodating to them. If teams are to produce the benefits of constant mutual adjustment, the needs of the members must be given as much consideration as the leader's. There are two ways that organizations may accommodate to this requirement.

Recruit Leaders for Members. Team work is a conflictual, emotionally taxing, and cognitively demanding form of work. Members need a team leader who is emotionally capable of facilitating the differentiation and the integration of ideas. Hackman and Walton[9] have characterized this quality as emotional maturity. Though it is beneficial for all members to have facilitation skills, it is useful for someone to have the assigned role of facilitation. To be effective at facilitation requires a whole host of skills such as listening, communicating, envisioning, inventing, negotiating, learning, and teaching.[10]

Beyond these skills, my research suggests some other qualities that team members look for in their leaders. It appears that a leader needs a profound commitment to the product or task in order to help a team tolerate the conflicts and weather the emotional lows in such work. He or she also needs recognized expertise and a reputation for integrity. These qualities enhance the potential for team effectiveness in several ways. The expertise enables the leader to influence all team members to contribute what they can with certainty that the team task will be accomplished. Externally, the expertise translates into the clout required to get the resources and support the team requires. A leader's integrity serves team members by ensuring that everyone will receive appropriate credit for the team performance, and thus motivating team members' willing contributions.

Allow Teams to Change Their Leadership.   Although many of the team members I interviewed agreed that the functions discussed above could be accomplished by the team itself and did not necessarily have to be assigned to a single person, they felt that cultural expectations made it easier and more efficient to assign them to a team leader. However, they also felt that if other members had the requisite skills and qualities, there were times when a team might feel the need or desire to change its leadership.

Having the authority to change or restructure their leadership gives teams greater responsibility as well as autonomy. It signals the importance of membership by recognizing both the rights and responsibilities that members individually and jointly have to their teams.

Change the Role of Functional Managers

Clearly, one of the ways to resolve the contradiction in the role of the functional managers is to give teams the assignment, authority, and autonomy to control themselves. This means that functional managers must surrender their authority to demand or direct the use of team members' time for the achievement of functional subgoals at the expense of achieving team goals. However, functional managers cannot be expected to give up this authority if they themselves continue to be held accountable by senior executives for the achievement of functional subgoals.

Part of the solution then is to alter the basis for allocating responsibility for achievement of divisional goals. If teams are given adequate support to achieve the integration necessary to ensure performance, they should be accountable for that performance, as discussed below. Because team performance depends upon specialized knowledge and expertise, the responsibility of functional managers could and should be supplying that expertise.

The role of supplier entails the development and coordination of resources, roles not new to functional management. However, removing responsibility for controlling resources permits more attention to be given to developing capacity. Such capacity may be developed in terms of updating one's own technical expertise or by devoting more time to identifying and recruiting new experts.

Altering the role of functional managers may be the most significant accommodation that an organization can make to team work. For it challenges the cherished bureaucratic notions of hierarchical prerogatives. In a time of scarce resources and rapid change, executives may well find this message of relinquishing control heretical and unworkable. We must keep in mind, though, that the need for more creative solutions that drives our interest in teams will not be fulfilled if teams are subject to stringent, externally imposed controls. However, this recommendation does not mean that organizations should not control teams, but that there is a preferable solution that maintains the balance between control and creativity: making teams accountable.

Hold Teams, Not Team Members, Accountable

In effect, the design of teams at OH&ESD made teams accountable. The other organizations were holding team members individually accountable. Why? I believe that this is partially due to the process of assimilation, which allows managers automatically to subordinate the team design to other, presumably given, features of the organization without seeing how those other features could be adjusted to accommodate the team process. It is also because there would be certain dysfunctional consequences of holding whole teams accountable. Organizations would have to be willing to punish whole teams, as well as to reward them. This is problematic if the reasons for team failure or mediocre performance are due to team members being preoccupied with important functional responsibilities. It also makes the bases for evaluation a more public issue, which can have both positive and negative results. For example, a more public evaluation of teams strictly on the basis of their performance may reduce some managerial discretion regarding individual professionals, thereby reducing managers' influence over "their own" people.

Two distinct ideas combine in my prescription to make teams, and not team members, accountable for their performance. The first idea is that teams, if held accountable, can provide better control over task performance than managers can. The second idea is that the appropriate unit of measurement for control of task performance is the team, not individual team members.

Give Teams Responsibility for Controlling the Task.   Managers have a tendency to insist on procedures and reports that give them a sense of control over the performance of critical tasks. Such practices are typically required of teams, even though they may divert attention and energy from other activities that would yield better, more timely information and therefore, presumably, more control over the work. Setting aside the concern about whether managers actually use such information to control the work or just the people, we must reckon with the important issue of these control mechanisms acting as a disincentive to provide accurate information. This occurs when managers, determined to achieve strategic goals, insist on unrealistic objectives and refuse to hear that these will not be met. The result is that managers are told what they want to hear and learn the real story only after the goal has been missed, when it's too late to make corrections. At BCD, for example, some team members confided that they had even concealed details about their progress from other team members to spare themselves some of the inevitable pressure and distraction from their tasks. The result was that critical information regarding the timing of product launch was inaccurate and the projections of return on investment for this product fell far short.

By contrast, accounts of teams working nights, weekends, and holidays to meet their own targets abounded at OH&ESD. Giving teams the authority and autonomy to establish their own objectives, budgets, and schedules provided the executive at OH&ESD with a much clearer sense of what the organization's performance would be. It also focused teams on their joint task by eliminating distractions from managers demanding subgoal reports. Finally, it generated the personal commitment to the team and its task that external control pressure obviates.

Suspend Individual Performance Evaluation.   Individual performance evaluation tends to be based on functional process measures. Examples include the number of units sold, the number of engineering changes, the cost of materials, and the number of warranty repairs. Such measures may be useful indicators of what is happening, and they can be very helpful targets for altering inputs to a team process, everything else being equal. But precisely because everything else is never equal, they are not reliable as predictors of the interdependent task performance. For example, a team member evaluated on the number of engineering change orders required on a particular design may have a tendency to resist a team's joint sense that certain changes could make a new product easier and cheaper to manufacture. In such an instance, assuming the product development team's joint sense is accurate, the team member's efforts to meet his or her individual performance objectives would look satisfactory but would be impeding the team's performance on the task. Individual, functional performance measures may also be inadequate measures of an individual's contribution to the team performance. In the case discussed earlier, effective team performance often requires individuals to contribute their expertise about how to make appropriate trade-offs in complex decisions, regardless of the effect that these trade-offs have on a subgoal or a milestone. Yet, because individual performance is assessed on these subgoals and milestones, they tend to develop a rigidity that leads to their subordinating what should have been the superordinate goal—like manufacturing a quality product at a lower cost.

Individual performance evaluation also tends to preserve the historical status structure of functions in an organization, which can undermine team effectiveness. If contribution to the team is measured individually, people may tend to see themselves as offering more than others strictly on the basis of their organizationally dominant expertise. This leads to overidentification with the functional area and the possibility of withholding contributions until or unless they can be credited to oneself.

Given then that *team* accountability has such a positive effect on task performance and *individual* accountability such negative impact, a counterconventional implication of this research is that individual performance evaluations should be suspended—at least until such time as it takes to test and confirm that individual performance appraisal does have a positive impact *on team performance*. Some would argue that the other major reason for individual performance evaluation is to allocate individual rewards that will motivate people to make efforts that result in high performance. However, in the case of a reciprocally interdependent task such as product development, the problems with allocating individual rewards are numerous and may cause more dysfunctional behavior than contribute to high individual performance. For example, how do you fairly compensate people if they're on more than one team or they've been on a team for varying lengths of time? Furthermore, individual rewards for team contributions tend to be small and are therefore unlikely to be sufficient to overcome the organizational and individual pressures on team members to differentiate. Finally, allocating different individual rewards among team members *should* be hard to do, and therefore, should be avoided. The point of a team is to integrate, that is, to create more than the sum of the parts. Contributions should be made with the team's good in mind rather than one's individual interests and when this occurs ideas are developed in ways that make it impossible to trace to individuals. If team members know that contributions will be individually rewarded, they are more likely to manage their contributions according to their own interests rather than the team's.

Others will argue that a suspension of individual performance evaluation will pose problems for attraction and retention of excellent performers, and for promoting the best performers into positions of greater organizational responsibility. This may be, but there are alternative (although perhaps not easier or cheaper) approaches to both these problems. What I propose here is an experimental comparison of the effects on team and organizational effectiveness with and without individual performance evaluations.

Some would say that a lack of individual feedback would produce mediocrity and lack of learning and development because people will not know where their actions have been ineffective. This need not be the case. Suspension of individual performance evaluations need not be accompanied by a suspension of feedback on performance. In fact, there is increasing evidence[11] that the *occurrence* of individual performance evaluations does not guarantee the delivery of feedback that results in improved performance. Indeed, it may be the case that more individual feedback *relevant* to task performance may be likelier to occur if teams and not individuals are the basis of evaluation.

Clearly, these six accommodations are not merely a set of techniques for managing teams, nor do they constitute a new program for team building. Rather, they amount to a prescription for significantly altering the organizational context. Some would argue that constraints like the competitive environment, the corporate strategy, the corporate culture, and financial markets severely limit any executive's ability to change the organizational context as dramatically as is proposed here. Of course, I agree that contextual variables will influence how readily such change can be implemented. It is reasonable to expect that, for some managers, the bureaucratic culture and ideology are so deeply engrained that implementing such change could mean career suicide. It is also possible that the pressure of financial markets would leave no space for the longer return on the investment in teams.

On the other hand, if it is true that to gain competitive advantage, companies must achieve simultaneous and substantial improvements in both quality and cost or in innovation and time to market, the decision *not* to accommodate to teams may ultimately prove even more perilous, both to the executive and the company. So the real question becomes, Where and how does one start to make such momentous changes?

Senior executives are naturally in the best position to start such initiatives, though even they are bound by the assumptions of the bureaucratic culture and the web of managerial and professional expectations that derive from it. However, recent research on organizational change[12] has documented an effective approach to fundamental organizational change. Beer, Eisenstat, and Spector propose that the change process should begin with numerous multilevel, multifunctional task force discussions of how a particular change would affect each part of the organization and move to a discussion of how implementation should be designed to minimize problems and maximize the potential for success. The authors also found that after this discussion and planning phase was completed, companies that followed a particular order of steps in their implementation experienced the change as most effective. That order, or "critical path" in the authors' terms, started by changing task behaviors and interactions, then focused on systems, followed by change in structures.

This critical path is very similar to the one that Hershock took at OH&ESD. He started with a series of strategic planning discussions in the division. Then he proceeded to create and train cross-functional teams. Gradually, over a total period of seven years, systems were changed to accommodate to teams, and structures were changing at the time that the research data were collected. Harvard Business School cases on G.E. Canada[13] and Quantum Corporation[14] also describe similar processes by which organizations incrementally adapted themselves to the needs of the team system they required to accomplish their strategic goals.

Middle managers at Wayne Division informally created coalitions to urge upper management to adopt new approaches to cross-functional collaboration. This growing interest converged with initiatives by the internal organizational development staff to explore teams as a vehicle for such collaboration. This set of managers effectively formed teams to promote the idea and to develop a design for the team system.

Team leaders and team members may conclude from this chapter that there is little they can do to improve their own team's performance because the most powerful influences on team interaction are features in the organizational context that are beyond their control. The Alpha team case offers an alternative view. That team managed to construct a new, albeit provisional, sense of mutual interdependence and personal commitment to the team and its task. Despite organizational influences that pushed team members in the opposite direction, they became a team and accomplished team work. The linguistic audit, profiles, and interventions described in chapter 7 provide a methodology for accomplishing similar ends.

AN AMERICAN MODEL OF TEAM WORK

At the beginning of this book, I reviewed numerous claims about the benefits and sheer necessity of work teams. Despite the pain, stress, conflict, and frustration that I have observed in and around teams, I remain convinced that team work is the only way to accomplish much of the work required to achieve the strategic goals of creating quality products and services and accelerating the speed by which those are delivered to the market. Therefore, I see it as critical that Americans learn how to create, support, and work in effective teams.

I have argued earlier that part of the problem with teams in U.S. companies is that organizations create teams by simply grafting them onto the existing structure. Teams are thus compelled to assimilate to the organization designed in accordance with the bureaucratic principles of hierarchy, control, functional division of labor, and individual accountability. These principles constrain teams, dooming them to failure. My research indicates that this assimilation occurs not through deliberate choice but as a result of lack of understanding about how different a form of work they are.

The lack of understanding about the nature of team work may occur because teams have been adopted in imitation of successful Asian, particularly Japanese, competitors. Adopting the form without considering how the design of work interacts with the design of the organization and the cultural expectations of individuals is a prescription for disappointment, to say the least. Numerous structural and cultural factors make the use of teams in Japanese firms a very different phenomenon from the introduction and use of teams of professional workers here in this country. If the strategic goals of American organizations and the nature of the work demand teams, then the solution to the gap between our ideals of teams and the reality chronicled here (and well known to most of us) lies in the design of, and commitment to, a uniquely American model of team work.

In the preceding pages, I have described such a model. It is American in the sense that it addresses itself to the cultural expectations that must be offset in order to motivate team work. It is also American in the sense that it draws on aspects of our history, heritage, and contemporary practices. Two of the features of this design are particularly tailored to American cultural sensibilities: the confrontational but consensual nature of the team interaction and the autonomy of choosing one's own work assignments.

Giving professional workers greater autonomy to choose their own work assignments is a radical change from current practice. In large corporations, adoption of this feature greatly amplifies the need for coordination and inevitably leads to greater costs, at least in the short term. A host of other changes in the organizational system described above would make it feasible to achieve both autonomy and coordination, while achieving effective cross-functional team work.

CONCLUSION

Team work, despite its overuse and fading cachet, remains the most effective way to accomplish the organizational tasks that require integration of diverse expertise and experience. Yet many companies have stalled in the development of teams, and many people who manage and work in teams have hit a plateau of frustration and skepticism. There is a pervasive sense of disappointment with what teams have produced and great uncertainty about the causes of, and solutions for, this problem.

This book argues that the gap between the ideal and the reality of team work is due to our failure to recognize and address the numerous paradoxes and contradictions that team work poses for individuals, teams, managers, and organizations. The central paradox of team work is that teams require both the differences among their members and the integration of those differences into a single product. For teams doing professional work, these requirements are met—or at least sought—in the process of team talk. Teams, unlike individual contributors, must talk to contribute and combine their expertise. Through their talk, teams must also manage the permanent tensions of diversity and interdependence. Coping with such tensions is difficult for individuals, especially in the U.S. culture; and that difficulty is compounded in the team context. Team talk reflects and shapes the way individual team members resolve these tensions.

The patterns of team talk are also significantly influenced by organizational structures, systems, and cultures that emphasize differences and inhibit integration. My research indicates that if organizations are to use professional teams effectively, they must remove the contradictions and barriers that impede team work. In effect, organizations and managers must accommodate themselves to the requirements of real team process.

However, the relationships among individuals, teams, organizations, and team talk are not linear or unidirectional. Indeed, this book has illuminated the reciprocal influence between individuals and teams and between teams and organizations. I have shown how, through the power of language, individuals can influence teams and teams can influence organizations. But in the final analysis, to realize their potential, teams both ensure and require organizational change. The changes required are daunting, particularly in light of the fact that both individual interests and organizational designs derive from the surrounding national culture. Nevertheless, organizations must consider whether there is any alternative to creating the conditions that will produce effective team work.

Appendix A

Research Methodology

The research methods used in the field project discussed in this book are anthropological and linguistic. Because this study was exploratory, I chose to collect extensive data at a small number of research sites. The data are rich and provide complex views of each organization. However, because the sites are few in number, my claims about "significant differences" are based not on statistical tests but on broad, observable patterns and plausible argument.

Extensive archival data were collected from the four Fortune 200 organizations that were sites for this research. Interview data were collected from the senior executives and functional heads in each division, as well as from the members of twelve product development teams. Altogether, approximately 250 people were interviewed. In three of the four organizations, I was also able to audiotape several team meetings and observe the daily activities of several team members. The meetings (and interviews) were recorded with the knowledge and consent of the participants. These data were analyzed using sociolinguistic and comparative analyses.

SOCIOLINGUISTIC ANALYSIS

Sociolinguistics is an interdisciplinary field of inquiry that focuses on human interaction to "account for the role that communicative phenomena play in the exercise of power and control and in the production and reproduction of social identity"[1] and social structure.[2]

The methodology is interpretive, integrating ethnographic information and recorded conversational data. The process begins with the sampling of real conversational exchanges, then proceeds to identifying empirical regularities in the discourse. The next step is to show how these patterns "contribute to participants' interpretations of each other's motives and intents".[3] By intent, however, sociolinguists refer not to a psychological state but to the observable interpretations of each other's language that participants display.[4] The specific theoretical concern determines how the linkage between sociolinguistic patterns and interactional effect is made.

My study was designed to explain how team work is accomplished conversationally, so I reviewed the sociolinguistic literature to expand Fairhurst and Chandler's[5] categorization scheme to include conversational forms that corresponded to the six dimensions of team interaction (see table A.1). I then listened to audiotapes and written transcripts of team interaction to identify episodes of negotiation. (Excerpts from transcripts of these episodes appear in chapters 3, 4, 5, and 6.) The next step was to analyze the interactions to determine how team identification, interdependence, power differentiation, social distance, conflict, and negotiation were being managed in each of the teams. Because the method is ethnographic and interpretive, and because language has enormous flexibility, new forms for displaying and accomplishing these team qualities were discovered in the analysis. These appear in table A.1 without citation.

Then the talk of each team was assessed in terms of the six key dimensions of team talk. As stated earlier, only one team—the Eurous team from the 3M Occupational Health Division—was so characterized by forms of team identification, interdependence, social closeness, collaborative conflict management, and win-win negotiation process that it clearly deserved to be considered a real team.

The pattern of similarities and differences among four organizational contexts when compared to patterns of team talk in each identified which differences make the difference between real teams and nominal ones. Strategic goals, the choice of assignment, the role of functional managers, the basis of team membership and leadership, and training were thus shown to relate most directly to the dimensions of team interaction that are critical to team task performance.

Linking interview data on employees' experiences and feelings, with descriptive data on the context with team interaction data, I was also able to provide plausible explanations for how those differences produce the observed differences in team work.

Table A.1 Linguistic forms and social functions.

Linguistic Forms	Sources
I. Identification	
A. *Functional Identification*	
Inclusive pronouns refer to functional group	Brown and Gilman, 1960
Reference to functional groups	
B. *Team Identification*	
Inclusive pronouns refer to team	Brown and Gilman, 1960
Reference to team	
II. Interdependence	
A. *Independence Forms*	
Explicit reference to independence	
Assertions of individual intent	Tannen, 1990
Failure to respond to questions	West, 1984
B. *Interdependence Forms*	
Acknowledgment of mutual interests	Tannen, 1990
Expressions of own needs	Tannen, 1990
Proposals of joint action	Goodwin, 1980
Soliciting of others' views and needs	Maltz and Borker, 1982
Explicit reference to interdependence	
III. Power Differentiation	
A. *High*	
Certainty	Berger and Bradac, 1982
Challenges	Rogers and Farace, 1975
Challenges to competence	Bogoch and Danet, 1987
Corrections	Jefferson, 1987
Directness	Berger and Bradac, 1982
Disconfirmation	Watzlawick, Beavin, and Jackson, 1967
Interruptions	Mishler and Waxler, 1968; West, 1984; Zimmerman and West, 1975
Leading questions	Labov and Fanshel, 1977

Table A.1 Continued

Linguistic Forms	Sources
Orders	Drake and Moberg, 1986; Rogers and Farace, 1975
Repetition of questions	Drew, 1989; O'Donnell, 1990
Topic change	Clark and Haviland, 1977; West, 1984
Verbal aggression (threats)	Miller, 1983
B. *Low*	
Apologies	Brown and Levinson, 1978
Disassociations of self from request	Brown and Levinson, 1978
Disclaimers	Hewitt and Stokes, 1975
Indirect questions	Brown and Levinson, 1978
Hedges	Lind and O'Barr, 1979; Lakoff, 1975
Politeness	Bradac and Mulac, 1984; Brown and Levinson, 1978
Stating one's debt to other	Drake and Moberg, 1986
IV. Social Distance	
A. *Social Distance Forms*	
Accounts using consultative or formal language	Scott and Lyman, 1968
Formal forms of address	Brown and Gilman, 1960
Excessive politeness	Drake and Moberg, 1986
Impersonal requests or assertions	Brown and Levinson, 1978
Hedges	Drake and Moberg, 1986
Literal response to question about relationship	Tannen, 1990
B. *Social Closeness Forms*	
Casual style, use of slang	Brown and Levinson, 1978
Use of nicknames	Brown and Levinson, 1978
Slurring of pronunciation or ellipsis	Morand, forthcoming
Claiming commonalities in group membership	Brown and Levinson, 1978
Claiming common views and seeking agreement	Brown and Levinson, 1978
Displaying knowledge and concern for others' wants	Brown and Levinson, 1978
Expressions of liking or admiration	Brown and Levinson, 1978
Expressions of reciprocity or cooperation	Brown and Gilman, 1960
Familiar address/nicknames	Brown and Levinson, 1978
Similar language	Drake and Moberg, 1986
V. Conflict Management Tactics	
A. *Forcing, Avoiding, Accommodating Forms*	
Directives	Vuchinich, 1990
Threats	Kochman, 1981
Acquiescence	Filley, 1975
Use of Power Differences	Filley, 1975

Table A.1 Continued

Linguistic Forms	*Sources*
Postponing or Delegating Decisions	Filley, 1975; Robbins, 1974
Voting	Robbins, 1974
B. *Confrontating, Collaborating Forms*	
Expression of interest, problem, need	Fisher and Ury, 1981; Follett, 1994
Questions seeking others' needs	Walton and McKersie, 1965
Syntheses of interests	Follett, 1995; Pruitt, 1983
Non-threatening tone to debates	
Restatement of dissenting views	Gray, 1989
Analysis of implications or consequences	
VI. Negotiation Process	
A. *Win-Lose Forms*	
Expressions of positions	Fisher and Ury, 1981
Lexicon of debt, concession	Donnellon and Gray, 1989
Use of power differences to win	O'Donnell, 1990
B. *Win-Win Forms*	
Reframing or reinterpreting in light of others' ideas	Follett, 1994; Donnellon and Gray, 1989
Expansion or emphasis of others' ideas	Maltz and Borker, 1982
Exploration of implications	Donnellon, Gray and Bougon, 1986
What-if questions	Fisher and Ury, 1981
Using objective criteria for resolution	

Note: Table adapted from Fairhurst and Chandler, 1989.

Appendix B

The Academic Context of This Research

"What accounts for differences in the effectiveness of task groups?" has been a persistent question in academic research over many decades. It is unnecessary for this appendix to review all the work that has been done to answer that question, McGrath's review of the subject is quite exhaustive.[1] Of more use is a description of recent or relevant work that addresses this question when applied to groups or teams at work.

Ironically, current strategic exigencies show that one of the most relevant answers to this question was presented in 1967 by organizational sociologist James Thompson.[2] The current and widespread emphasis[3] on time to market and on quality have altered the interdependencies among the various functions or departments of many organizations. Formerly, most large, complex organizations designed workflows sequentially and arrayed work units so that all units were dependent on the units "upstream" in the workflow—those that created their inputs—but not on "downstream" units—those that received their outputs. Thompson characterized this relationship as "sequential interdependence."[4]

Now, in the effort to meet multiple strategic goals simultaneously, new information is produced in the process of action. These informational outputs of each functional unit then necessarily become inputs to the others. For example, in order to accelerate work cycles without sacrificing quality, manufacturing must give feedback to design engineering on the outcomes of the design decisions, and this information must be input to the next iteration of design. The relationship among the functional departments as they take action to meet the organization's goals has thus become "reciprocally interdependent."[5]

To coordinate in a relationship of reciprocal interdependence requires constant communication and continuous mutual adjustment to the information produced in the work process and this can be effectively achieved only by a small work group or team.[6] By extrapolation, Thompson's answer to the question of what accounts for differences in effectiveness of the teams would no doubt be that the nature of the task shapes a team's effectiveness.

Generally speaking, there are three current theories about determinants of effectiveness in teams. One theory favored by managers and consultants[7] argues that effectiveness of teams is ensured by creating a team culture. This theory identifies the steps that teams must take to create a shared set of understandings about their work, such as agreeing on their goals, establishing clear responsibilities, and creating appropriate procedures and measurements.

A second theory argues that team design is critical to achieving the desired process.[8] The design features should include certain kinds of tasks and members. The group task should require members to use relatively high-level skills; be a whole and meaningful piece of work with a visible outcome of significant consequences for other people; provide members with substantial autonomy for deciding about how they do the work; and provide regular, trustworthy feedback about how well the group is performing. The members should have high task-relevant expertise and interpersonal as well as task skills. They should be moderately diverse, and the group should be just large enough to do the work. The team design should also require that teams build group norms that support self-regulation, situational monitoring and assessment, and strategy planning.

This theory also identifies aspects of the organizational context that are likely to affect team performance,[9] including challenging, specific performance objectives; positive consequences for excellent performance; rewards and objectives that focus on group, not individual, behavior; training and consultation to supplement members' task expertise; clarity about the parameters of the performance situation; and access to data about likely consequences of alternative strategies.

The third theory proposes that team performance depends upon the active management of both team and organizational contexts by team members.[10] For example, Ancona and Caldwell identified a set of roles—beyond technical experts or process facilitators—that teams need to create and fulfill in order to manage their environment.[11] These included scouts who collected data from the environment, sentinels who protect the team from unwanted incursions, and ambassadors who work externally to create goodwill for the team.

The research presented in the preceding chapters was an attempt to be comprehensive, to draw on existing theory, and combine it with inductive observation and deductive reasoning to make sense of the whole experience of team work.

Notes

CHAPTER I

1. *Fortune* reporter Dumaine (1990) offers numerous examples of this relationship. On the other hand, Adler and Cole (1993) provide recent data on the satisfaction of workers at Volvo's famous Uddevalla plant that suggest otherwise.

2. LaBier (1986).

3. Although the evidence is ambiguous, researchers have long argued that groups are the critical building block of organizations. They produce more creative solutions (Osborn, 1957), make better decisions (Davis, 1973), improve the implementation of decisions, and increase commitment (Hoffman, 1979; Hackman, 1987; Cohen and Ledford, 1991). Work teams have also been identified (Lawrence and Lorsch, 1967) as one of several mechanisms for integrating the differentiated perspectives on the environment that are likely to develop as a function of specialization within a firm. It has also been argued (Thompson, 1967) that certain tasks require teams because they can be accomplished only through constant mutual adjustment to the information provided by each team member. Donnellon and Scully (1994) explain why teams are an essential component of the postbureaucratic organization.

4. Cohen and Ledford (1991), Dumaine (1990), and Pfeffer (1994).

5. Dumaine (1994) and "The trouble with teams," *The Economist* (1994).

6. Ibid.

7. Ibid.

8. Bower and Hout (1988) and Stalk (1988).

9. Organizational sociologist Thompson characterized this relationship as "reciprocal interdependence" and the former as "sequential interdependence" (1967).

10. I use the word "need" here rather than the stronger "require" in the recognition that other forms could be used to do such tasks as product development. Indeed, until recently other forms, such as sequential work-flows through discrete work units, were found to be quite effective—when the strategic goals were focused essentially on efficiency measures like low cost. However, recent requirements for acceleration in work cycles of all types has created the need for an organizational form that integrates information from various parts of the organization efficiently and effectively.

11. Hackman (1987), Hackman and Walton (1986), Katzenbach and Smith (1993), Larson and LaFasto (1989), and Parker (1994).

12. This distinction must be made because team work for other types of employees does not necessarily entail ongoing communication. In a manufacturing context, for example, a team of employees typically contributes physical effort or expertise to the accomplishment of the task of assembling a car. Although communication would have been necessary at some point in order for all team members to understand their roles, it is not required on an ongoing basis for the teams to work. It is also important to recognize that many employees who are not part of the professional or managerial work force are nevertheless knowledge workers for whom team work may well be a linguistic matter. Such knowledge workers include technicians and customer service representatives, to name a few.

13. Gumperz and Cook-Gumperz (1982), Molotch and Boden (1985), and West (1984).

14. See Garfinkel (1967) on culture and Pike (1967) on language.

15. Pragmatics is a specialized field of linguistics that examines the social effects of language. See Watzlawick, Beavin, and Jackson (1967) for further discussion.

16. Goodenough (1964).

17. Tannen (1990) and (1994a).

18. Fairhurst and Chandler (1989).

19. Linde (1988).

20. Hymes (1964).

21. Gumperz and Cook-Gumperz (1982), p. 16.

22. West (1984).

23. Gumperz and Cook-Gumperz (1982).

24. Fairhurst and Chandler (1989).

25. Schneider and De Meyer (1991).

26. See Cox (1993) and Gentile (1995) for useful discussions of the organizational dynamics due to ethnic and other types of diversity.

27. See Katzenbach and Smith (1993) for further discussion.

28. People will argue that this definition of the word is too restrictive, that there are teams of people who have the same expertise. I would argue that the word "group" adequately refers to such sets, and more importantly, that there are conceptual and practical differences between groups of people with similar knowledge bases or responsibilities and those with different (or distributed) expertise. Integrating different expertise in the service of a common goals is a much more difficult, and in today's business firms a more important, task.

29. *The American Heritage Dictionary,* New College Edition (1975), p. 950.

30. Smith and Berg (1987), p. 15.

31. Lawrence and Lorsch (1967) coined the labels *differentiation* and *integration* as references to the relationship of organizational departments to one another. However, those labels with the attendant meanings that Lawrence and Lorsch gave them (i.e., to develop and use different expertise and to combine that expertise to a shared goal, respectively) apply as well to relationships of team members to one another.

32. Smith and Berg (1987).

33. Ibid, pp. 99–100.

34. Hofstede (1980).

35. Smith and Berg (1987), p. 90.

36. Kahn et al. (1964) and Alderfer (1977).

37. Smith and Berg (1987), p. 140.

38. Janis (1972).

39. Smith and Berg (1987), p. 143.

40. Ibid, p. 115.

41. Dougherty (1992), p. 180.

42. Ibid.

43. Drucker (1992).

CHAPTER 2

1. See Appendix A for additional information on this research.

2. Sherif and Sherif (1953).

3. Lawrence and Lorsch (1967).

4. Dougherty (1992).

5. Some researchers (Tajfel, 1981; Gudykunst, 1986) have also argued that exaggeration of between-group differences can also provide evidence of the strength of the group identification.

6. Tannen (1990).

7. Goodwin (1980).

8. Maltz and Borker (1982).

9. Tannen (1990).

10. West (1984).

11. Asch (1951), Lewin (1953), and Bales and Cohen (1979).

12. Steiner (1966 and 1972).

13. Davis (1980).

14. Collins (1981).

15. Expressions of certainty (Berger and Bradac, 1982); challenges (Rogers and Farace, 1975; Bogoch and Danet, 1987); corrections (Jefferson, 1987); disconfirmation (Watzlawick, Beavin, and Jackson, 1967); interruptions (Mishler and Waxler, 1968; West, 1984); orders (Drake and Moberg, 1986; Rogers and Farace, 1975); topic change (West, 1984); questions (Drew, 1989); and verbal aggression (Miller, 1983).

16. Apologies (Brown and Levinson, 1978); disclaimers (Hewitt and Stokes, 1975); hedges (Lind and O'Barr, 1979; O'Barr, 1982; Lakoff, 1975); indirect questions and requests (Brown and Levinson, 1978); question intonation (Lakoff, 1975; O'Barr, 1982); politeness (Brown and Levinson, 1978); minimizing imposition or stating one's debt to the target (Brown and Levinson, 1978; Drake and Moberg, 1986).

17. Brown and Levinson (1978); Collins (1981); Baxter (1984); Drake and Moberg (1986); Fairhurst and Chandler (1989).

18. Drake and Moberg (1986).

19. Casual style of speech, slang, nicknames or firstnames as form of address, claiming commonality or displaying concern (Brown and Levinson, 1978); similar linguistic usages (Drake and Moberg, 1986); humor (Brown and Ford, 1961).

20. Formal language (Scott and Lyman, 1968); disagreement (Brown and Levinson, 1978); disconfirmation (Watzlawick, Beavin, and Jackson, 1967); and literal response to questions about relationship (Tannen, 1990).

21. Janis (1972).

22. Filley (1975 and 1978), Robbins (1974), and Ruble and Thomas (1976).

23. Lawrence and Lorsch (1967) proposed that conforming differences was a critical step in the collaborative resolution of differences. Other, collaborative tactics are required to create integrative solutions (Pruitt, 1983).

24. Vuchinich (1990).

25. Follett (1995) and Fisher and Ury (1981).

26. Walton and McKersie (1965).

27. Pruitt (1983), p. 35.

28. Fisher and Ury (1981).

29. Donnellon and Gray (1989).

30. Maltz and Borker (1982).

31. Donnellon, Gray, and Bougon (1986).

32. Follett (1995), Maltz and Borker (1982), and Donnellon and Gray (1989).

PART II

1. This is a set of cultural and design features used to provide a description of each organization developed as the field study proceeded.

CHAPTER 3

1. The data for this research were collected six months after the establishment of the teams, when they were in a hiatus. The task of preparing the annual implementation plans for each product had been accomplished, and presentations to the operating committee had just concluded. The division president reported that the product plans had been done ahead of schedule, and as a result the division's strategic planning and budgeting were also proceeding well. Though most of the team members spoke as if the teams had a broader, ongoing mandate to manage the products, the conflict in the operating committee about the role and authority of teams was not yet resolved. Everyone understood that the functioning of the teams would change now that the urgency of the annual planning had subsided, but it was not yet clear what teams would do or how they would operate. Some teams had scheduled meetings for the following month, while others awaited further direction from the operating committee.

2. See Emerson (1962) for a discussion of power and dependency.

3. According to Drake and Moberg's model of influence (1986), if such willingness to share power is displayed linguistically, it may have the effect of reducing attention otherwise accorded to questionable displays of power. Thus, it may also have served to focus attention on the task itself.

CHAPTER 4

1. Mannix (1993).

2. Fisher and Ury (1981).

3. A noteworthy contribution to solving this prevalent problem is Meyer's (1994) article in which he argues that the best measures of team performance are not functional but cross-functional.

CHAPTER 5

1. West (1984).

CHAPTER 6

1. Mitchell (1989).

2. *3M 1988 Annual Report: Sustaining Profitable Growth.*

3. "OH&SP Action Teams," *3M Manager: Special Report,* February 1988, 6–7.

4. "OH&SP Action Teams," 7.

5. Sociolinguist Pomerantz (1975) found that speakers show a clear preference to agree with a prior speaker's assessment, even if this agreement is in form only. They show this sociolinguistic preference in the grammatical forms of their responses to assessments. For example, in response to a question containing an assessment like "Don't you think it's too late for a movie?" people will more likely say "Yes" than "No." However, those respondents who want to go will typically add a phrase like "unless it's short."

6. Peters in *California Management Review* (1991) and Drucker in *Wall Street Journal* (1992).

7. Bateson (1972).

PART III

1. Hackman and Walton (1986).

2. Smith and Berg (1987).

CHAPTER 7

1. Dyer (1987) and Larson and LaFasto (1989).

2. Hackman (1987).

3. Tannen (1986).

4. Ibid.

5. Organizational forces are major influences on team members' sense of identification and of interdependence. When reporting lines, work assignments, and career paths tend to remain within a functional organizational unit, employees develop a strong identification with the functional group. This identification is even stronger if it converges with educational specialization. The perception of interdependence is created through the performance evaluation and reward systems (formal and informal) of an organization. For example, team members may feel somewhat interdependent with their teammates if "team player" traits are included in their

performance evaluation forms, but feel far more dependent on their functional managers for a number of reasons. The most promising career path may be functional; the formal procedure of evaluation may not require the functional manager to seek "team player" data for the review; or the informal practice may be to collect the data but incorporate them only if it suits the functional manager.

6. Neale and Bazerman (1991).

7. Fisher et al. (1992).

8. See Lewicki and Litterer (1985) on negotiation tactics producing a sense of greater interdependence and integration.

9. Janis (1972).

10. Katzenbach and Smith (1993).

CHAPTER 8

1. Klein (1994).

2. Crawford (1992).

3. Hackman and Oldham (1980).

4. Takeuchi and Nonaka (1986) and Bower and Hout (1988).

5. Ancona and Caldwell (1987), Gersick (1988), and Ancona, Friedman, and Kolb (1991).

6. See Donnellon and Margolis (1994) for further discussion of such managerial dilemmas.

7. This recommendation is consistent with the implications of a study by Meyers and Wilemon (1989) that recommended efforts to achieve "an organizationwide commitment to learning" on teams.

8. Manz, Keating, and Donnellon (1990).

9. Hackman and Walton (1986).

10. Ibid.

11. Murphy and Cleveland (1991).

12. Beer, Eisenstat, and Spector (1990).

13. Applegate and Cash (1989).

14. Wheelwright and Christensen (1992).

APPENDIX A

1. Gumperz and Cook-Gumperz (1982), p. 1.

2. Molotch and Boden (1985).

3. Gumperz and Cook-Gumperz (1982), p. 16.

4. West (1984).

5. Fairhurst and Chandler (1989).

APPENDIX B

1. McGrath (1984).

2. Thompson (1967).

3. See Stalk (1988) and Bower and Hout (1988).

4. Thompson (1967), p. 54.

5. Ibid, p. 58.

6. Ibid, p. 58.

7. Dyer (1987), Larson and LaFasto (1989), Katzenbach and Smith (1993), and Parker (1994).

8. Hackman (1987).

9. Hackman and Walton (1986).

10. Gladstein (1984), Ancona (1990), and Ancona and Caldwell (1987 and 1992).

11. Ancona and Caldwell (1992).

References

Adler, Paul S., and Cole, Robert E. 1993. Designed for learning: A tale of two auto plants. *Sloan Management Review,* spring:85–94.

Alderfer, Clay. 1977. Group and intergroup relations. In J. R. Hackman and J. L. Suttle (Eds.), *Improving life at work*. Santa Monica, Calif.: Goodyear.

The American Heritage Dictionary, New College Edition. 1975. Boston: American Heritage Publishing Co, Inc., and Houghton Mifflin Co.

Ancona, D. G. 1990. Outward bound: Strategies for team survival in an organization. *Academy of Management Journal* 33(2):334–365.

Ancona, Deborah G., and Caldwell, David F. 1987. Management issues facing new product teams in high-technology companies. *Advances in Industrial and Labor Relations* 4:199–221.

———. 1990. Improving the performance of new product teams. *Research in Technology Management,* March–April: 25–29.

———. (1992). Cross-functional teams: Blessing or curse for new product development. In T. A. Kochan and M. Useem (Eds.), *Transforming organizations*. New York: Oxford University Press.

Ancona, Deborah G., Friedman, Raymond F. and Kolb, Deborah M. 1991. The group and what happens on the way to "Yes." *Negotiation Journal,* April:155–173.

Applegate, L. M., and Cash, J. I., Jr. 1989. General Electric Canada: Designing a new organization. Case 9:189–238. Boston: Harvard Business School.

Asch, S. 1951. Effects of group pressure upon the modification and distortion of judgment. In H. Guetzkow (Ed.), *Groups, leadership, and men.* Pittsburgh: Carnegie Press.

Bales, R. F., and Cohen, S. P. 1979. *SYMLOG: A system for multilevel observation of groups.* New York: Free Press.

Bateson, G. 1972. *Steps to an ecology of mind.* New York: Ballantine.

Baxter, L. A. 1984. An investigation of compliance-gaining as politeness. *Human Communication Research* 10:427–456.

Beer, Michael, Eisenstat, Russell A., and Spector, B. 1990. *The critical path to corporate renewal.* Boston: Harvard Business School Press.

Berger, C. R. and Bradac, J. J. 1982. *Language and social knowledge: Uncertainty in interpersonal relations.* London: Edward Arnold.

Bettenhausen, K. L., and Murnighan, J. K. 1985. The emergence of norms in competitive decision-making groups. *Administrative Science Quarterly* 30:350–372.

Blau, Peter. 1964. *Exchange and power in social life.* New York: Wiley.

Bogoch, B. and Danet, B. 1987. Challenge and control in lawyer-client interaction. *Text* 4(1–3):249–295.

Bower, Joseph, and Hout, Thomas. 1988. Fast-cycle capability for competitive power. *Harvard Business Review,* November–December: 110–118.

Bradac, J. J., and Mulac, A. 1984. Attributional consequences of powerful and powerless speech styles in a crisis-intervention context. *Journal of Language and Social Pyschology* 3:1–19.

Brown, Penelope, and Levinson, S. 1978. Universals in language usage: politeness phenomena. In E. N. Goody (Ed.), *Questions and politeness: Strategies in social interaction.* Cambridge, England: Cambridge University Press.

Brown, R., and Ford, M. 1961. Address in American English. *Journal of Abnormal and Social Psychology* 62:375–385.

Brown, R., and Gilman, A. 1960. The pronouns of power and solidarity. In T. Sebeok (Ed.), *Style in language.* New York: Free Press.

Clark, H. H., and Haviland, S. W. 1977. Comprehension and the given-new contact. In R. O. Freedle (Ed.), *Discourse production and comprehension* (Vol. 1). Norwood, N.J.: Ablex.

Cohen, Allan, and Bradford, David. 1990. *Influence without authority.* New York: Wiley and Son.

Cohen, S. G., and Ledford, G. E., Jr. 1991. *The effectiveness of self managing teams: A quasi-experiment.* CEO Publication G91-6(191), Los Angeles: Center for Creative Organizations, University of California.

Collins, Randall. 1981. On the microfoundations of macrosociology. *American Journal of Sociology* 86:984-1014.

Cox, Taylor. 1993. *Cultural diversity at work.* San Francisco: Berrett-Koehler.

Crawford, C. M. 1992. The hidden costs of accelerated product development. *The Journal of Product Innovation Management* 9:188–199.

Davis, J. H. 1973. Group decision and social interaction: A theory of social decision schemes. *Psychological Review* 80:97–125.

———. 1980. Group decision and procedural justice. In M. Fishbein (Ed.), *Progress in Social Psychology* (Vol. 1). Hillsdale, N.J.: Erlbaum.

Deming, W. E. 1982. *Quality, productivity, and competitive position.* Cambridge, Mass.: MIT Center for Advanced Engineering Study.

Donnellon, Anne. 1987. *Management as a conversational process.* Unpublished dissertation, Penn State University.

———. 1994. Team work: Linguistic models of negotiating differences. In B. Sheppard, R. Lewicki, and R. Bies (Eds.), *Research on negotiations in organizations* (Vol. 4). Greenwich, Conn.: JAI Press.

Donnellon, Anne, and Gray, Barbara. 1989. *An interactive theory of reframing in negotiation.* Unpublished manuscript.

Donnellon, Anne, Gray, Barbara, and Bougon, Michel B. 1986. Communication, meaning, and organized action. *Administrative Science Quarterly* 31:43–55.

Donnellon, Anne, and Margolis, Joshua. 1994. The delicate art of designing interdisciplinary teams. *Design Management Journal* 5:8–14.

Donnellon, Anne, and Scully, Maureen. 1994. Teams, evaluation, and reward: Will the post-bureacratic organization be post-meritocratic? In C. Heckscher and A. Donnellon (Eds.), *The Post-bureacratic Organization.* Thousand Oaks, Calif.: Sage Publications.

Dougherty, Deborah. 1992. Interpretive barriers to successful product innovation in large firms. *Organization Science* 3(2):179–202.

Drake, B. H., and Moberg, D. J. 1986. Communicating influence attempts in dyads: Linguistic sedatives and palliatives. *Academy of Management Journal* 11(3):567–584.

Drew, P. 1989. Recalling someone from the past. In D. Roger and P. Bull (Eds.), *Conversation: An interdisciplinary perspective.* Clevedon, England: Multilingual Matters.

Drucker, Peter. 1992 There's more than one kind of team. *The Wall Street Journal,* 11 February, A16.

Dumaine, Brian. 1990. Who needs a boss? *Fortune,* May 7:52–59.

———. 1994. The trouble with teams. *Fortune,* 5 September: 86–90.

Dyer, William G. 1987. *Team Building,* 2d ed. Reading, Mass.: Addison-Wesley.

Emerson, Richard M. 1962. Power-dependence relationships. *American Sociological Review* 27:31–41.

Fairhurst, Gail, and Chandler, Theresa. 1989. Social structure in leader-member interaction. *Communication Monographs* 56:215–239.

Filley, A. C. 1975. *Interpersonal conflict resolution.* Glenview, Ill.: Scott, Foresman.

———. 1978. Some normative issues in conflict management. *California Management Review* 71:61–66.

Fisher, Roger, and Ury, William. 1981. *Getting to yes.* Boston: Houghton Mifflin.

Fisher, Roger, Ury, William, and Patton, Bruce. 1992. *Getting to yes,* revised edition. Boston: Houghton Mifflin.

Follett, Mary Parker. 1995. Constructive conflict. In Pauline Graham (Ed.), *Mary Parker Follett: Prophet of management.* Boston: Harvard Business School Press, 1995.

Garfinkel, H. 1967. *Studies in ethnomethodology.* Englewood Cliffs, N.J.: Prentice-Hall.

Gentile, Mary C. 1995. *Managerial excellence through diversity.* Burr Ridge, Ill.: Richard D. Irwin.

Gersick, Connie J. G. 1988. Time and transition in work teams: Toward a new model of group development. *Academy of Management Journal* 41:4–41.

Gersick, Connie J. G., and Hackman, J. Richard. 1990. Habitual routines in task-performing groups. *Organizational Behavior and Human Decision Processes* 47:65–97.

Gladstein, Deborah L. 1984. Groups in context: A model of task group effectiveness. *Administrative Science Quarterly* 29(4):499–517.

Glaser, B., and Strauss, A. 1967. *The discovery of grounded theory.* Chicago: Aldine.

Goffman, Erving. 1974. *Frame analysis.* Cambridge, Mass.: Harvard University Press.

Goodenough, Ward. 1964. Cultural anthropology and linguistics. In D. Hymes (ed.), *Language in culture and society.* New York: Harper & Row.

Goodwin, Marjorie. 1980. Directive-response speech sequences in girls' and boys' task activities. In S. McConnell-Ginet, R. Borker, and N. Furman (Eds.), *Women and language in literature and society.* New York: Praeger.

Gray, Barbara. 1989. *Collaboration*. San Francisco: Jossey-Bass.

Gudykunst, W. 1986. Toward a theory of intergroup communication. In W. Gudykunst (Ed.), *Intergroup Communication*. London: Edward Arnold.

Gumperz, J. J., and Cook-Gumperz, J. 1982. Interethnic communication in committee negotiation. In J. J. Gumperz (Ed.). *Language and social identity*, 145–162. Cambridge, England: Cambridge University Press.

Hackman, J. R. 1987. The design of work teams. In J. W. Lorsch (Ed.), *Handbook of Organizational Behavior*, 315–342. Englewood Cliffs, NJ: Prentice-Hall.

———, ed. 1990. *Groups that work (and those that don't)*. San Francisco: Jossey-Bass.

Hackman, J. R., and Morris, C. G. 1978. Group process and group effectiveness: A reappraisal. In L. Berkowitz (Ed.), *Group Processes*. New York: Academic Press.

Hackman, J. R., and Oldham, Gregory R. 1980. *Work redesign*. Reading, Mass.: Addison-Wesley.

Hackman, J. R., and Walton, R. E. 1986. Leading Groups in organizations. In P. S. Goodman (Ed.), *Designing effective work groups*. San Francisco: Jossey-Bass.

Hamel, Gary, and Prahalad, C. K. 1989. Strategic intent. *Harvard Business Review*, May–June:63–76.

Hardaker, Maurice, and Ward, Bryan K. 1987. How to make a team work. *Harvard Business Review*, November–December: 112–120.

Hewitt, J. P., and Stokes, R. 1975. Disclaimers. *American Sociological Review* 40:1–11.

Hirschhorn, Larry. 1990. *Managing in the new team environment*. Reading, Mass.: Addison-Wesley.

Hoffman, L. R., ed. 1979. *The group problem solving process: Studies of a valence model*. New York: Praeger.

Hofstede, Geert. 1980. *Culture's consequences*. Beverly Hills, Calif.: Sage Publications.

Husband, C. 1977. News media, language and race relations: A case study in identity maintenance. In H. Giles (Ed.), *Language, ethnicity and intergroup relations*. London: Academic Press.

Hymes, Dell. 1964. Introduction: Toward ethnographies of communication. In J. J. Gumperz and D. Hymes (Eds.), *The ethnography of communication*. Washington, D.C.: American Anthropological Association.

Janis, Irving. 1972. *Victims of groupthink*. Boston: Houghton-Mifflin.

Jefferson, Gail. 1987. On exposed and embedded correction in conversation. In G. Button and J. Lee (Eds.), *Talk and social organization.* Clevedon, England: Multilingual Matters.

Kahn, R. L., et al. 1964. *Organizational stress: Studies in role conflict and ambiguity.* New York: Wiley.

Kanter, Rosabeth Moss. 1989. The new managerial work. *Harvard Business Review,* November–December:85–92.

Kaplan, Robert. 1979. The conspicuous absence of evidence that process consultation enhances task performance. *Journal of Applied Behavioral Science* 15:346–60.

Katzenbach, Jon R., and Smith, Douglas K. 1993. *The wisdom of teams.* Boston: Harvard Business School Press.

Keidel, Robert. 1984. Baseball, football, and basketball: Models for business. *Organizational Dynamics,* winter:5–18.

Klein, Janice. 1994. The paradox of quality management: Commitment, ownership, and control. In C. Heckscher and A. Donnellon (Eds.), *The post-bureaucratic organization.* Thousand Oaks, Calif.: Sage Publications.

Kochman, Thomas. 1981. *Black and white styles in conflict.* Chicago: University of Chicago Press.

LaBier, D. 1986. *Modern madness: The emotional fallout of success.* Reading, Mass.: Addison-Wesley.

Labov, William, and Fanshel, David. 1977. *Therapeutic discourse: Psychotherapy as conversation.* New York: Academic Press.

Lakoff, R. 1975. *Language and woman's place.* New York: Harper & Row.

Larson, Carl E., and LaFasto, Frank. 1989. *TeamWork: What must go right/What can go wrong.* Newbury Park: Sage Publications.

Larson, E. W., and Gobeli, D. H. 1988. Organizing for product development projects. *The Journal of Product Innovation Management* 5:180–190.

Lawrence, P. R., and Lorsch, J. W. 1967. *Organization and environment.* Boston: Harvard University Press.

Lax, D. A., and Sebenius, J. K. 1986. *The manager as negotiator.* New York: Free Press.

Lewicki, Roy and Litterer, Joseph A. 1985. *Negotiation.* Homewood, Ill.: Irwin.

Lewin, K. 1953. Studies in group decision. In D. Cartwright and A. Zander (Eds.), *Group dynamics: Research and theory.* Evanston, Ill.: Row, Peterson.

Lind, E. A., and O'Barr, W. M. 1979. The social significance of speech in the courtroom. In H. Giles and R. N. St. Clair (Eds.), *Language and social psychology.* Baltimore: University Park Press.

Linde, Charlotte. 1988. The quantitative study of communicative success: Politeness and accidents in aviation discourse. *Language in Society* 17:375–99.

Maltz, Daniel N., and Borker, Ruth A. 1982. A Cultural Approach to Male-Female Miscommunication. In J. J. Gumperz (Ed.), *Language and social identity.* Cambridge, England: Cambridge University Press.

Mannix, Elizabeth A. 1993. Organizations as resource dilemmas: The effect of power balance on coalition formation in small groups. *Organizational Behavior and Human Processes* 55(1):1–22.

Manz, Charles, Keating, David, and Donnellon, Anne. 1990. Preparing for an organizational change to employee self-management: The managerial transition. *Organizational Dynamics,* autumn:15–26.

McGrath, Joseph. 1984. *Groups: Interaction and performance.* Englewood Cliffs, N.J.: Prentice-Hall.

Meyer, Christopher. 1994. How the right measures help teams excel. *Harvard Business Review,* May–June:95–103.

Meyers, P. W., and Wilemon, D. 1989. Learning in new technology development teams. *The Journal of Product Innovation Management* 6:79–88.

Miles, M. B., and Huberman, A. M. 1983. *Qualitative data analysis.* Newbury Park, Calif: Sage Publications.

Miller, J. G. 1983. Culture and the development of everyday social explanations. *Journal of Personality and Social Psychology* 46(5):961–978.

Mishler, E. G., and Waxler, N. E. 1968. *Interaction in families: An experimental study of family processes and schizophrenia.* New York: Wiley.

Mitchell, Russell. 1989. Masters of innovation. *Business Week:* 10 April, 58–63.

Molotch, H. L., and Boden, Dierdre. 1985. Talking social structure: Discourse, domination and the watergate hearings. *American Sociological Review* 50:273–288.

Morand, David A. Forthcoming. Dominance, deference, and egalitarianism in organizational interaction: A sociolinguistic analysis of power and politeness. *Organization Science.*

Murphy, Kevin, and Cleveland, June N. 1991. *Performance appraisal: An organizational perspective.* Boston: Allyn-Bacon.

Neale, Margaret, and Bazerman, Max. 1991. *Cognition and rationality in negotiation.* New York: Free Press.

O'Barr, W. M. 1982. *Linguistic evidence.* New York: Academic Press.

O'Donnell, Katherine. 1990. Difference and dominance: How labor and management talk conflict. In A.D. Grimshaw (Ed.), *Conflict talk.* Cambridge, Cambridge University Press.

OH&SP Action Teams. 1988. *3M manager: Special report,* February:6–7.

Osborn, A. F. 1957. *Applied imagination,* rev. ed. New York: Scribner's.

Parker, Glenn. 1994. *Crossfunctional teams.* San Francisco: Jossey-Bass.

Peters, Tom. 1991. Get innovative or get dead, part II. *California Management Review* 33(2):9–23.

Pfeffer, Jeffrey. 1994. *Competitive advantage through people.* Boston: Harvard Business School Press.

Piaget, J. 1952. *The origins of intelligence in children* (Margaret Cook, trans.). New York: International Universities Press (original French ed., 1936).

Pike, K. 1967. *Language in relation to a unified theory of the structure of human behavior.* The Hague: Mouton.

Pinto, M. B. and Pinto, J. K. 1990. Project team communication and cross-functional cooperation in new program development. *The Journal of Product Innovation Management* 7:200–212.

Pomerantz, Anita M. 1975. *Second assessments: A study of some features of agreements/disagreements.* Ph.D. dissertation. University of California, Irvine.

Pruitt, Dean. 1983. Achieving integrative solutions. In M. Bazerman and R. Lewicki (Eds.), *Negotiating in organizations.* Beverly Hills: Sage.

Reich, Robert. 1987. Entrepreneurship reconsidered: The team as hero. *Harvard Business Review,* May–June:77–83.

Robbins, S.P. 1974. *Managing organizational conflict: A nontraditional approach.* Englewood Cliffs, N.J.: Prentice-Hall.

Rogers, L. E., and Farace, R. V. 1975. Relational communication analysis: New measures and procedures. *Human Communication Research* 1:222–239.

Ruble, T. L., and Thomas, K. 1976. Support for a two-dimensional model of conflict behavior. *Organizational Behavior and Human Performance* 16:145.

Sacks, H., Schegloff, E., and Jefferson, G. 1974. A simplest systematics for the organization of turn-taking in conversation. *Language* 50:696–735.

Schiffrin, Deborah. 1990. The management of a cooperative self during argument: The role of opinion and stories. In A. D. Grimshaw (Ed.), *Conflict talk.* Cambridge, England: Cambridge University Press.

Schneider, Susan, and De Meyer, Arnoud. 1991. Interpreting and responding to strategic issues: The impact of national culture. *Strategic Management Journal* 12:307–320.

Scott, M. B., and Lyman, S. M. 1968. Accounts: inquiries in the social construction of reality. American Sociological Review, 33:46–62.

Sherif, M., and Sherif, C. 1953. Groups in harmony and tension. New York: Harper.

Sluzki, Carlos E. 1992. Transformations: A blueprint for narrative changes in therapy. *Family Process* 31:217–230.

Smith, Kenwyn K., and Berg, David N. 1987. Paradoxes of group life. San Francisco: Jossey-Bass.

Stalk, George, Jr. 1988. Time—the next source of competitive advantage. *Harvard Business Review,* July–August:41–53.

Steiner, I. D. 1966. Models for inferring relationships between group size and potential group productivity. *Behavioral Science* 11:273–283.

————. 1972. Group process and productivity. New York: Academic Press.

Strauss, Anselm. 1978. *Negotiations.* San Francisco: Jossey-Bass.

Takeuchi, H., and Nonaka, I. 1986. The new product development game. *Harvard Business Review,* January–February: 137–146.

Tajfel, H. 1981. *Human categories and social groups.* Cambridge, England: Cambridge University Press.

Tannen, D. 1979. What's in a frame? Surface evidence for underlying expectations. In R. O. Freedie (Ed.), *New directions in discourse processing.* Norwood, N.J.: Ablex.

————. 1986. *That's not what I meant.* New York: Ballantine Books.

————. 1990. *You just don't understand.* New York: William Morrow.

————. 1994a. *Talking from 9 to 5.* New York: William Morrow.

————. 1994b. How to give orders like a man. *The New York Times Sunday Magazine,* 28 August:46–49.

Thampain, H. J. 1990. Managing technologically innovative team efforts toward new product success. *The Journal of Product Innovation Management* 7:5–18.

Thompson, J. D. 1967. Organizations in action. New York: McGraw-Hill.

The trouble with teams. 1995. *The Economist,* 14 January:61.

Vuchinich, Samuel. 1990. The sequential organization of closing in verbal family conflict. In A. Grimshaw (Ed.), *Conflict talk.* Cambridge, England: Cambridge University Press.

Walton, Richard E. 1987. *Managing conflict,* 2d ed. Reading, Mass.: Addison-Wesley.

Walton, Richard E., and McKersie, Robert. 1965. *A behavioral theory of labor negotiations.* New York: McGraw-Hill.

Watzlawick, P., Beavin, J. H., and Jackson, D. D. 1967. *Pragmatics of human communication: A study of international patterns, pathologies, and paradoxes.* New York: Norton.

West, C. 1984. *Routine complications.* Bloomington: University of Indiana Press.

Wheelwright, S. C., and Christensen C. M. 1992. *Quantum Corporation: Business and product teams.* Case 9-692-023. Boston: Harvard Business School.

Whetten, D. A., and Cameron, K. S. 1984. *Developing management skills.* Glenview, Ill.: Scott, Foresman and Company.

Zimmerman, Don H., and West, Candace. 1975. Sex roles, interruptions and silences in conversation. In Barrie Thorne and Noancy Henley (Eds.), *Language and sex: Difference and dominance.* Rowley, Mass.: Newbury House.

Index

About the Author

Anne Donnellon is an associate professor in the management division at Babson College in Wellesley, Massachusetts. She teaches cross-functional team work, organizational design, and cross-cultural management in Babson's MBA and executive education programs. She has published many articles in journals such as *Administrative Science Quarterly, Organizational Dynamics, Journal of Management, Journal of Product Innovation Management,* and *Journal of Social Issues.* Donnellon has also authored chapters in *The Portable MBA in Management, Research in Negotiations in Organizations,* and *The Post-Bureaucratic Organization,* which she co-edited with Charles Heckscher. She has also written best-selling cases for Harvard Business School, where she was previously on the faculty. Her current research focuses on evaluating and rewarding teams and cross-cultural team work.